BOOZE

Books by James H. Gray

The Winter Years
Men Against the Desert
The Boy from Winnipeg
Red Lights on the Prairies

BOOZE

The Impact of Whisky
on the Prairie West

James H. Gray

Macmillan of Canada/Toronto

ISBN 0-7705-0893-6

Printed in Canada by The Alger Press Limited
for The Macmillan Company of Canada Limited
70 Bond Street, Toronto 2

For G. V. F.

*Friend, mentor, and door-opener
to a writing career*

Contents

List of illustrations   ix
Preface   xi

Belly up to the bar, boys!   1
The law and the prophets   20
The lesser breeds, and wife-beaters   38
What good were laws without loopholes?   52
The slogan that won the west   69
Prohibition: where it worked, where it didn't   89
Yorkton, where Harry planted the money tree   109
Here it is, you come and get it   128
Sue the bastards!   150
In the Customs Department, who told the truth?   166
The first crack in the dike   190
How it all ended — with governments as booze-pushers   203

Appendix   222
Footnotes   227
Index   235

Illustrations

(between pages 80 and 81)

1. Pledge card *(Eric Knowles and the Saskatoon Public Library)*
2. Headquarters Saloon, 1885 *(Manitoba Archives)*
3. The executive of the W.C.T.U., 1908 *(Glenbow-Alberta Institute)*
4. Nellie McClung *(Glenbow-Alberta Institute)*
5. Calgary House, 1883 *(Glenbow-Alberta Institute)*
6. The bar of the Alberta Hotel, Calgary *(Glenbow-Alberta Institute)*
7,8,9. Hotel bars in High River, Alberta *(Glenbow-Alberta Institute)*
10. The Alberta Hotel bar, Crossfield, Alberta *(Glenbow-Alberta Institute)*
11. Weston Liquor House, Winnipeg
12. The bar of the Windsor Hotel, Saskatoon *(Glenbow-Alberta Institute)*
13. Pool hall, Estevan, Saskatchewan *(Archives of Saskatchewan)*
14. "Positively No Credit Given at this Bar" *(Saskatoon Public Library)*
15. The Wainwright Hotel *(Glenbow-Alberta Institute)*

16. The elegant bar of the Edmonton Hotel *(Provincial Museum and Archives of Alberta)*
17. The Imperial Hotel, Lagenburg, Saskatchewan *(Archives of Saskatchewan)*
18. The W.C.T.U. Convention, Tofield, Alberta, May 1916 *(Glenbow-Alberta Institute)*
19. Sunday School Prohibition float, Calgary *(Glenbow-Alberta Institute)*
20. Harry and Sam Bronfman *(Montreal Star-Canada Wide)*
21. A still seized by the R.C.M.P. *(Archives of Saskatchewan)*
22. A still seized near Edmonton in 1919 *(Glenbow-Alberta Institute)*

Preface

With the completion of *Booze* I have reached the end of a quintet of prairie histories I never intended to write in the first place. It has been a case of one book leading to another and another and another. *The Winter Years* was a first-person memoir of the life of people on unemployment relief in the cities of the west during the great depression. It led into a natural sequel, *Men Against the Desert*, which dealt with the struggle of the farmers to survive during the dust-bowl era so vividly described as the "dirty thirties". In *The Boy from Winnipeg* two steps backward were taken into the lives of the people in the urban environment of the population crush of the period before the First World War. Out of it grew *Red Lights on the Prairies,* an examination of the effect of the brothel-booze syndrome on the urban pioneers of prairie Canada. This final work traces the evolution of the Temperance-Prohibition movement through the same era of mass immigration.

John Buchan once wrote that those who do not remember the past will find themselves doomed to repeat it. If there are any people who have engaged in a massive conspiracy to bury their past, it is the people of western Canada. This has made the assembly of this work more difficult than it otherwise would have been.

To those who have managed to reach three score and ten, this book may seem overly cluttered with explanations which, to senior citizens, may seem unnecessary. But during my research I was somewhat dismayed to find how few younger Canadians were aware that there had been a Prohibition era in Canada. To them, Prohibition was something which the Americans invented and which led to the development of their gangster era. They thought vaguely that Canada had a small part in it as a supplier of liquor to the rum-runners who took it into the United States and sold it to Al Capone.

An author who can assume that his readers have a working knowledge of the manner in which their country developed can get on with his story. As one who is fearful of making such an assumption, I have perhaps been guilty of expanding on subsidiary aspects of the main theme. In expiation, I have tried to concentrate on people and avoid politics except where it is absolutely essential to the events being described, a procedure which was followed in my other books.

To anyone interested in pursuing my irrelevancies further, I have relied mainly on four sources of material. The old newspaper files are storehouses of excellent stuff which frequently led to the flushing out of survivors of important events whose recollections of things past added a touch of spice to the mixture. The reports of royal commissions, lawsuits, and legislative committees were also mined with considerable profit. I was able to get into communication through conversation and correspondence with a score of men and women who were there when it happened, some of whom had a hand in making things happen. Finally, I have drawn heavily on my personal experiences as a boy in the middle of the booze problem in Winnipeg, and as a newspaper reporter at the end of the era.

On several occasions efforts to provide more than sketchy documentation for some of the most fascinating aspects of the early booze problems have proved abortive. One example was a fruitless search for material with which to further expand on the payday drunks that developed from the custom of cashing pay-cheques in the bars. In 1935, while covering the labour beat for the *Winnipeg Free Press,* I wrote a two-part history of the Winnipeg labour movement for the paper's magazine section. In gathering material, I spent hours in conversation with Bob Russell and Allan Meikle at the One Big Union and with Charles Foster and his cribbage-playing cronies in the office of the Unemployed Railway Men's Association in the Labor Temple. Half their stories of pre-First World War misadventures seemed to start with their storming into the Stock Exchange Hotel near the C.P.R. shops, or into the saloons at Main Street and Higgins Avenue, to cash their monthly pay-cheques. They all recalled the days when demand for payment of wages by the week and in cash was a burning issue among trade-unionists and Prohibitionists alike. Yet the story of this long agitation, save for minor references in the *Labor Gazette,* seems lost to trade-union history.

I should make special mention of the fact that this work covers only the prairie provinces. Indeed, I have ceded the Crowsnest Pass area of Alberta to British Columbia. The story of the impact of booze on British Columbia would make a book in itself, and the wild and carefree Crowsnest Pass would fill a good third of it, for it was more part of British Columbia history than that of the prairies. The big-time Calgary whisky dealers were more orientated toward British Columbia than toward Saskatchewan. Frank Webster, for example, who ran a job polishing spittoons in a Calgary hotel into the ownership of three of the best hotels in town, was said to have made his fortune in Crowsnest Pass during the period of legal exporting to the United States. The Royal Commission on Customs and Excise, which provided a wealth of material for the Manitoba and Saskatchewan chapters, skimmed over British Columbia without leaving much factual residue.

Once again I am most deeply indebted to the co-operative and helpful staffs of the public libraries in Winnipeg, Regina, Saskatoon,

Moose Jaw, and Calgary; to the archivists and their staffs in the Manitoba and Saskatchewan Archives; and to the Glenbow-Alberta Institute in Calgary. And I must add a word of appreciation for Helen Purdy in Regina and Helen Watkins in Winnipeg; Dr. Sam Wynn and H. M. Jackson in Yorkton; George Burnett of Glen Ewen, Saskatchewan; Ken John of Estevan, Saskatchewan; the former Chief of Police, Malcolm Boyd, of Calgary; and Inspector George Logan of Regina; and their many former clients on the other side of the law whose wish is to remain anonymous.

JAMES H. GRAY
Calgary, 1972

BOOZE

Belly up to the bar, boys!

The name of the game was whisky. Whisky was the force which impelled the American fur traders into the Canadian west; and it was the liquid lorelei that lured the Indians to the trading posts and their own destruction. Whisky kept the embers of American annexation smouldering in The Dutchman's bar in Winnipeg in the 1860s and it hurried the dispatch of the North West Mounted Police to the western plains to evict the American whisky traders; whisky fuelled the engines of the political machines and corroded their steering mechanisms; whisky oiled the escalators to political success and greased the skids to oblivion.

From Winnipeg to the Rockies, whisky kept the prairies in a ferment for fifty years. Other causes flared brightly for a decade or two and expired. The crusade against whisky went on and on. The Prohibitionist zealots may have let their attention wander occasionally to the espousal of woman suffrage, the eradication of prostitution, or the adoption of the Single Tax. In the end they always came back to the anti-whisky crusade, usually trailing converts picked up along the way from the other movements. It was natural that this would be so. For the deeply religious Methodists, Baptists, and Presbyterians who pioneered the settlement of the west, strong drink was more, much more, than a challenge. Whisky to the fundamentalist Protestants was what pork was to Muslims and Jews, animal flesh was to Hindus, and coffee and tobacco were to Mormons. Not only was booze an abomination to their religion, it was both a millstone grinding on their business interests and, in the rural areas, a threat to their physical existence.

For sheer intensity of conviction and staying power over the long haul no other prairie mass movement ever equalled the Prohibition crusade. And yet the excitement and the political infighting that marked the long assault on the demon rum was hardly more boisterous than the uproar that developed after Prohibition became the law of the land. Then, as governments occasionally did their best to enforce the law, they were heckled continually by the Prohibitionists. While the Temperance spokesmen were demanding more adequate enforcement, clutches of doctors, druggists, lawyers, judges, and free-lance assuagers of the public thirst were conspiring to reduce the law to absurdity. Out of all this there developed a bootlegging industry that kept the newspapers supplied with headlines and provided both Wets and Drys with oratorical ammunition with which to bombard the nearest legislature.

Time, as it has a way of doing, has worked its magic in creating a Prohibition era mythology out of the polemic flotsam drifting in the backwaters of aging memories. Uncountable thousands of western Canadians are convinced that Prohibition either was foisted upon the country by the Borden government during the First World War or was the result of granting voting rights to women while the men were off at war. As a corollary there is the belief that an outraged and enlightened populace voted out Prohibition at the first opportunity. It is believed that Prohibition, in the words of a C.B.C. interviewer,[1] "turned Saskatchewan into the rum-running capital of the world", and as a result broke down law enforcement and ushered in an era of corruption, violence, drunkenness, and debauchery.

There is little foundation in fact for any of the legends and in some of them not even a grain of truth. Not only did the people of the prairies vote for Prohibition with unbounded enthusiasm in 1916, they returned to the polls with equal zest four years later, long after the troops were home, to vote to stem the flow of booze across provincial borders. And when, three years still later, they again returned to the polls to vote for government control as a substitute for total Prohibition, their verdict was defiantly against any return to the *status quo ante* of wide-open bars. The rum-runners, contrary to legend, were usually the personification of restrained circumspection. They seldom arrived for their cargoes before nightfall, and were nowhere to be seen with the coming of dawn.[2] That there were infrequent robberies of country banks along the American border cannot be denied. No evidence can be produced, however, to connect the bank robbers with the rum-runners.

As for the legendary failure of Prohibition, it not only ushered in the most law-abiding era in prairie history, it marked the end of the maleficent impact of wide-open boozing on urban family life. The pauperizing effect of the pre-Prohibition saloons on the working class of the frontier cities is difficult to document specifically; but would be as difficult to exaggerate. All too frequently on paydays and holidays downtown streets became animated replicas of Hogarth prints into which it was unsafe for women and children to venture.[3] All this, the factual as well as the fictional, was pre-ordained by the nature of the country, the nature of the people, and the pattern of settlement that developed. Which of the three ranked first in importance would be difficult to determine. But a start can be made where everything began — in the Winnipeg of the 1870s in the early years that followed Louis Riel's Red River insurrection. Winnipeg was a turbulent, rowdy, bawdy town of 100 in 1870; 215 in 1871; 1,467 in 1872; 3,700 by 1874; and

5,000 in 1875. It was a turbulent, rowdy, and bawdy town that thought nothing of tar-and-feathering a speaker of the legislature,[4] or threatening mob violence to the attorney general of the province. It was a turbulent, rowdy, and bawdy town whose mould had been set by the free-traders of the 1850s when they broke the Hudson's Bay Company's trading monopoly in the Red River Valley; by the belligerent Canadians of the 1860s; and by the first rush of the Ontario homesteaders and railroad builders of the 1870s.

Winnipeg had begun life as a jumping-off place for the fur-trading posts farther west and north. Despite its phenomenal post-Riel growth, it remained a jumping-off place for most of its first half-century. What was more, it was from the Winnipeg mould that the other cities of western Canada were cast as jumping-off places for later waves of immigrants. And they too were turbulent, rowdy, and bawdy towns to which the homesteaders returned for boozy relaxation and libidinous diversion.

Winnipeg's growth, like the settlement of the west, was characterized by incredible booms and shattering collapses. Such a pattern was perhaps inevitable, given the vast expanse of uninhabited nothingness that was prairie Canada and the surge-pause, surge-pause inflow of population. As Manitoba settled down after the Riel trouble on the Red River, the first invasion came from Ontario.[5] Then the group settlements led by the Mennonites and the Icelanders started, and, a decade after Riel, Ontario and Minnesota alike were gripped by the "Manitoba fever" which sent thousands of new citizens to Winnipeg over the newly completed railway from St. Paul. It not only carried the homesteaders and their equipment and furnishings, but brought in a wild miscellany of promoters, tradesmen, financiers, entrepreneurs, skilled craftsmen, and strong-backed navvies. From a clutter of rude clapboard shacks and stores scattered above the Water Street docks, Winnipeg exploded overnight into a frontier metropolis. The sawmills, brickyards, and quarries worked dawn-to-dark shifts and still fell far short of filling the demand for building materials. Soon the wreckers were following the builders as Main Street shacks were demolished to make way for three- and four-storey brick and stone hotels, stores, and office structures. As the boom of 1880-2 ran its course the frenzied promotion of the real estate speculators pushed the price of Main Street property from $100 a foot frontage with no takers to $2,500 a foot with buyers clamouring for it. Sub-division promoters were everywhere, carving up the landscape into twenty-five-foot lots to the far horizons. It all added up to the greatest boom in Winnipeg's history.

In no other aspect was the boom more pronounced than in the rash of jerry-built hotels that soon dotted the Winnipeg environs. This was perhaps an obvious development on two counts. Sleeping room for the immigrants was the most essential service Winnipeg was expected to provide. Hotel-keeping was the easiest business anybody with a few hundred dollars in cash could get into. Indeed, there is little doubt that many of the hotels were the accidental result of early arrivals turning their homes into lodging houses.

In the 1860s the settlement got along with five hotels. The hand-somest was the Canadian Pacific, a three-storey brick structure on Main Street near the Fort Garry gate. The most popular was George Emmering's American Hotel, known far and wide as "The Dutch-man's", near what would become the corner of Portage Avenue and Main Street.[6] Henry McKinney's Royal Hotel was near the corner of Water Street, while Browse's and O'Lone's were closer to the Red River docks. All were geared to the rough and ready patronage of the buffalo-hunting frontier era then nearing its end. In a word, their emphasis was heavy on booze and light on rooms. Patrons who over-estimated their capacity for the rot-gut that passed for whisky were perfectly welcome to sleep off their stupor on the floor where they dropped.

Of the earliest hotels themselves, few descriptions survive. But from the random snatches of evidence that have turned up, it can be safely assumed that they were as typical of the frontier as the people who ran and patronized them. Bob O'Lone, for example, died in a brawl in his own saloon. Miss Bella McLean, who arrived in Winnipeg in 1873 to go missionarying for the Wesleyan Methodist Church, described Browse's Hotel in her diary. She reported being met at the Red River dock by three clergymen who escorted her to the hotel which was "an oblong structure of brick with floors carpeted with native mud, black as coal". All Winnipeg floors of the era were "carpeted with native mud" after every rainstorm and for weeks following spring thaws. Winnipeg streets became completely impass-able when the incredibly adhesive black soil of the Red River Valley was mixed with water and turned into instant glue. Inelegant as it was, however, Browse's Hotel was clearly the least rowdy accom-

modation Winnipeg could offer a visiting lady missionary.[7] Charlie
Mair, the only Ontario lyric poet who was ever horse-whipped on a
Winnipeg street by a matron who took umbrage at his writings,
reported that he had been driven from his room at The Dutchman's
by the round-the-clock uproar in the hotel's saloon.

The Royal, The Dutchman's, and O'Lone's all disappeared in the
early stages of the Manitoba boom, to be replaced by more and
bigger but by no means better hostelries. A decade after Riel, Winnipeg could boast of thirty-two hotels to serve a population of less
than 8,000. By 1881, that number had doubled to sixty-four, most
of them with saloons attached, along with five breweries and
twenty-four wine and liquor stores, fifteen of them on Main Street.
Henderson's Directory, which naturally sought to put the best possible gloss on the city for its first issue in 1883, noted with pride:

> It is unnecessary to say much about the hotels of Win-
> nipeg. It is a fact beyond dispute that no city in the uni-
> verse of the same size possesses so many and so commo-
> dious homes for the travelling public and no where does a
> floating population take more advantage of these houses.
> Fifteen houses in the city are capable of accommodating
> over 100 guests and five can house comfortably 150.

During 1882 the number of hotels in operation peaked at eighty-
six, along with sixty-four grocery stores selling whisky by the bottle.
Henderson's Directory to the contrary, only the widest poetic
licence would have permitted most of the hostelries to be identified
as hotels. Chief of Police D. B. Murray's assessment was that "many
hotels are resorts for thieves and blackguards and are hotbeds for
drunkenness. . . . They would better be described," he said, "as
cesspools operating under the guise of hotels."[8] The chief provincial
licence commissioner in January 1883 listed a score of hotels by
name which were unfit for occupation, but they still got licences to
operate because of the desperate needs of the incoming settlers for
accommodation.[9] In a city whose population had jumped from
8,000 in 1881 to 16,000 in 1882 the incomers often had to beg for
sleeping space on the floors of unfinished buildings.

For the settlers who were bound for homesteads in western Manitoba and the Northwest Territories, Winnipeg was a place to leave

with all possible haste. But for the Winnipeg real estate salesmen, merchants, outfitters, con-men, and sundry scalawags, the settlers represented an ephemeral money crop which had to be harvested before it left the town. For the building tradesmen of Ontario, Winnipeg was a Valhalla where stonemasons, carpenters, and painters could earn up to five dollars a day. For the newspapers of eastern Canada, Winnipeg was an assignment for their most imaginative reporters, whose colourful and hyperbolic dispatches of one week might be exceeded by the realities of the next.

Winnipeg's new city hall, rushed to completion during the previous winter, collapsed in a heap and had to be replaced in the spring of 1883. The city council was so riddled with cliques that it seldom completed a vote on anything important without reversing itself, or becoming involved in a legal hassle with the mayor over his veto powers. Its police court was run by a magistrate who regarded shouted insults, spectator applause, and a stench-filled court room as an acceptable norm. His was an institution which everybody seemed to hold in contempt, particularly the drunks, brawlers, and prostitutes who were almost its only customers. [10]

And yet this squalling infant of a city, so out of control in many ways, was populated by as deeply religious, as God-fearing, and as fundamentalist Christian a people as existed anywhere. It was only after the collapse of the land boom of 1882 that the character of the settlers, whose arrival caused the boom, began to emerge. The fly-by-night promoters bound up their financial wounds and left. The town settled down to the harsh realities of frontier life and a return to the Puritan ethic of hard work. It was a change that was made without rancour. Nobody really had come to Winnipeg expecting to find streets paved with gold. They had come to escape the confining environment of rural Ontario, to find and make places for themselves with whatever muscle, skill, and intelligence they had been endowed. Only the incurably optimistic would ever have left for Manitoba in the first place, and of such enduring quality was the optimism with which they were imbued that it was passed from generation to generation. If success were the reward, for hard work, frugality, and determination, success would be theirs!

All this was only to have been expected from the religious persuasions of the early settlers which are set forth in the tabulation below: [11]

*Religions
of the population*

Denomination	1881	1891
Anglican	2,373	6,854
Baptist	—	1,045
Congregationalist	111	1,050
Jewish	—	645
Lutheran	292	2,291
Methodist	371	4,310
Presbyterian	2,365	5,952
Roman Catholic	1,020	2,470

Within this decade the evangelical-fundamentalist Protestants clearly emerged as the dominant religious force within the community. Under their influence, Winnipeg would soon become the most tightly closed city on the continent on Sundays. So deeply held were their sabbatarian convictions that it was sixty years before Manitoba farmers, despite imminent threats of hail, rust, or grasshoppers, were able to bring themselves to thresh their grain on Sunday.

The dedication of the early settlers to strict Sunday observance was as good a measure as any of the piety of the population. The C.P.R. line was hardly in business before there were ministerial protests against its operation on Sunday. The company's contention that moving immigrants to their homesteads was a work of necessity which the Lord's Day Act permitted was challenged in several pulpits. The railway bowed to public opinion and agreed to dispatch no trains from Winnipeg on Sunday, with the exception of emergency trains to restore traffic after collisions, wrecks, and derailments, of which there were many.

Railway construction on Sunday was held to be illegal. Five workmen from Prince Edward Island who were fired for refusing to work on Sunday east of Winnipeg sued the contractor for damages and won.[12] West of the city the *Marquette Review* blasted the railway for employing Jews in the railway gravel pit, doing the same work on Sundays as they did on week-days. While Winnipeg was a roistering town for six days, even its bars were tightly shut on Sundays. Church attendance, dressed always in "Sunday best", was expected of all church members. Even the non-believers were expected to dress in their best for Sunday afternoon strolling when the weather permitted.

This was the age in which Protestant religious precepts were still being drawn from Calvin, Knox, Wesley, and Jonathan Edwards. It was an era before the ripples from Charles Darwin and the Huxley-Gladstone debates began to lap at the portals of Christian theology. The belief in hellfire and damnation was as firmly held as the belief in salvation by faith in Christ, coupled with an unshakable faith in the perfectibility of all creatures made in the image of God. The existence of the wide-open bars and Winnipeg's seemingly easy toleration of prostitution were as hateful to the pious immigrants to Manitoba as the ale-house of Boston had been to Cotton Mather.

"Alas," Mather wrote, "men have their estates devoured, their names devoured, their hours devoured and their souls devoured when they are so besotted that they are not in their element except when tippling at such houses. When a man is bewitched — what usually becomes of him? He is a gone man and when he comes to die he will cry out as many have done 'Ale-houses are hell-houses! Ale-houses are hell-houses!' "[13]

The Protestant clergymen of Winnipeg were strict teetotallers in their personal lives and enthusiastic members of their new Manitoba Temperance Alliance, formed in 1883. In the attitude of the clergymen, as in the title of their organization, "Temperance" had not yet evolved into "Prohibition". That would come only after fifteen years of total frustration at the hands of Canadian politicians, of all political stripes, sizes and shades of cozenage.

In 1883, the guardians of Winnipeg morality, clerical and lay alike, would still have settled for a slight indication that liquor regulations would be enforced. Canada at that moment was going through one of its earliest constitutional crises, one that arose from a Privy Council decision in the Russell case. Russell was an Ontario saloon-keeper who had been arrested for violation of the province's liquor control act. He argued that Ontario's act was in conflict with the Canada Temperance Act which the Macdonald government had passed in 1878. The Privy Council ruled in 1882 that Russell's whisky-selling was engagement in "trade and commerce" which fell within the jurisdiction of the federal government. The effect of the decision was to worsen the chaotic condition already prevailing, for it brought all provincial liquor legislation into question.

One of the earliest enactments of the Manitoba legislature had been a law to regulate and control the liquor traffic. Under its charter, the Winnipeg city council also had power to license hotels and other business establishments. The province set up a Board of Licence Commissioners whose duty it was to establish and enforce licensing regulations of all kinds. This board decided that saloon licences should be confined to hotels, that to qualify for a dispensing licence a hotel should have at least ten rooms, that hours of sale would be from 7 a.m. to 11 p.m., and that there should be no more than one hotel licence issued for every three hundred of population. Provision was also made for the sale of whisky by the bottle in grocery stores and by the case through licensed wholesale liquor dealers. Winnipeg also passed a licence by-law which was intended to regulate conditions within the bars. During the boom everybody with a ten- or twelve-roomed house rushed to get into the hotel business, and all efforts to regulate the behaviour of the saloons collapsed as the courts split their legal hairs into the finest filaments.[14] Winnipeg, they ruled in 1883, had power only to license, not to regulate.

When nightly riots developed in the Main Street bistros, police action was limited to arresting the evictees as they were bounced from the bars into the perpetually self-renewing quagmire that was Main Street most of the year. As Chief Murray explained, his force functioned more as a shepherding agency than as one concerned with incarcerative action against drunks, even though they jailed more than 2,000 of them in 1882.[15] There had been a problem with the policemen themselves becoming intoxicated, so after several were fired for being drunk on duty they were forbidden to enter the bars except in cases where brawling got completely out of hand. Nor did they pay any attention to ordinary drunks on the streets. They would even make sure the lurching imbibers were headed in the general direction of home and often guided them around mud holes at street intersections. Only when the belligerent drunks turned into disturbers of the peace of the streets were they escorted to the city jail, an unspeakably odoriferous drunk tank.

If the police had arrested all the drunks in sight, there would not have been a room in the city large enough to accommodate them.

But because of the lenient attitude which constitutional uncertainty forced upon the police, maintaining a semblance of order on the streets became increasingly difficult, not only in Winnipeg but everywhere else. In Portage la Prairie, for example, things got so badly out of hand that the police decided to haul the barkeepers into court under a town by-law. All were convicted and fined. They appealed the conviction, and won acquittal on the grounds the regulations were *ultra vires*, and the appeal judge ordered judgment for costs against the magistrate who had presided at their trial. To save the magistrate's home from seizure, the Manitoba Temperance Alliance in an emergency convention undertook to raise the required $1,500. [16]

The Privy Council decision in the Russell case raised serious questions about whether Manitoba could license whisky sellers, let alone establish rules of conduct. There was even doubt as to whether a licence could be cancelled for cause once it had been issued. Winnipeg's most notorious dive of the 1880s — the "Turf and Wine Vault" of Brady and Parsons — was frequently the scene of brawling, thievery, and drunk-rolling, against which only token action could be taken. So in booming Winnipeg, regulation of the liquor trade was easily stated. It was non-existent. The only restraint upon outrageous behaviour in the saloons was the one imposed by the conscience of the owner.

The notorious elasticity of the bar managers' consciences soon became an abomination not only to the reverend clergy of Winnipeg but to the entire commercial establishment as well. And what an Establishment it was! As W. L. Morton has emphasized, the leading citizens of Manitoba in the main cared nothing for Manitoba; their entire capacity for caring was filled with passionate concern for Winnipeg. One of the great puzzles of Canadian history must surely be this: Here was this wind-blown, dust-coated, mud-caked, flood-prone, ice-encrusted near-nothing of a town in the middle of nowhere; yet it somehow managed to infuse not only its first settlers but the thousands who came after with visions of building a new Jerusalem at the confluence of the Red and Assiniboine rivers. To the Ashdowns, McArthurs, McIntyres, Macmillans, Robinsons, Alloways, Hammonds, Bannatynes, Macdonalds, Luxtons, McDermots, and Ryans, to be a Winnipegger was to be something indefinably special. [17]

The existence of the wall-to-wall hotel saloons on Main and Market and Queen streets they regarded as a blot on their city's proud
escutcheon. While the newcomers were throwing their money away
on booze, they were erecting stone-walled emporiums of trade, and
building sawmills and flour mills, iron works, tanneries, and banks.
At the same time they were funding the construction of churches
and denominational schools, colleges, and hospitals, and stirring up
the city council with appeals for expansion of services and, of
course, greater economy and lower taxes. The achievement of financial success, moreover, was as much a part of their religion as the
Apostles' Creed. For them the moral of the parable of the talents
came instantly to life. Theirs would have been a profound "Amen!"
to the sentiments expressed in a sermon on success and failure by the
Rev. J. B. Silcox at the Congregational church. Nine out of ten
failed, Silcox declared, because they lacked the integrity and the
moral fibre that Christianity alone could provide. The unrestrained
boozing that went on in the bars was obvious evidence of unchristian
depravity. It was also an affront to their business interests and their
frugal Scottish instincts.

To Winnipeg merchants, bankers, real estate developers, and
newspaper editors, every dollar that passed across the bars for booze
represented a dead loss to the community. This opinion was shared
by other communities as well. For example, the *Hamilton Times*
blamed the tightness of the money supply in Ontario on the wastage
of the country's substance on booze in far-off Winnipeg.

> Those who make money on real estate celebrate by buy-
> ing champagne. Those who lose drown their sorrows in
> whisky. Either way money sent out to develop the
> country, goes instead into dissipation and that helps to
> account for the capital stringency here.

The *Winnipeg Times* agreed that far too much money was being
spent on whisky in Winnipeg. But no Winnipeg editor would ever
allow eastern criticism, no matter how valid, to go unanswered. [18]

> It was recently reported [the *Times* noted] that we had
> spent $5.80 per capita last year on spirituous liquors. Let
> us concede that that was $5 per capita too much. But the

Lieutenant Governor of Ontario recently led a party of 14 men and a boy from Prince Arthur's Landing to Winnipeg and return via Chicago. On that five week journey a total of $5,300 was spent on whisky and cigars. That was more whisky than Sir George Nares' party consumed on its two-year expedition to the North Pole. It worked out, moreover to $65 per head per week or $3,250 per capita per year.

Whatever else could be blamed on the whisky consumption of Winnipeg, the *Times* argued, it could hardly be blamed for the entire capital shortage in Ontario.

The Winnipeg Establishment, however, was beset by one problem that never developed in other western cities. It centred on the sale of whisky by grocery stores. In the Winnipeg saloons booze sold for "two-bits a slug" — twenty-five cents for two ounces of whisky or rum, which were equally popular. Often whisky was taken with a five-cent glass of beer for a chaser. Liquor came in bottles of two sizes — Imperial quarts and "reputed" quarts. A "reputed" quart was equivalent to an American "fifth" or roughly to a twenty-six-ounce Canadian bottle. For a normal one-bottle-a-day drinker the cost of an evening's sojourn at a bar with a "reputed" quart would be $3.25. The imbiber could get the same quantity of whisky for $1 or $1.15 a bottle at any of the sixty-four groceries licensed to sell it. To the Winnipeg clergymen, the groceries were often seen as a greater threat to public morality than the bars.[19] There was no law to prevent a grocery store customer from opening a bottle of booze in the store, knocking back a couple of shots, and passing the bottle to the other customers. The "first class drinking men" of the era adhered to a rather rigid drinking code. No one drank alone — a wise precaution in face of the risk inherent in the quality of the booze and the saloon environment. No one bought a drink for himself without buying one for a friend. No one accepted a drink from a friend without buying him one in return. No one deserted an unconscious drinking companion. Though not strictly adhered to in grocery-store drinking, the drinking man's code was not completely ignored there either.

The stores differed from the bars in one important respect: there were usually more than enough bags, boxes, and barrels around so that the drinkers could sit in reasonable comfort while they polished off their booze. That was never possible in the bars, which made but two faint concessions to customer comfort. The fancier places provided the drinkers with a rail on which they could rest one foot while they leaned against the bar. The other convenience was a collection of randomly placed spittoons in whose general direction the drinkers could squirt the surplus juice that developed from the cuds of chewing tobacco they kept in their jaws while they drank. As the accuracy of the chewers declined with alcoholic intake, more juice landed on the floor than hit the receptacles. The more fastidious hotelmen sought to minimize the mess by increasing the size and the number of cuspidors. Some even placed loose tin sheets under the receptacles to catch the mis-aimed spit. Nothing, however, could prevent the permanent scarring of the barroom floors, or the permeation of the rooms with the indelicate aroma of chewed tobacco and stale beer. Aside from the foot-rails and spittoons, the barrooms of the west were devoid of furniture. There were no chairs or tables, seldom even coat-racks or hooks.

The Winnipeg bars were designed for but a single purpose — for stand-up drinking. Drinking was for the purpose of "getting drunk", almost never for relaxing conversation. For the congenially inclined, the grocery stores would have been preferable to the bars without the substantial savings in the cost of drinking; financial considerations made them doubly so.

The universal practice of treating, however, brought the problem of excessive drunkenness into the residential areas instead of confining it to the Main Street hotel strip. Grocery drinking with attendant rowdy behaviour, moreover, was done in full view of the women and children who were in and out of the stores on shopping excursions. Many a father who went down to the corner for a bag of potatoes returned listing badly to starboard from the alcoholic ballast he had taken aboard at the store. Clearly, in the eyes of the clergy, the whisky-selling grocers were an undermining force in the bosom of their parishes.

To the business community, the whisky-selling grocery stores were rat-holes down which their own profits drained. When hungover carpenters, bricklayers, plasterers, millwrights, and tinsmiths sent down to the grocer's for bottles of booze, productivity dropped, mistakes increased, and costly accidents multiplied. The workman who fell off a scaffold and broke a leg could be replaced, but the lost time and lost production caused by the accident was beyond recovery. There was hardly a building contractor, factory foreman, or material supplier in Winnipeg who would not have voted to outlaw the sale of booze in grocery stores.

To the pillars of the churches who dominated the banking, real estate, and retail business, booze was a double-pronged menace to the future of the city they loved. Neither the drinking workmen nor their families could really afford the luxury of drunkenness. If they did not need the money being spent on booze for food and clothing, they needed it to provide housing accommodation for themselves and their families, if, as, and when their families were brought to the west or otherwise acquired.

The merchants in turn needed the steady flow of cash across their counters to satisfy their creditors back east. Despite the boom, the newly established storekeepers lived in a perpetual credit squeeze. The bulk of the retail trade was done on credit and few retailers had the resources required by the type of business they were in. It frequently happened that the more business they did the more serious their capital shortage became. At the height of the boom, a dozen butcher shops took an advertisement in the *Winnipeg Times* to announce that beginning at once none of them would do any more business on credit.[20] Clearly under boom conditions carrying the accounts of even reliable customers was a problem. When too much pay of too many customers disappeared into the saloons, accounts receivable were transformed into bad debts.

The financiers saw the problem somewhat differently. What the west needed was not consumer spending alone but rapidly increasing supplies of long-term credit which would finance the construction of all the immense new warehouses, factories, and commercial and office buildings the city needed. Winnipeg's reputation as a shrine to Bacchus, coupled with the disreputable appearance of many of its boozeries, to say nothing of its streets, reflected an image ill-designed to attract prudent investment capital. It was no accident, therefore, that when the first Temperance campaign was organized by the clergy it drew enthusiastic response from the Winnipeg business community and was applauded by the newspapers. In the years that followed, as the Temperance movement became a crusade for total Prohibition, business and the press never wavered in their support.

No one, so far as can be discovered, ever attempted to tot up Winnipeg's booze bill during the first great boom. Certainly it must have been a town with a monumental thirst. How else could the doubling of the number of hotel bars between 1880 and 1881 be explained? That thirst was the result, in part at least, of the descent upon the town of thousands of building tradesmen from Ontario who had been lured west by reports of wages of upwards of five dollars a day. Many left their families at home in the east and intended to return when construction ended for the winter. Many others were young single men, free of parental restraints for the first time. Such was the incredible housing famine in Winnipeg that the only escape from the overcrowded lodging houses was into the brothels, poolrooms, and bars. It could well be argued that the Winnipeg thirst developed simply from the availability of standing room in the bars and poolrooms. In any event the first nose count and public-opinion poll of drinking Winnipeg was undertaken during the first week of June 1883 by the Rev. A. A. Cameron, a Baptist minister.[21]

During the preceding months there were intermittent agitations by the clergy to force the saloons to close earlier on Saturday nights. When they stayed open until midnight and later, far too many of the pew holders were still too drunk on Sunday morning to make it to church with their families. The Rev. Mr. Cameron decided to find out for himself what was going on at the bars on Saturday night and did a spot check of no less than thirty of them. He found them jammed with thirsty patrons struggling to hold places at the bar long enough to be served and get their drinks inside them before being jostled aside. By actual count, Cameron reported that the drinkers ranged in numbers from twenty to thirty in the smaller places to over a hundred and fifty in the larger hotels. When his count reached one thousand he called it a night, with two-thirds of the bistros still unvisited. As he questioned the drinkers Cameron noted a curious unanimity in their responses. Why were they content to spend their Saturday nights in such vile surroundings, placing their very souls in jeopardy? "Where else," they asked, "is there to go, what else is there to do?" The answers, of course, were "nowhere" and "nothing". These answers provided the Rev. Mr. Cameron with a topic for a sermon the following week. If Christian Winnipeg was to save its sons from lives of drunken debauchery, and their souls from the devil, the churches must do something to provide alternative recreational facilities to those being supplied by the bars and pool rooms. His message went unheeded, of course, but the conditions he publicized were an important factor in getting the first ecumenical movement in the west off the ground.

Some weeks prior to Cameron's survey, the Manitoba branch of the Dominion Temperance Alliance had held a meeting at which representatives of both the Roman Catholic and the Anglican churches attended along with the Evangelical Protestants. Such Protestant luminaries as Dr. D. M. Gordon and Dr. C. P. Pitblado for the Presbyterians, Dr. J. B. Silcox for the Congregationalists, and Dr. W. L. Rutledge and the Rev. J. E. Starr for the Methodists, were joined by Archbishop Taché and Father Patrick Cowley for the Roman Catholics and Canon Matheson and Archdeacon Pinkham for the Anglicans. With complete harmony and unanimity they worked out a Temperance program to press upon the provincial government.

The ecumenical program called for early closing of the bars on Saturday evening to provide adequate overnight sobering-up time, and amendment of the licensing regulations to restrict the whisky trade to legitimate hotels. They wanted any licensed hotel to contain a minimum of twenty rooms, and to qualify, a room had to have a minimum of one hundred square feet and an outside window. They asked for an end to grocery-store whisky selling, and provision for interdicting confirmed drunkards and for cancellation of licences for cause. They also wanted the number of licences granted limited to one for every five hundred inhabitants.

The submission of the Temperance advocates was endorsed by the government licence commissioners, and when the constitutional tangle over jurisdiction was ironed out some years later most of the reforms they asked for were adopted, at least in part. On one point, however, the Manitoba government would give no ground. It refused to further the cause of Temperance by limiting the number of hotels, particularly in the country. The small-town hotels were vital to the settlement of the surrounding farmland. Before the branch lines were extended from the mainlines, many settlers lived fifteen to twenty miles from a rail point. Given the climate of the prairies, overnight accommodation for both man and beast was a categorical imperative. So thinly spread, however, was the farm population that no small-town hotel could have survived for long on the room trade of the settlers. Bar profits were conceded to be absolutely essential to keep the hotels in business. Unhappily, many of the small-town hotel bars turned out to be as great a threat to both the moral and the financial well-being of their communities as those in Winnipeg were.

Nevertheless the ecumenical Temperance movement of 1883 did succeed in supplying the pressure which in the end blotted out some of the worst aspects of uncontrolled boozing. That the movement itself failed to survive cannot be attributed to lack of conviction in the cause, or discouragement with their achievement. It was blown apart by the Protestant-Catholic hatreds that developed over the famous Manitoba Schools Question.

The collapse of the boom did not reduce Winnipeg to anything approaching an enclave of sobriety, but it did put half the hotels out of business and set events in motion which reduced the booze problem to more manageable proportions. A sharp drop in wage rates, from five dollars a day in 1882 to two dollars a day in 1883, was fatal to the smaller hotels. There was a lot less money in circulation, and the influx of seasonal workers slowed to a trickle. The Canadian Pacific Railway, until 1883, had used Winnipeg as a kind of sorting pen for construction materials, construction crews, and incoming settlers. By 1883 it was running its trains through to Regina and Calgary, setting off construction booms there and easing the demand for hotel space in Winnipeg. Many of the hotels that were thrown up in preceding years had been as rickety in their financing as they were in structure. The summer of 1883 was enlivened by pitched battles on Main Street between rival bailiffs seeking to seize hotel furniture on behalf of rival creditors.[22] The hotels, even more than the commercial establishments, were numbed by the severe credit freeze that followed the collapse of the real estate boom.

The long depression which settled over the west following the collapse of the Winnipeg boom strengthened rather than weakened the Temperance movement. Most of the itinerant construction workers disappeared and their places were taken by family men who settled permanently in the main centres. There they worked for low wages and frequently suffered long sieges of winter unemployment. Where it had once been argued that the community could not afford the wastage of money spent on booze, the argument was now brought down to a very personal level. The workman who could not resist dropping into the saloon on payday might quite literally be taking food off the family table. So in times of low economic activity the clergymen became more and more concerned with the social evils of boozing and less concerned with the sinful aspects.

The conversion from Temperance to Prohibition was still somewhat in the future, and the emphasis was on education and ameliorative measures rather than toward government coercion. Vigorous efforts were made to get the church-going drinkers to sign total abstinence pledges and to carry a pledge card to help beat off friends seeking to lure them into bars. No record was kept of the number of pledges signed, kept or broken. But the campaign could hardly have been an outstanding success. It was followed by one to get the church-going drinkers to join the Anti-Treating League. Membership was free, and all a drinker had to do was sign a pledge to stop accepting proffered drinks at the bars and to stop buying drinks for others. Nothing much came of that campaign, either, and it, like the total abstinence pledge, was filed and forgotten when the drive for Prohibition got into high gear.

The law
and the prophets

When the time came for Sir John A. Macdonald to sit back and contemplate his nation-building handiwork he must have felt a certain kinship with the apartment-dwelling father whose small daughter won a pony in a raffle. When the euphoria passed both faced the most compelling questions: How are we going to keep it, and who is going to look after it? For Sir John A. the problems attached to looking after the 2,300,000 square miles of territory he had acquired from the Hudson's Bay Company were as vexing as any that could

confront an apartment-dwelling pony winner. There may even have
been times when he would have been tempted to trade the whole of
the prairie west for a Shetland pony.

The bungled madhouse that had developed on the Red River in
1870 would have driven a sober prime minister to drink. The Riel
business was barely out of the way when other trouble erupted
farther west. American traders had brazenly moved into Canadian
territory with their whisky forts. American wolfers had hunted
down and murdered Canadian Indians. Here and there isolated
homesteaders were terrorized by wandering bands of Indians. From
the reports drifting back from the west, it was a moot point whether
the Indians would themselves be wiped out by smallpox and poisonous booze before they killed each other off in drunken orgies. The
Rev. John McDougall, the Methodist missionary, reported that in
the winter of 1873-4 there were forty-two fatalities among the
Blackfoot bands following drinking bouts.

Save for the scattered fur-trading posts between Manitoba and the
Rocky Mountains, western Canada was almost as empty in fact as it
was on the map. If the west was ever to be settled, some security for
the settlers and their property had to be provided, particularly if the
Indians were to be driven off their lands and onto reserves so that the
white settlers could occupy them. Sir John decided that a battalion
of soldiers on horseback would be about right for the job. He intro-
duced a bill to establish the North West Mounted Rifles in the spring
of 1873.

The news of Canada's intentions soon reached Washington, where
it set off protests in Congress and in the Washington press. What right
did Canada have to put an armed force on the American border? The
uneasiness was reflected in the Canadian Parliament. Sir John, in a
momentary flash of inspiration, grabbed his pen and stroked out the
words "Mounted Rifles" and inserted the words "Mounted Police".
The change of title was followed by changes in nomenclature.[1] The
lieutenant-colonel became a commissioner, superintendent-inspec-
tors replaced captains, sub-inspectors replaced lieutenants. Chief
constables were edited in and sergeants edited out, corporals became
constables, and privates were sub-constables. Rates of pay remained
the same — seventy-five cents a day for constables, fifty cents for
sub-constables, and up to $2,600 a year for the commissioner. The
men all got food, shelter, one uniform a year, and the right to a

160-acre land grant when their three-year enlistment expired.[2]

Whose idea it was to clothe the force in the brightest-coloured uniform imaginable is not altogether clear. Colonel P. Robertson-Ross is reported to have recommended the scarlet tunics because the red coats worn by the Wolseley Expedition had particularly impressed the natives. In view of the tight-fistedness of early governments with public funds for expenditures in the west, a more likely explanation is that there was a surplus stock of red coats on hand in the quartermaster's stores, leftovers from some British regiment.

Though the Canadian government was prepared to change names to placate the Americans, it was clearly not prepared to compromise on things that mattered. The make-up of the North West Mounted Police was as thoroughly military as the North West Mounted Rifles would have been. The first Mounted Police Commissioner, Lt.-Col. George A. French, was a graduate of Sandhurst, Woolwich, and the Royal Irish Constabulary. Major J. M. Walsh, the acting adjutant, had served in the Prescott Cavalry Regiment. Superintendent C. F. Young was an officer in the 50th Foot Guards. Colonel J. F. Macleod was the assistant brigade major of the Wolseley Expedition. The recruits who were signed on in Ontario were, where possible, men with British military experience or Canadian militia training. That was a mistake the force laboured under for a decade. The first force was largely a collection of greenhorns, totally unaccustomed to hardship or hard work, and lacking in whatever qualities it took to take the bitter western weather in stride. In their subsequent reports, one superintendent after another stressed the need for recruiting strong-backed farm boys who were accustomed to outside labour under adverse conditions and who knew how to take proper care of horses.

This military force in everything but name — 150 strong at first — made its way in 1873 to Fort Garry over the old Dawson Trail and spent the winter in training there. The following spring it joined a second group that came by train from Toronto via the United States to Fort Dufferin south of Winnipeg. The great trek westward to Fort Whoop-up began with 318 men, 339 horses, 142 oxen, an assortment of arms, a herd of beef for meat, and 73 wagons filled with other supplies. It would be difficult to imagine anything quite as preposterous as this tenderfoot army setting out to wipe out the far-flung whisky trade with the Indians, to protect the border from incursions of American outlaws, to keep peace between warring

Indian factions, and to persuade the Indians to hive themselves away on special reserves to be created for them. Yet on every count the North West Mounted Police accomplished its objectives, and did so with amazing ease and completeness.

The minuscule size of the force in contrast to the size of its assignment was an early indication of the lack of comprehension on the part of eastern politicians of the expanse of their western domain. It was a deficiency that survived to exacerbate east-west relations for fifty years. In the two decades after the force was established, the debates on N.W.M.P. appropriations were frequently highlighted by demands from eastern members for a reduction in the size of the force and equally insistent demands from prairie members for an increase in its strength.[3]

The eight-hundred-mile safari from Dufferin to Whoop-up is an authentic Canadian saga of hardship and frustration that has been told and retold. It was in the last stage of this journey that the force came upon Jerry Potts, the Scots-Piegan half-breed guide who probably contributed as much to the pacification of the west as all the N.W.M.P. commissioners combined. Without him as guide, interpreter, and counsellor, a much different story might have been told. It was Potts who led the Mounties to their primary objective, the trading post at Fort Whoop-up where the American traders plied the Indians with whisky in exchange for their furs. The whisky traders had been warned of the approach of the force and the mere word that it was coming was enough to frighten them clear out of the country. The war against the American invaders was won without a shot being fired.

One of Adam Archibald's first acts as lieutenant-governor had been to pass an order-in-council establishing total Prohibition in the Northwest Territories. Due to some error in form, the order was declared *ultra vires* and had to be re-enacted in 1873.[4] It gave anybody who found anybody anywhere in the Territories with whisky in his possession the power to confiscate and destroy the booze and to arrest the owner. Few more all-encompassing statutes have ever been passed in Canada, even in wartime emergencies. But the Mounties' efforts to enforce this law were a different matter. In that undertaking they lost the war itself and most of the battles in it. Those who wanted alcoholic beverages, and they were many in the frontier west, readily found the ways and means to get them.

Failure to enforce Prohibition can by no means be blamed on the

Mounties alone. It is quite conceivable that the force could have enforced the Order-in-Council of 1873. By the time the N.W.M.P. were settled into their duties, however, the 1873 Order-in-Council was replaced by the Northwest Territories Act of 1875, in which section 74 covered the control of intoxicating liquors. Importation, sale, or possession of liquor was still under a general prohibition, except when imported under permit from the lieutenant-governor. Conceivably, this exception might well have permitted the establishment of saloons, but the authorities interpreted the exception as applying strictly to liquor imported by individuals for personal consumption. Otherwise possession of liquor was still prohibited, as, of course, was sale within the Territories.

As the control system evolved, so did the means of circumventing the regulations. In the settlements that were springing up everywhere, the registration desks of the frontier hotels doubled as bars. Under the permit system neither the town drunks nor the incoming settlers had much difficulty in slaking their thirsts. When drinking got out of hand, as it frequently did, a general clamour was set off for stricter law enforcement.

Building forts, running off the whisky traders, sorting out the Indians, and getting a border patrol system in operation occupied the Mounties for their first half-decade. During that period the white population within the N.W.M.P. jurisdiction rose steadily from a bare five thousand to better than ten thousand. Once most of the Indians were safely out of the way, the Mounties evolved into symbols of security for the white settlers who were taking up the land. They kept the peace in the towns, hunted down horse thieves, arrested settlers who set grass fires, broke up fights, rounded up and jailed lunatics, and ran confidence men and common thugs out of the country. Overriding all else in consumption of time and effort, however, was the enforcement of Prohibition. Booze was not only a working preoccupation, it was a continuing disruptive element within the force itself. When the Mounties were not chasing whisky smugglers across the prairies, arresting white men caught plying Indians with alcohol, or riding herd on disorderly drunks in the towns and villages, they were themselves getting roaring drunk in their barracks.[5] On one occasion in 1886, "H" Troop in Lethbridge got its back pay and went on a prolonged collective binge that terrorized the town. There was another time at Fort Macleod when a couple of drunken Mounties who had run out of money held up a visitor from Saskatoon on the main street of the town, relieved him of his wallet, and went back to the hotel to continue their spree.[6]

In carrying out their diverse duties the Mounties were aided by a curiously all-embracing legal code. The North West Mounted Police was not only an enforcer of the law, it was the law. The force could search and make arrests without warrant. A prisoner so arrested was brought before a senior officer who could try him at once or remand him in custody. If convicted the accused would be incarcerated in the cells of the Mounted Police barracks for the duration of his sentence. So well did the force combine the roles of policeman, judge, and jailer that they transformed the so-called wild west into an idyllic countryside almost devoid of violent crime.[7]

The respect, the genuine regard the homesteaders had for the Mounties, in all respects save one, was universal. Their efforts to enforce the unenforceable liquor laws brought them into contempt in the towns and villages and seriously undermined the relations between the force and the people. It was not so much that the prohibitory statute was opposed by the majority of the people; indeed, it was probably favoured by most of the homesteaders from Ontario and by many of the Protestant majorities of the urban centres. But the law rubbed abrasively on racist sores with which most Anglo-Saxon settlers were afflicted. Prohibition was all right for Indians, but it was clearly an affront to the racial superiority of the "whites" — even if they had no desire to drink. There were those who would concede that it was also fitting to impose Prohibition on the Ruthenians and other sub-species who turned to mayhem and worse under the influence of alcohol. But to treat a white man like an Indian!

In most public agitations a financial interest can usually be uncovered by diligent digging. With the Mounties it lay right in the open for everybody to see. The word for it was "moieties". In order to ease the task of law enforcement the Government of Canada had made provision for the payment of moieties — one-half the fine — to informers.[8]

The reward-paying to informers might have raised no hackles if the payments had not gone to the Mounties who laid the charges or made the arrests. Fines in liquor cases ordinarily ran from fifty to one hundred dollars, from which the informing constable's share

would be equal to a couple of months' pay. That, in the eyes of the
drinkers, could be incentive enough to make a recreant policeman
bend the truth or even fabricate evidence. The Mounted Police inspectors themselves recognized the risk and ultimately recommended the abolition of moiety distribution to policemen. On the
other hand, without some public assistance in obtaining information, the force was spread so thinly over the prairies that wholesale
violation of the law could have occurred without their discovering it.
But here too avarice might have been a motivation behind the words
passed to the Mounties by one settler informing against his neighbour. The combination of moiety payments and the prosecutor-
judge-jailer role of the Mounties led to the first public protest meeting in the Territories at Calgary in December of 1884.[9]

Earlier in the year the Rev. J. W. Dyke, the pastor of the Methodist Church, had preached a couple of fire-eating sermons against
the whisky trade. He described the bars of Calgary as an unmitigated
evil and the vilest curse of citizenship. Taking dead aim at the agitation to repeal the permit system, he said that adoption of a saloon-
licensing system would "take bread from the mouths of children . . .
incite murder . . . loose a foul viper's brood of wretched evil". He
urged his listeners to enlist in the battle against the liquor trade "for
the sake of your wives, children, God, the church and humanity".
The newly established *Calgary Herald* gave the Reverend Mr. Dyke
two full columns on its front page.[10]

The speech undoubtedly caught the eye of Colonel William
Herchmer, who was in charge of the local Mounted Police detachment. A series of raids on both hotels and private homes was staged
that fall and some stiff sentences were handed out. As one element in
the town burned inwardly over public boozing, another boiled over
with rage against the Mounties for trying to enforce the liquor law.
Colonel Herchmer was set upon one night and beaten unconscious
as he passed the old Calgary House. Calmer elements, led by Mayor
George Murdock, called the entire town, all 450 residents, to attend
a letting-off-steam meeting at the Boynton Hall.[11]

After a night of speech-making the capacity crowd got around to
passing a resolution for dispatch to the Territorial Council. Among
the points carried unanimously by the meeting were: Great injustice
was caused by the arbitrary searching of private homes by policemen
looking for liquor; as a result of giving informers half the fine a great

deal of perjury was being committed. The demands of the meeting included: That no member of the N.W.M.P. should have power to enter a private dwelling without a warrant; that all civil power be removed from the police and a stipendiary magistrate be appointed; that no member of the N.W.M.P. be permitted to obtain an informer's share of fines imposed. The Territorial Council yielded on the second demand and appointed a stipendiary magistrate, who turned out to be a near-despot who jailed the local editor and a member of the town council and appointed a second mayor and a second town council to office. On the other points — search and seize without warrant, and the payment of moieties to policemen — the government refused to budge.[12]

Moieties or no, there is no doubt that the Mounties presided over one of the most tranquil areas extant. In their annual reports the commissioners and superintendents seldom found anything interestingly violent to comment upon. A reading of the annual reports of the commissioners quickly demonstrates the trivial nature of the law-breaking with which the Mounties had to contend once they had the Indians filed away on the reserves.[13] It is clear that what were later identified in N.W.M.P. statistics as "offenses against religion and morals" made up well over half the work the Mounties were called upon to do. In 1884, for example, liquor offences alone accounted for 257 of the 596 cases prosecuted by the Mounties. The figures themselves are striking proof of the law-abiding nature of the west when, with a strength of three hundred-odd, the Mounties made an average of only two arrests per man during the year.

Nevertheless, as long as weather permitted, the Mounties had more than enough work to occupy their time. They organized patrols that took them back and forth across the prairie in all directions. They sealed off the old trails over which the whisky traders brought their contraband into the country. They assisted the new settlers and ranchers in locating livestock. They made enough arrests to demonstrate to the population that the laws would be enforced. Once winter set in and the force was idle in barracks, it was another story. As Kipling once noticed, "single men in barracks don't grow into plaster saints." Neither did Mounted Policemen in any of the western forts. They were, in fact, far from the knights errant in scarlet tunics their latter-day aggrandizers made them out to be. The individual Mounties had as much trouble with booze, and with sex,

as any of the Kipling heroes. Composed as the force was of inexperi-
enced greenhorns, many of them still in their teens, it was inevitable
that the carousing of the Mounties would attract public attention,
and questions were frequently asked in Parliament. The following
comments are by Sir John A. Macdonald to the session of 1881:

> The men now receive 40 cents per day during the first year
> and 50 cents per day during the other four years of ser-
> vice. The old rates were 50 cents . . . and 75 cents. . . . The
> pay was originally very large [*sic*] fixed at a time when it
> was new, and when the difficulties of going through the
> unknown country were perhaps exaggerated. But the pay
> was so good that there was a rush of men to the force; we
> found great pressure brought to send up gentlemen's sons
> — educated men of broken habits — and the force was to
> some extent made to serve the purpose of an inebriate
> asylum. . . . There is still a good deal of drinking. . . .

The Prime Minister went on to hope that the appointment of a
cadre of disciplinarians to the higher command of the force would
bring its drinking problem down to manageable size. But from the
number of eruptions during the next decade, the internal struggle
with the demon rum was far from over. Nicholas Flood Davin reported drunken orgies at the N.W.M.P. barracks in Regina in 1883
and continued his attacks on the force in Parliament. In February
1886, the *Macleod Gazette* protested:

> For two or three days the shouts of drunken men have
> disturbed the quiet citizens. The pistol act was repeated
> but this time it was some policeman on a painting expedi-
> tion. But really, this blazing away with a pistol whenever a
> man gets drunk, whether it be in the hands of a policeman
> or a civilian, is getting monotonous and must be put down
> with a high hand.

It is abundantly clear from these and other references that both
the tastes and the appetites of the North West Mounted Police were
in deep conflict with the objectives of the Territories Prohibition
Act. And the act itself was in conflict with the principle so strongly

held by the government of Manitoba, that the urban hotels required what profit they could make from selling whisky to balance the losses they took on room rental and meals. The first Dewdney administration of the Northwest Territories certainly wanted to do everything possible to speed the settlement of the west. Whether by accident or by design, the type of liquor permit system it devised made enforcement by the Mounties almost impossible, even for a force dedicated to that end, which it certainly was not.

Under the revised system, upon the obtaining of a permit a Territorial resident could send to Winnipeg or Brandon for a quart, half-gallon, or gallon of whisky, rum, or brandy. The permit was neither numbered nor dated. When the expressman delivered the booze the customer could either drink it at home or deposit it at the hotel bar, where it might be handier for casual nipping. It was essential, as proof against prosecution, for the permit to accompany the liquor. When the booze was gone the permit was retained and so, frequently, was the bottle. The latter could be filled with liquor imported by the barrel by smugglers from the United States and sold for about half the price of the bottled stuff from Manitoba — one dollar a quart compared with three dollars. The permits and bottles could also be left at the bars so that the hotel keeper would always have enough paper on hand to cover all the stock the Mounties could find in his place.

So the hotel-building pattern which was established in Winnipeg was followed generally as the new towns sprang up along the C.P.R. tracks, and cities grew at Regina, Moose Jaw, and Calgary. None of the new towns bothered to hire town policemen, and there simply were not enough Mounties in the country to serve them all. The liquor law, therefore, was not something about which anybody was doing very much of anything. There was booze available, but on a quietly *sub rosa* basis, in all the hotels along the line. Unless nudged into action by the reverend clergy, the Mounties generally turned blind eyes to the small-town liquor traffic.

In the main the Mounties concentrated on the rum-runners who brought contraband into the Territories from Manitoba, North Dakota, or Montana. Incoming train passengers were patted for suspicious bulges, and unusually heavy baggage was opened and inspected. The penalty for being caught was loss of the liquor, which was poured down the drain. The largest hauls were made in the over-the-border trade, for across vast stretches of the prairie there was no place to hide when a Mounted Police patrol was attracted by the dust kicked up by a bull train laden with whisky. This happened frequently enough to make a show, statistically, in the tabulated reports of annual seizures. When such seizures were effected, regulations required that the liquor be taken to the nearest post, where it was spilled on the ground under supervision of superior officers.

There are widely believed legends in the west that in most of the Mounted Police posts the spilling was done in a carefully selected spot where earth-covered containers were previously installed to catch the booze. Such was the quality of the liquor sold in the west that nobody seemed overly concerned about drinking stuff that had filtered through a foot of mud and a couple of discarded horse blankets.[14]

In the earliest days of settlement, there was surprisingly little agitation over the liquor question on the part of the clergy in the Northwest Territories. One explanation may be that except for the wide-open boozing that went on in Regina, Moose Jaw, Medicine Hat, Lethbridge, Calgary, and Edmonton, drinking was not that important a problem in the rural areas. For one thing, the struggle to survive which the original homesteaders were waging was so bitter and prolonged that there was neither the time nor the inclination for drinking. With rare exceptions, the social gospel, the concern with earthly things, had not yet become an important aspect of Protestant preaching. The text for the sermons was invariably biblical, the content designed to reinforce faith in the dogma of the church. The focus, in short, was very sharply on the hereafter.[15]

Total abstinence was still very much a part of the Congregationalist, Methodist, Presbyterian, and Baptist faiths, at least as far as the clergy themselves were concerned. Certainly it was a behaviour pattern which they held out to their followers as a route to salvation. The thunderers against distilled damnation, such as Silcox and Cameron in Winnipeg, James Duncan and D. C. Johnson in Prince Albert, Charles McKillop in Lethbridge, and J. W. Dyke in Calgary, were the very odd exceptions. Indeed, there was an impression abroad that the church members took a rather dim view of ministers who concerned themselves with such mundane problems. In 1883, for example, Silcox preached sermons in which he denounced the theatre, the popular publishers, and the whisky trade, along with an attack on segregated prostitution. One of his followers wrote a letter to the *Times* in which he criticized Silcox and any other minister who wandered from strictly religious topics. It was not the function of any minister, he wrote, to seek to popularize himself with his congregation by becoming involved in social issues. Boozing in the larger towns was certainly an important, if neglected, social issue of the 1880s. It was so serious in Calgary that on one occasion the town council petitioned the Territorial Council to stop issuing permits to local people. In response the council did put Calgary out of bounds for some weeks. In general, expressed concern over the liquor problem came from the newspapers and the N.W.M.P., and in both cases the concern was related to the difficulty of enforcing the law rather than with boozing *per se*.

Commissioner Herchmer in his *Annual Report* for 1887 summed up the situation this way:

LIQUOR LAWS

The enforcement of the North-West prohibitory law is more difficult than ever, the sympathy of many of the settlers being generally against us in this matter. Large quantities of liquor have been seized and spilt, but a great deal more illicit liquor has undoubtedly been used under the cloak of the permit system. Liquor is run into the country in every conceivable manner, in barrels of sugar, salt, and as ginger ale, and even in neatly constructed imitation eggs, and respectable people, who otherwise are honest, will resort to every device to evade the liquor laws, and when caught they have generally the quantity covered by their permits. It is really curious the extraordinary length of time some holders of permits can keep their liquor.

The permit system should be done away with in the first place if the law is to be enforced, and the law itself should be cleared of the technicalities that have enabled so many to escape punishment this last year.

The importation and manufacture of a good article of lager beer, under stringent Inland Revenue regulations,

would, in my opinion greatly assist the satisfactory settlement of this vexed question. Nearly all the opprobrium
that has been cast upon the Police generally, and my
management in particular, can be directly traced to public
sentiment on the attempt to enforce this law.

By this time absolute power had been removed from the Mounties, a sprinkling of stipendiary magistrates was scattered through
the Territories, and there was a Territorial Court en Banc to hear
appeals from Mounted Police and magisterial decisions. The higher
courts all but destroyed the ability of the Mounties to enforce the
Prohibition law. The situation was described by Superintendent
J. H. McIllree of the Calgary detachment in his *Annual Report* of
1888:

There is no doubt that the time has arrived for some
change in the liquor laws. At the present time the existing
law is not obeyed or respected by the mass of the inhabitants of this part of the North-West. It is evaded and set at
naught by very many. The country has changed in so
many ways since the North-West Act was passed that I
consider it is necessary either to do one of two things — to
allow intoxicants into the Territories under licence or
otherwise, or to amend the Act so that its provisions
cannot be misinterpreted. At present in Calgary it is
almost impossible to get a conviction by a magistrate for
infractions of the North-West Territories Act sustained. In
the first place, every effort is made by the opposing counsel to have the conviction quashed on some error in form
of proceedings or legal technicality, which is often successful — indeed, is successful in every case where there is
the slightest error, though Section 100 of the Act states
that no seizure, prosecution, conviction or commitment
under the Act shall be invalid for want of form, so long as
the same is according to the true intent and meaning of
the Act. Then it has been ruled in the Supreme Court that
there is no penalty attached by the Act to "having liquor
in possession", and that if liquor is legally brought into
the Territories the holder can give his permit to whom he

pleases. Under these rulings it is almost impossible to get a conviction sustained.

The present law does not work as it should; certainly not in this section. Of course, everyone knows whisky is sold in nearly every saloon in Calgary. I see that a Calgary member in the Council Chamber at Regina stated the consumption of whisky in Calgary was fifty gallons a day. It may be so; I know there is a great deal consumed, and that the great mass of the inhabitants are in opposition to the law. We get no sympathy or assistance to uphold the law; on the contrary, every obstacle is put in our way. Every case of infraction of the North-West Territories Intoxicant Act that is brought to light is, of course, the work of members of our force. The local police take no notice of this liquor traffic. The saloons are searched at intervals, but every saloon has its hiding place, and if intoxicants are found a permit is at once produced, either in the saloon keeper's name or, what is just as good here, the name of one of his friends. My men, endeavouring to do their duty, are made a laughing stock of, and accordingly it is not a popular duty with them.

Since the 1st December, 1887, there have been seized and destroyed in this district 840 gallons of intoxicants. This does not include beer, of which some was spilt. Much of the liquor was good, coming from Montreal, and put up in half-gallon glass bottles. This amount of liquor destroyed represents a great waste of money. If the value of the liquor be taken, and to it added the value of vessels containing it, with freight charges, etc., it will be found to reach a large amount. If the existing law is to remain in force many alterations should be made, to enable those to whom the enforcement is entrusted to have a greater chance to secure convictions than at present. The evil is increasing rapidly and less regard is paid daily to the provisions of the Act. Under existing circumstances, there is not the slightest incentive for a policeman to try to do his duty in this particular. A man is looked upon as a martyr if he is arrested for a breach of the Act. The Act, if intended to be enforced, should be changed, so that its provisions

cannot be twisted and misinterpreted, and if the evidence
is sufficient to prove the offence there should be no loophole for the offender to escape.

The decade-long agitation of the Mounted Police for changes in
the liquor law that would make their job easier must surely be
unique in Canadian history. In other circumstances one might well
imagine an appropriate cabinet minister firing off a directive to the
force to stop complaining and get on with the job it was hired to do
and paid to do. Nothing like that happened, perhaps because the
authorities in Ottawa had no more sympathy with the Prohibition
statute than the Mounted Police themselves. It is interesting to
speculate what might have happened if the force had been as dominated by confirmed teetotallers as it was by confirmed drinkers.

The agitation of the Mounted Police against the liquor law serves
to highlight the sharp contrast which prevailed between conditions
in Manitoba and those in the Territories. By the end of the 1880s,
Manitoba settlements had begun to shed a good deal of their frontier
roughness. The towns were turning from mere concentration on
maintaining a subsistence economy to concern for the quality of life.
Though a compulsory school-attendance act would have to wait
until 1916, even the meanest hamlets of Manitoba now had their
own schools functioning under inspectors employed by the Department of Education.

Settlement in what was to become Saskatchewan and Alberta
lagged a full generation behind that in Manitoba. The population was
still floating and scattered. In Manitoba many of the towns had built
permanent churches and were served by resident clergymen. The
frontier tended to get along with student preachers, summer visitors,
and ministers who covered several communities. In Manitoba the
deeply held Temperance tenets of the Protestant clergymen were
moving beyond "Temperance" to the embracement of total Prohibition of alcohol as a solution to the booze problems which afflicted
most of the settlement. Just about every community had its town
drunk. The merchants had long since discovered that drinking
farmers were poor credit risks. In the period of poor crops through
which the province had passed, the economic loss of local purchasing
power to the whisky trade became a fetching Temperance argument.
At rock bottom, however, the most potent of all forces which

worked for Prohibition was religious conviction, and the stronger the Protestant denominations became in rural Manitoba the louder the agitation grew for some means of drying up the province.

In the Territories, however, there was no such organized group as the Dominion Temperance Alliance or the Women's Christian Temperance Union. And there was Prohibition, of a sort. All that was wrong was that it was a law with too many loopholes, and was getting only half-hearted enforcement from the only law-enforcement agency in the Territories. As previously noted, the Mounties, instead of vigorously enforcing the law, spent their time explaining why a policeman's lot was not a happy one.

What part the persistent agitation by the Mounted Police against the permit system had in its ultimate repeal is difficult to assess. But in 1891 the government did repeal the Prohibition section of the Northwest Territories Act, and turned responsibility for the liquor problem over to the Northwest Territories Council. In 1892 the council enacted regulations which permitted the establishment of licensed saloons and provided for the enforcement of closing laws and other regulations by Territorial liquor inspectors.

According to Commissioner Herchmer, things immediately went from bad to worse. Drunkenness increased everywhere. Under the permit system the saloons had exercised considerable caution in deciding to whom they would sell their booze. Because of the system of kicking back half the fines to informers, a strange customer in search of a drink was suspect until he could be vouched for. In addition the bartenders had tended to ease up on serving obvious drunks to avoid calling attention to their establishments. But with the new law, restraints were off, and the thorny problem of Indians becoming addicted to alcohol was intensified as half-breeds with the necessary cash were able to buy liquor for their Indian friends. As for enforcement, Superintendent Constantine of the Regina detachment made this comment in 1899:

LIQUOR LAW

The prevailing idea (no doubt largely inculcated by the reading of the ordinance) that the law regulates the sale of liquor and tends to the decrease of drunkenness is farcical to the last degree. It really seems to increase and encourage it. Where there is a policeman stationed who is certain to insist on prosecution, care is taken by the vendors of liquor, but where there is not, or when his back is turned, wholesale drunkenness goes on. More particularly during the autumn when the proceeds of the harvest are being sold and the chances of a rake-off are greater. That the system of inspection is so arranged as to prevent this is a comfortable fiction. The inspector* as a rule will not move until some one reports a breach of the ordinance, furnishing witnesses, &c. Then when all the work in connection with the case is done and some one else has to bear the so-called odium of the prosecution, the inspector may prosecute and incidentally collect fees for so doing.

Some of the lower class places are sanctuaries from arrest for vagrancy for characters who would otherwise find their way to jail if not provided with a refuge.

Wide-open boozeries had become general in most of the larger towns of the west by the time mass migration began with the turn of the century. The hotel saloons existed in a three-way enforcement vacuum. The casual neglect of the Mounties was matched by the lethargic enforcement by the hopelessly understaffed liquor police, and the local police, where they existed at all, fell naturally into an attitude of benign indifference. A local policeman, indeed, was near the bottom of the list of essential employees to be hired by most Territorial communities. Certainly he ranked far below the fire chief and the town clerk in importance. In any event he would probably be too occupied with his other multifarious duties to waste his time on the overloaded saloon patrons. There was one good thing about drunkenness in the eyes of the town constables: it was a problem that usually solved itself if it was ignored. The timid soul who became John L. Sullivan after tarrying at the bar would inevitably be ejected from the bistro by superior force. He might challenge everybody in sight on the street, but if left alone he would probably fall

---

*Once the new Territorial licensing law was enacted the Mounties turned their backs on the booze business. Enforcement of the Territorial ordinance became the responsibility of the Northwest Territories Liquor Inspectors. Only when drinking led to the commission of offences under the Criminal Code did the Mounties become involved.

down somewhere and lapse into unconsciousness. Usually, if it had rained recently, that would be in the mud hole where a sidewalk would have been, if the standard plank catwalk in front of the hotel had extended past the vacant lot next door to the store beyond, which it seldom, if ever, did.

The lesser breeds, and wife-beaters

In its lack of social sensitivity, the whisky era of the prairie provinces could be compared unfavourably with almost any era in the history of western civilization. Insensitivity has always been a concomitant of frontier life; living so close to the minimum level of existence leaves little time for the tender emotions or the elevation of compassion to a significant level in human relationships. The bitterly prolonged struggle for survival in the root-hog-or-die economy could well have blunted whatever social consciousness the settlers had when they came to the west, and understandably so.

The crudeness of any environment must eventually rub off on the inhabitants. The crudeness of the prairie environment could hardly have been exaggerated. For the settlers within the Palliser Triangle, the most fortunate were those who, in the beginning, chose the sod huts for homes instead of trying to carpenter regular houses together out of the green and rough lumber available. The huts were made by piling up squares of hand-cut prairie sod and roofed with more sod laid on poplar poles, and they provided warmth against the winter. The ship-lap shacks turned into wind-swept refrigerators with the first frosts.

City dwellings were not much of an improvement. They too were utterly inadequate to cope with the climate in an age before insulation was invented. Sanitary conditions within the towns verged on the unspeakable. Herds of pigs wandered at large and cows grazed the streets and lanes. The disposal of stable manure was still a vexing problem long after the towns had evolved into cities. Typhoid fever was endemic to all the cities, and hospitals were filled to capacity every fall as the water supplies became contaminated. Fear of small-pox hung like a pall over the settlements, and such was the level of medical diagnosis that in Winnipeg children with chicken pox were often sent to the smallpox pesthouse.[1] When delirium seized the stricken patients they were chained to their beds and at least one woman was burned to death when her bedding caught fire from an overheated stove. Medical services were almost non-existent on the frontier; only recent graduates or aging alcoholics among the medics would have exchanged a lucrative practice in Ontario or Minnesota for what the Canadian west had to offer.

Within the cities and towns, physical conditions improved as rapidly, of course, as an energetic, enterprising, and profit-mad populace could make them. As quickly as they could afford it, the merchants moved out of their crude frame houses in the business districts into substantial brick houses on the outskirts. Downtown streets bloomed with brick and stone structures and the newly rich gave free rein to an appetite for conspicuous expenditure on the trappings of affluence.

In the sharpest of contrast, the social consciousness of rich and poor alike developed at a snail's pace, if in fact it developed at all. Indeed the Victorian era was drawing rapidly toward its close before the first signs of humanitarian concerns became identifiable in western Canada. Until then these concerns, if they existed at all, were well hidden by the militant Protestant pietists who were determined that their behavioural code would be enforced on the whole population for their own good, whether they wanted it or not. And it was done with the conviction that theirs was the only true religion and that they, as Anglo-Saxon Protestants, were God's chosen people, chosen to have sway over all other lesser breeds beyond the pale.[2] When the Reverend Mr. Silcox thundered from his Congregationalist pulpit that the Anglo-Saxon race ruled the world because it had maintained its racial purity, neither his congregation nor his fellow ministers considered entering any kind of a caveat. This attitude was reinforced by the immigration of thousands of Orangemen from Ontario, and by even greater numbers of equally devout Methodists, Baptists, and Presbyterians from the United States.

Where the Roman Catholics fitted into all this is difficult to determine. As the settlements grew and newspapers sprang up, the complete dominance of Protestantism became very clear indeed. Almost without exception, the newspapers gave their space freely to the Protestant churches and secret societies, such as the Masonic Order, the Loyal Orange Lodges, the Foresters, the Knights of Pythias, etc. Any preacher who would take the trouble to write out his sermon for the local editors would have it reproduced, sometimes verbatim. On the other hand the only time the existence of the Roman Catholics was noticed was when a bishop or other high-ranking cleric turned up at a Temperance mass meeting. They did this infrequently because Temperance crusading was, by and large, a Protestant monopoly.

From the attitude of the Protestant clergy toward boozing, it might have been concluded that "original sin" was not partaking of the fruit of the tree of knowledge but converting the fruit into potable alcohol. The newspapers, again almost without exception, faithfully mirrored the clergy in their attitude toward strong drink. As the clergy moved gradually from a Temperance to a Prohibition stance, so did the newspapers. The Protestants were preoccupied with whisky-drinking to the exclusion of all other social problems. There is indeed little evidence of anybody's interest in, or even awareness of, any other social problems, save, of course, prostitution which was regarded as a subsidiary of the booze problem.

From a social point of view, the frontier west would compare unfavourably with Dickens' London. The west did not even have workhouses to which the destitute could be sent. When there was no work, people went hungry, except during periods of mass winter unemployment when the cities did provide handouts of food. There were no school attendance laws and children could be put to work at any age. Such things as Juvenile Courts were unknown, and in 1907 a twelve-year-old boy who had been sentenced to two years' imprisonment at hard labour arrived in Edmonton from Regina to begin his term.[3] Lunacy was treated as a crime. People with mental disorders were arrested, charged in open court with being lunatics at large, and sentenced to indefinite confinement in the jails. Suicides were reported in gory details, along with the names of the deceased and speculation about the reason for the act.

In no other area was the insensitivity of the times more apparent than in the attitudes of the Anglo-Saxon majority to the other races, beginning with the Indians. The original concept of rounding up the Indians and imprisoning them on reserves was borrowed from the Americans, who had been persecuting the natives and confiscating their lands for a hundred years. When the Canadian Indians wandered off the newly established reserves they became the target of abuse from the recently arrived white settlers. The *Macleod Gazette*, voice of the newcomers to southern Alberta, concluded in 1887 that the reserve idea was all wrong, not because it segregated the Indians on land of their own but because it did not do the job properly. There was no law, it complained, that would keep the Indians on the reserves. They insisted on visiting the areas of settlement, where they fell in with "degraded whites". They were an unmitigated nuisance for they frequently killed ranchers' cattle, trafficked in prostitution with their women, and disturbed the peace and quiet of the towns. What should be done, in the opinion of the *Gazette,* was for the government to gather up all the Indians in the Territories, find a remote area somewhere north of Red Deer, and convert it into a reserve where all the Indians could be sequestered permanently, far from civilization.

In 1889 the Indians were still hanging around the cities, and the murder of an Indian prostitute in Calgary served to underline the rancorous attitude of the whites toward the Indians. William Fisk, a local blacksmith turned gambler, had, at the end of a three-day drunk, murdered an Indian prostitute identified only as Rosalie. The bestial nature of the killing had those privy to it comparing it with the Jack-the-Ripper cases. It was indeed, as the *Weekly Herald* described it, "a murder most foul" which was much too revolting for the testimony at the trial to be published.

Fisk was a member of a highly respected Ontario family but was himself of little account. His family retained Frank Tyrrell, a noted eastern criminal lawyer with twenty-one murder acquittals to his credit, to defend him. In Calgary, when Fisk was ordered to trial for the murder, there was considerable public grumbling over the laying of a murder charge against a white man when the deceased was "only an Indian". When the time came to bury Rosalie, who was a Roman Catholic, the local priest refused to allow interment to take place in the Roman Catholic cemetery because "she had died in sin". The Indian Affairs Department took over, provided a handsome coffin, and buried her in the Protestant cemetery.[4]

In his opening statement to the jury the crown prosecutor, J. R. Costigan, taking note of public opinion, castigated those who subscribed "to the doctrine being enunciated in certain quarters that Rosalie was only a squaw and that her death did not matter much". He urged the jury to ignore such a horrible belief. Rosalie, he said, was a human being and very dear to her mother and father, and she was a Christian into the bargain.

From the evidence adduced at the trial, there was not a flicker of doubt of Fisk's guilt. When the jury came into the courtroom after being locked up for the previous night and announced its verdict of "not guilty" the judge was so shocked he refused to accept it. He sent the jurors back to reconsider. When they came back they reported being hopelessly split, so they were discharged and a new trial was ordered. In the interim the *Calgary Tribune* and the *Edmonton Bulletin* took turns blasting the jury for bringing the entire judicial process into disrepute. The *Tribune*, on the eve of Fisk's second trial, wrote a long editorial which began:

> The idea that seems to possess the minds of some people because a crime or an offense is committed against an Indian, therefore the crime is lesser, is inhuman in the

extreme. . . . The life of that unfortunate girl will have to be answered for by some one before the Great Judge, before whom all must appear.

The *Calgary Herald,* being more restrained, said only that the tragic event was just more proof of the absolute necessity of keeping the Indians out of the cities and towns. For one thing, they did not spend enough money to make their patronage worth while. It concluded that some strict permit system must be devised so that the Indians could not leave the reserves without permission of those in charge.

At Fisk's second trial Judge Rouleau in his opening charge echoed the prosecutor's appeal at the previous trial, that prejudice against the Indians should be disregarded. This time the jury paid attention and brought in a verdict of manslaughter, for which Fisk was sent to prison for fourteen years at hard labour. The Calgary Jack-the-Ripper case was one of the few occasions when the white establishment raised their voices on the western frontier on behalf of the Indians.

As a general rule, the Indians were ignored by press and pulpit except when the home missionaries for the Catholic and Protestant churches became embroiled in arguments over whose school the reserve children should attend.

The favourite whipping-boys of the media, though the churches ignored them, were the Chinese. The Chinese, who had been imported to build the Canadian Pacific Railway, were treated with contemptuous brutality. "Cleaning out the Chinks" became a common phrase of the small-town toughs and livery-stable loafers. When they got sufficiently imbued with whisky courage, they would gang up in an invasion of a Chinese restaurant or laundry and wreck the place, and in the riot that developed it was usually the Chinese who were arrested.

The teamsters' union at Fernie once threatened its members with expulsion if they were caught eating in a restaurant employing Chinese help.[5] One of the early laws passed by Saskatchewan when it achieved provincial status banned the employment of white women in "any establishment operated by a Chinaman".[6] A Moose Jaw restaurant owner challenged the law and carried it to the Supreme Court of Canada, which upheld the law. Lethbridge and

Medicine Hat both had regulations forbidding the employment of
Chinese or Japanese on civic works. As late as 1907, the *Edmonton
Journal,* could carry a long exposé on life in Chinatown in Van-
couver which led off with this paragraph:

> Let not the sympathy of the tenderhearted be aroused by
> these poor Chinks. They do not live like rats from force of
> circumstances. They prefer the stench and filth of their
> vile surroundings. They prefer the squalor because it is
> cheaper to live in filth than in cleanliness.[7]

A month later, the *Lethbridge Herald* attacked the Chinese in this
editorial:

> The Alberta Government would be well advised if it
> passed legislation making it impossible for Japanese and
> Chinese to vote in this province. Make these yellow men
> realize they are not going to have any influence on our
> affairs. They have no right to compete with white labor
> and they have no right to compete with white voters.

Only a small step above the Chinese in the Canadian pecking order
were the newly arrived immigrants from central Europe, identified
usually as Ruthenians or Galicians. Most of the time they were
treated by the press as non-persons. Thus, when the *Lethbridge
News* published the casualty list of the Frank Slide in May of 1903, it
named the miners who had lost their lives and "10 foreigners, names
unknown". Nobody bothered with the names of foreigners. The
Medicine Hat News always played the stories concerning foreigners
for laughs:[8]

> Several Galicians rounded up over the week-end for being
> drunk and disorderly were fined $3 each. A court observer
> who tried to pronounce their names put his jaw out of
> joint.

The life style of the Ruthenians became the concern of the
Women's Christian Temperance Union as well as of the newspapers.
At the 1905 convention of the W.C.T.U. the Manitoba branch intro-

duced a resolution calling attention to child marriages among certain colonies of Galicians and Poles:

> There is a regular traffic between the would-be grooms and the fathers of the children whereby the wife seeker can have the pick of the family for prices ranging from $25 to $100. The children have nothing to say and are put up for auction to the highest bidder.
>
> What is most distressing is that these practices have the approval of the churches because they are sanctified at the altar. It is said that in European countries from which these people come the practice of selling the bride to the groom is a very usual one and is responsible for much of the depravity that is prevalent among these people. In Canada are wanted neither the morals nor the ideals which exist among the debased populations of Europe.[9]

It was the accepted custom of the newspapers to identify nationalities in all reports of unfavourable circumstances. On the other hand, on heroic occasions the British nationality of the heroes was brought suitably to the fore. In 1909 the *Edmonton Bulletin* reported a terrible collision in the English Channel with considerable loss of life. The headline atop page one read: "British Pluck in Hour of Danger." When the *Titanic* was sunk on her maiden voyage in 1912, the *Saskatoon Star* headlined its story: "Men of Anglo-Saxon race face death in heroic manner".

As the migrants from central Europe began settling in numbers they were quickly caught up in the Temperance campaigns. Most of those of peasant stock had been accustomed in their homeland to making enough vodka for their own use from potatoes and grain screenings. They continued the practice in Canada and most of the stories about illegal stills dotting the countryside were ethnically slanted. To wit: "Mounties raid Galician still". In the uproar over enforcement of the liquor laws, special emphasis was always placed on the illegal activities of "the foreigners". That term, of course, included Jews, who eventually became the prime target for the racial jibes of the Prohibitionists.

The *Moose Jaw Times* summed up the drinking habits of the people in this way: "Among the Canadians there are many who do not drink at all. Among the French there are very few who do not drink. Among the Germans and Half-breeds there are absolutely none at all."

Though the extent of wife-beating is difficult to document because of the reluctance of the victims to press charges, there can be little doubt that the attitude of many of the Anglo-Saxons toward their womenfolk was somewhat less than knightly. The women on the Canadian frontier had no rights which their husbands, or anyone else for that matter, were bound to respect. The synonym for "wife" was chattel. There was no Dower Act. A husband could sell a farm on which his wife had shared the labour for a lifetime, pocket the entire proceeds, and walk out on his wife and family with impunity. On the other hand, if an abused wife chose to escape from a brutal husband in the company of another man, the husband could have the pair arrested and the wife returned by force. There were no laws for the protection of children, save for the law against incest. For tosspot husbands, wife-beating was a frequent offshoot of over-indulgence. Such stories as these are legion:

The school-teacher at the town of Duff, Saskatchewan, was walking home late one evening when he caught up with the father of one of his pupils lurching along under a too-heavy load of booze. He had fallen a couple of times and was obviously in need of assistance. The teacher provided a shoulder and helped the man to his house and in through the back door. It was well past supper time and the dishes had been cleared from the kitchen table. When the drunk spied the empty table he let out a roar at his wife:

"Where the hell is my supper?" he demanded. "I've told you a thousand times I want my supper when I get home!"

With that he staggered against the kitchen door, reached behind it and felt around until his hand grasped a three-foot length of rope with a couple of knots in one end which he kept on a hook on the door. Clasping the rope end in his fist, he lashed out at his wife and began to whip her around the back and head until the school-teacher interfered. The latter got the man outside, took the rope from him, and gave him a thorough thrashing. Then he departed with the warning that if the drunk ever laid a hand on his wife again he would administer a worse beating.

Did the warning have any effect? "I doubt it," the teacher recalled, "though he never did it again with that rope because I took it with me. But what astounded me about the whole performance was the way that woman behaved. When she saw him reaching for that rope she just turned her back and stood there, as if getting rope-whipped by a drunken husband was an everyday occurrence."[10]

Wife-beaters tended to be slow learners from all such experiences, as a case in Belmont, Manitoba, demonstrated. There the repeated acts of brutality of one of the citizens became such a public scandal that the more sober residents formed a posse, caught the wife-beater in the act, and gave him a strong dose of his own medicine. They accompanied it with the warning that if he ever repeated his attack on his wife he would be ridden out of town on a rail. The wife-beater nursed his wounds overnight and the following day tried to drown his humiliation in booze. With the inevitable result. He went home and started in on his wife where he had left off the day before. Neighbours called the vigilantes, who came running. They manhandled the drunk onto a fence rail, tied him securely, doused him with hot tar, beat him enthusiastically as he was carried to the edge of town, and then turned him loose with the warning that if he ever came back a worse fate would await him. Whether he ever tempted that fate is unknown.[11] That, unfortunately, is the way most wife-beating episodes are left; the final answer is seldom supplied.

In a Dominion City, Manitoba, case, however, there is a happy ending, of sorts. At the turn of the century, Dr. Murrough O'Brien was the justice of the peace as well as the coroner and medical health officer of the town. When he was called upon to patch up the cuts and contusions of the victim of Dominion City's most notorious wife-beater, he tried to persuade her to lay charges against her husband. She always refused, usually with the explanation that her wounds had come from horse kicks and other accidents. O'Brien in the end lost patience and conned the friendly local strongman to helping put an end to the beatings. In addition to his ability to perform feats of strength the Dominion City Atlas also took great pride in his pugilistic ability. One day while the doctor was dressing the wounds of the beaten wife the strongman wandered in and was quick to agree with the doctor that the wife-beater needed a dose of his own medicine.

"He'll get it one of these days," the doctor said, "because he has been bragging what a great fighter he is. In fact he has been bragging about how he is going to lick you if he ever gets the chance."

"Oh, he has, has he?" the strongman snarled as he exploded out of the doctor's office and down the street.

"I got the woman a place to stay for the night," the doctor said, "and was just getting ready for bed when I had a caller. It was the wife-beater. He was the most beaten man you ever saw. Setting his broken jaw was a pleasure I would not have missed for anything. That fellow left his wife alone after that."[12]

If he did, he must have been the exception, for when the wife-beaters did get into the police court news it was usually as repeaters. A record of some kind was established in Winnipeg where one man appeared in court for the forty-seventh time in fifteen years on charges of drunkenness and wife-beating. He was sent to jail for two months with the warning that the next appearance would bring the lash. [13]

Only a minor fraction of wife-beaters ever had to face the humiliation of a court appearance, however. Most women preferred to suffer in silence rather than undergo the embarrassment of admitting publicly that they had married a wife-beater. The women not only accepted their sorry status, they seemed at times to resent the efforts of those who sought to change things for the better. As Nellie McClung noted during the great Prohibition crusade, it was always the wife of the town drunkard who was loudest in her protests that demanding votes for women was an affront to her husband's judgment.

It was intrinsic in the creed of the Protestant settlers of western Canada that it was the love of whisky and not of gold that was the root of all evil. In the periodic eruption of the clergy against the toleration of prostitution, this "social evil" was usually linked with illegal boozing. It was, it can be conceded at once, a comparatively simple step to isolate the whisky base of a great many problems of the times. There was for example the near civil war which erupted in 1881 between the postage-stamp province of Manitoba and Ontario over where the Manitoba-Ontario boundary was located.

Under federal law, as it applied in 1881, it was illegal to have liquor for sale near public works. This act was enforced in the wilderness between Winnipeg and Fort William during the early stages of construction of the Canadian Pacific Railway. The federal government, for reasons never spelled out, withdrew the application of the act from the railway and within a matter of weeks the whole region was flooded with whisky. Between the Whitemouth River and Wabagoon Lake, a distance of one hundred and sixty miles, it was estimated that eight hundred gallons of liquor was being sold a month, to the two thousand men employed on the right of way. Drunkenness became such a menace to railway construction that the Manitoba government decided to take a hand. On August 15, 1881, the Lieutenant-Governor of Manitoba signed a proclamation extending the laws of Manitoba to the disputed territory, of which the town of Rat Portage (later Kenora) was the construction centre.

Manitoba then extended its licence law to the territory and granted several hotel and wholesale liquor licences to residents of Rat Portage. A clash with Ontario came quickly. Ontario magistrates refused to recognize the licences on the ground that Manitoba had no jurisdiction over the territory. Manitoba retaliated by sending its own policemen to Rat Portage to enforce the law. The police of each province took to arresting the police officials of the other. The assaults and counter-assaults made headlines for the Winnipeg newspapers who sent their correspondents to Rat Portage. The following description of the uproar is from Alexander Begg, the historian of the Red River Valley:

> The newspaper reports of these teapot tempests are highly entertaining. The Conservative papers described the Ontario officials and their following as "rowdies", "toughs", etc., and declared that "every rough in Rat Portage was with the Grits in hopes of free whiskey and pay as specials", — and the soubriquets of some of the "specials" would certainly warrant such a contention, as we find among them such distinguished characters as "Black Jim Reddy of Montana", "Charley Bull-Pup", "Boston O'Brien, the Slugger", "Patsy Roach", and "Al Mulligan, the Bad Man". The Liberal journals represented every act of the Ontario authorities as being backed up by the efforts of "the respectable citizens" and characterized their opponents as "Tory miscreants" and the posse comitatus as a "lawless gang". The position of affairs was aptly

described by a correspondent who stated that on 27th
July, "Dominion Commissioner McCabe with two policemen, Ontario Magistrate Burdon with twenty-five policemen, and Stipendiary Magistrate Brenton with fifteen
policemen, acting on behalf of Manitoba, have been
arresting each other all day, and the people have been
siding, some with one party and some with another, to the
imminent danger of the peace and of loss of life." On the
following day the Manitoba jail was set on fire, it was
stated, by "Mowat's lambs". [14]

Eventually the governments of Manitoba and Ontario got together and agreed to mediate the jurisdictional problem by referring
it to the Privy Council. Rat Portage remained the boozing and
carousing centre for the construction workers until their track-lay-
ing took them too far away. Thereafter they were supplied by the
tent-hotels that preceded and followed the track-layers as they
worked westward.

The extent to which the governments of Ontario and Manitoba
owed their places of power to booze would be an interesting speculation. Certainly in western Canada whisky was a recognized persuader
which was used copiously by both parties on election day. It was
supplied in many instances by the brewers' and distillers' agents,
who also kept a careful eye on the Wet or Dry sympathies of the
candidates. It was a rare election on the prairies which was not
followed by charges of corruption and the use of liquor as a prime
persuader.

In justification of their seeming neglect of social problems, the
clergy of the whisky era might well have argued that they were
concentrating on the eradication of the fundamental cause of human
misery, not putting patches on its effects. They never put it in precisely these terms, but it could well have been argued that there
would be no wife-beating without booze; there would be no children
going hungry to bed and bootless to school without booze; political
corruption could not exist without booze; disorderly streets and
crimes of all kinds had an alcoholic basis; without the economic and
social wastage of alcoholic indulgence the brotherhood of man
would be possible. So they concentrated their attention on a single

target — Temperance, unaware perhaps of the intolerance, racism, and bigotry that were often the nether side of their movement.

Nor were the clergy alone in their belief in the blissful life which could be achieved with the banishment of John Barleycorn from the land. In the first waves of migration both from Ontario and from the United States, thousands of devout settlers turned their backs on the land available around Winnipeg and moved beyond the first boundary of Manitoba to land in the eastern area of the Northwest Territories. They did so because they understood that Prohibition prevailed there, and they, like the promoters of the Saskatoon Temperance Colony, were determined to settle where whisky was not available and hence was not a problem. They were scarcely located, however, before Manitoba reached out and took them in, when, in 1881, its boundary was shifted two degrees to the west from the 99th to beyond the 101st parallel.

A measure of the depths of conviction of the Temperance settlers of Manitoba can be gained from the fact that for the next fifty years western Manitoba was a hotbed of Prohibitionist sentiment. In every vote that was taken on the subject, the people of western Manitoba rallied to the cause of total abstinence with enough power, in the early days at least, to overcome the opposite sentiment that developed in the urban centres to the east.

What good were laws without loopholes?

The struggle of the pioneers of western Canada against the evils of untrammelled boozing proved long and difficult. It began in earnest in Prince Albert in 1880 with the formation of the first Total Abstinence League, the forerunner of the Rock Lake Total Abstinence Society, which was formed by a group of settlers from Ontario in southwestern Manitoba in 1883. In Winnipeg, the early campaigns led by Silcox, Pitblado, and Cameron were all intent on eradicating the worst evils of intoxication and not liquor itself. It was only when they were thwarted at every turn that the western Temperance leaders turned strongly to Prohibition.

Prohibitionist sentiment, cross-fertilized as it was by revulsion at the human cost of drunkenness and the perfervid Protestant religious opposition to alcohol, grew much stronger much earlier in the eastern provinces. As early as 1875, a resolution calling for the investigation of national Prohibition passed by a vote of seventy-two to nine in the House of Commons and twenty-five to seventeen in the Senate. In 1878 Parliament passed the Scott Act which enabled any city or municipality to vote itself Dry. During the next decade sixty-two communities in the east went Dry but by 1892 only thirty-two of the local option areas were left. Enforcement difficulties and the inflow of booze from outside had done in the others.[1] In 1870 anti-whisky sentiment in Ontario was strong enough to turn the Wolseley Expedition to the Red River into a Temperance experiment. It took no liquor along and on the long and arduous march through northwestern Ontario the men were served tea instead of whisky.[2]

The Canadian Temperance movements both east and west leaned heavily on the United States for both inspiration and ammunition. Frances Willard, who was the driving force of the W.C.T.U. in the United States, came to Canada in 1886 to help get the organization started here. Thereafter a great deal of the printed propaganda of the American Temperance organizations was imported and widely distributed in Canada. Prairie newspapers, which tended to run all the free handouts they could get, regularly opened their columns to W.C.T.U. propaganda from the United States. Mostly they favoured horror stories about families burned or frozen to death, or children dying of neglect, while the father was drinking himself into the gutter.

In this mass of material, one book stands out. It was written by Timothy Shay Arthur, the author of *Ten Nights in a Barroom*. With the unlikely title of *Strong Drink; and the Curse and the Cure*, it carried the sub-title *What Shall we do to be Saved from the Demon Drink?* The book was published originally in the United States in 1877 and was reprinted in Canada by Oberhaltzer and Co. of Berlin, Ontario.

The first half of *Strong Drink* is a novel about the fall and redemption of a variety of drunkards and reads like a serialized transcript of a beginners'-night confessional at an Alcoholics Anonymous meeting. The second half is an extensively researched report on the rescue asylums for inebriates that were then operating in various states. His closing chapters are a long elaboration on the Alcoholics Anonymous thesis — that alcoholism is an incurable disease which can only be arrested by the help of God and total abstinence. It was written a good sixty years before A.A. came into existence. Arthur cited copiously from the experiences and the opinions of a score of medical men who had run hundreds of drunkards through their institutions. They all subscribed to the Alcoholics Anonymous conviction — only total abstinence can save an alcoholic — but Arthur took it one step further in the final sentence in his 675-page book: "The curse is upon us and there is but one cure; *total abstinence,* by the help of God for the individual; and *Prohibition* by the State."

Arthur was one of the most prolific writers of his time; he churned out more than a hundred morality books, published a Temperance magazine, and frequently took to the lecture platform. His double-edged solution caught on more slowly in western Canada than it did in the United States, and for several reasons. The paucity of population in the Territories, scattered as it was over so vast a territory, did not lend itself to mass agitations. Prohibition, as a social goal, had become tarnished west of Manitoba by the long argument over the permit system and enforcement difficulties. The replacement of the permit system by the hotel bar system was a defeat for the Temperance movement, and recovery from that defeat was slow. The Arthur slogan, however, helped the Protestant clergymen who led the struggle against intoxication to wage their war on three fronts. They could do missionary work among the drunks — get them to sign total abstinence pledges and join the anti-treating crusades; they could exert pressure on governments to tighten and extend control of the saloons with a vague idea that in the end they might achieve Prohibition by attrition; they could press for the enactment of prohibitory laws at the provincial and national levels.

Whether they opted for all-out Prohibition or were willing to settle for Temperance, the reformers seldom got what they thought they were getting from the politicians. Somehow, when the offerings were translated into legislative action they lost on the swings what they had gained on the roundabouts. Even when the legislatures did nothing it could turn out disastrously for the Temperance forces.

That happened in the Territories in 1887 when Joseph Royal became lieutenant-governor. Some Temperance advocates, including high officers of the N.W.M.P., had been advocating the legalizing of the sale of beer as an alternative to whisky sold under permit. Royal legalized the sale of four-per-cent beer, but also made permits to import whisky much easier to obtain. As a result, importation of liquor into the Northwest Territories zoomed from 21,636 gallons in 1887 to 151,628 gallons in 1889.

The Temperance zealots fought back as best they could. They petitioned the Executive Council to bring Joe Royal to time. Nothing happened. They took up even larger petitions and fired them off to Ottawa. Again nothing happened. Eventually Ottawa decided that self-government should be extended to the Territories and enacted legislation to provide for an elective legislature and cabinet government. The election was held in December 1891, and the Temperance people worked hard to elect a Prohibitionist majority. Unfortunately the argument over booze got sidetracked by another even more passionate issue — the language question.

The original Northwest Territories Act provided for two official languages, but as the Legislative Council was overwhelmingly English-speaking, it opted for unilingualism and voted to abandon French. The Canadian Parliament, after a lot of soul-searching, decided to go along with the request from the west for the deletion of French as an official language for the Territorial government, but not until after an election was held. The question therefore became one for the electors and they gave a substantial majority to the one-language supporters, among whom there was only a small group of Prohibitionist advocates. When the question of regulating the liquor traffic came before the new legislature, it opted for a licence system very much like the one in use in Manitoba, i.e., licensing hotel saloons.[3]

Manitoba's attention in the late 1880s was also distracted by other issues which pushed booze into the background. It took the province years to get over the after-effects of the real estate boom of 1881-2. In 1887 Winnipeg was taking over subdivision after subdivision for unpaid taxes. Lots that once sold for fifty dollars a foot frontage went begging at fifty dollars each. A firebug on the loose in Winnipeg was turning the settlement into a nightmare for insurance adjusters. Within a matter of weeks the Rossin House, London

House, and the Queen's Hotel all went up in flames, and an entire Main Street business block burned down. The province itself was in desperate financial trouble, confounded by problems with railway promoters.[4]

The liquor question was not a priority matter when Manitoba electors went to the polls in 1888 to elect a new Liberal government headed by Thomas Greenway. And for the next couple of years it was decidedly subsidiary to the uproar over language rights and school rights which arose when Joe Martin exploded his Manitoba Schools Question time-bomb in 1889. Nevertheless, and particularly in the rural areas, the same people who were blood-and-guts proponents of a one-language (English) province with non-sectarian public schools were also among the most dedicated Orange Lodge—Protestant—Prohibitionists. They numbered, among their leaders, the young attorney general of the province, Clifford Sifton.

Just prior to the election of 1892, the Prohibitionists turned up at Sifton's office with a petition for a plebiscite on the question of Prohibition to be held along with the election. This, they said, would settle the matter of where the public stood on the liquor problem. Sifton supported the idea and when a private member brought in a bill to hold the plebiscite it passed the legislature with little opposition. There was, of course, uncertainty over whether the province had the authority under the B.N.A. Act to enforce Prohibition even if the vote was substantially in favour. When the vote turned out to be two and a half to one in favour of banishing alcohol from the province — 18,637 for, and 7,115 against — the Temperance organizations began to press for immediate enactment of province-wide Prohibition. When nothing happened the cry went up that the Greenway government had promised such a law if the plebiscite passed and on that promise had got the solid Dry support which turned the tide so strongly in its favour. Naturally, Sifton and the other government spokesmen denied giving any such commitment.[5]

The pressure from the Drys mounted and eventually the government decided upon a course of action. It had Sifton draft a memorial which would transfer the problem to the doorstep of the federal government. The memorial recited that the people of Manitoba by a substantial majority had voted in favour of a law totally prohibiting the importation, manufacture, or sale of intoxicating liquors; that the legislature had a duty to take steps to carry out the will of the electors; that while there were doubts that the province had power to enact total Prohibition there was no doubt that Ottawa had full power to legislate. It therefore called on the federal government to pass such a law and promised to supplement whatever law Ottawa passed with provincial legislation, if that was deemed necessary.

Sifton piloted the memorial through the house with a speech that was an almost perfect summary of the position which Prohibitionists would ultimately come to take. Only an act of complete Prohibition would meet the needs of Manitoba, he said. Manitobans did not want several acts of Parliament governing the liquor traffic, but absolute Prohibition of every description of liquor. A partial Prohibitionary law which might be within the power of the province could not be enforced. The only law that could be was one which totally out-lawed rather than regulated the liquor traffic, that made it unlawful to have, to make, or to import it. Then, he said, the traffic would die out of itself because the self-respecting people would respect the law. Sifton's memorial passed the legislature with but a single dis-senting vote and was sent to Ottawa. It was never heard of again.

The next step was for Manitoba to arrange to have a Prohibition law drafted and sent to the Privy Council for adjudication. That judgment came back in 1894 and was so ambiguous that the prov-ince had to hire one of the country's top lawyers, Edward Blake, to explain it. When nobody within the provincial government could understand Blake's explanation either, the matter was allowed to die, as Sifton's memorial to Ottawa had expired.[6]

The Conservative party which was in power in Ottawa in 1894 was in no mood to become entangled in any memorial from Manitoba. It was a Liberal Manitoba that had already forced the federal Conserva-tives to become hopelessly embroiled in its public schools legisla-tion. In its threshing around to find a solution to the vexed problem which would satisfy the Roman Catholic hierarchy while not offend-ing the Ontario Orangemen, the Conservative party disintegrated and Sir Wilfrid Laurier and the Liberals came to power in 1896.

Laurier was soon faced with a dilemma almost as painful as the one that Sir John Thompson and Sir Mackenzie Bowell had had to struggle with: what to do about the steadily rising pressure from the Maritimes, Ontario, Manitoba, and the Protestant enclave in Quebec for a national Prohibition law — a proposal that was anathema to the French Canadians of Quebec. Laurier decided to buy some peace and quiet from the Prohibitionist agitation by promising a national plebiscite.[7] It was held in September 1898, with the following result:

Province	For Prohibition	Against Prohibition	Majority For	Majority Against
Ontario	154,498	115,284	39,214	—
Quebec	28,436	122,760	—	94,324
Nova Scotia	34,678	5,370	29,308	—
New Brunswick	26,919	9,575	17,344	—
Prince Edward Is.	9,461	1,146	8,315	—
Manitoba	12,419	2,978	9,441	—
British Columbia	5,731	4,756	975	—
Northwest Territories	6,238	2,824	3,414	—
Total	278,380	264,693	108,011	94,324

Net Majority for Prohibition 13,687

By another method of stating the results, taking the Territories for convenience as a province, the vote stood as follows:

	For	Against	Majority
Provinces	7	1	6
Constituencies	125	81	44
Representatives	128	85	43

This remarkable vote hints at rather than spells out the strength of the Prohibition movement in Canada. For one thing, the franchise was confined to adult male British subjects over twenty-one years of age. Thus the aggressively vocal legions of the Women's Christian Temperance Union were not permitted to cast ballots. The vote was taken in September when most of the farmers, who were the backbone of the Dry movement, were busy with the harvest. None of the usual inducements were offered to get the voters to the polls. There was no free booze near the polling booths, no patronage jobs hanging on the results, no massive rallies with political luminaries to fetch crowds, no agents on the streets with marked ballots which corruptible voters could carry into the polling booth, collecting two dollars when they came out and produced the unmarked ballot they had received. Yet almost forty-five per cent of the eligible electors went to the polls and gave a majority for Prohibition in every province save Quebec.

The overwhelming Dry vote of Manitoba and the Northwest Territories produced a quick reaction. Manitoba almost immediately petitioned Ottawa to grant the province whatever additional powers it might need to get on with the business of suppressing the whisky trade. Elsewhere the ecstatic Temperance leaders waited confidently for the federal government to bring in legislation to establish national Prohibition. With six of the provinces and the Territories all showing such strong support, they had reason for confidence. They did not count on Sir Wilfrid Laurier's arithmetic. He quickly demonstrated to his own satisfaction, if not to theirs, that the vote was in fact a defeat for Prohibition. The measure, he pointed out, got only twenty-three per cent of the electorate to support it. Hence no good purpose would be served by even discussing the imposition of such a measure on the Canadian people.[8] For the Drys, it was back to the drawing boards again.

For the Manitoba Temperance leaders, Laurier's reaction was most disappointing. In the recent past the Liberals who supported the Greenway government had been much friendlier toward them than the Conservative opposition which was then led by R.P. Roblin. After the Greenway administration took office it rewrote and tightened the liquor licence act. Interdiction of confirmed drunkards became more widely used. It changed the regulations covering local option voting so that only resident electors were eligible. Previously the franchise had extended to absentee landlords and this had led to illegal voting. The closing hours of the saloons were reduced from 11.30 on weekdays and 10 p.m. on Saturdays to 11 p.m. and 8 p.m. respectively. As the regulations were tightened Roblin was quick to protest:

> The present legislation is so far ahead of public sentiment that the general public will not undertake to see to the punishment of infractions of the regulations, and the men who do the work of informing on behalf of the temperance associations are the lowest and most contemptible characters to be found in the community. . . . Authorities are agreed that sumptuary laws of the past have signally failed to accomplish their ends, and the only way in

which temperance principles can be inculcated is by moral
suasion. . . .

Whether Roblin or Greenway was more in tune with public opinion can perhaps be gauged by the resounding majority the Drys
rolled up in Manitoba in the Laurier referendum. In any event the
Liberals kept tightening regulations and managed by 1899 to reduce
the number of annual licences issued to 167 from the 218 issued in
1887, and this despite a fourfold increase in population.

With Laurier's rejection of the 1898 plebiscite, the Manitoba Conservatives reversed their position and rushed to cast their nets in the
Prohibitionist waters. Roblin was persuaded to vacate the party
leadership and was replaced by Hugh John Macdonald, Sir John A.'s
son and a prominent Winnipeg lawyer, whose sympathies were as
Dry as Roblin's were Wet. At the convention which elected Macdonald, the Conservative party adopted an unequivocal Prohibitionist plank.

> A measure will be adopted to give effect to the will of the
> people regarding prohibition of the liquor traffic, which
> measure should go as far in the direction of prohibition as
> the powers of the province will allow.[10]

While Roblin remained discreetly in the background, Macdonald
toured the countryside and repeated the platform pledge at every
opportunity, captivating the large audiences he attracted by the
warmth of his personality, his authentic Conservative image, and his
sympathy with the Protestant principles of the Loyal Orange Lodge.
In the election of 1899 the Conservatives swept the entire southwest
of the province — the heartland of Temperance, Orangeism, and
Anglo-Saxondom — and emerged with twenty-three seats to the
Liberals' fifteen. Only Greenway himself managed to save a southwestern seat.

Soon after the election Macdonald called in J. A. M. Aikins, one of
the ablest and most respected of Manitoba lawyers and a Temperance leader of note. Together they drafted what came ultimately to
be known as the "Macdonald Act" and the "Prohibitionists' Magna
Charta". In view of what was to come later, Macdonald's words in
moving first reading of his liquor act are perhaps worth resurrecting.

Some few months ago representatives of the Conservative party met in convention in Winnipeg to frame a platform on which that party was to go before the electors and ask their support in the election that terminated so happily on the 7th of December last. That Convention saw fit to place in the platform a plank in favour of Prohibition, that, if successful, we would at once enact a prohibitory law, going as far as the powers of the Province would allow, and having done that, we would apply to the Parliament of Canada for power to enact absolute Prohibition, which we cannot at present do. The moment that plank went into the platform, and we as a party went before the country asking for support on that plank, coupled with others, my course was clear, to carry out honestly the pledge made to the people. Nothing can more lower a public man and a party than to have it supposed by the people that specific definite pledges are like pie-crust, made to be broken.

. . . No other course was open but to carry out the pledge made when we asked for the suffrages of the people. If we broke our pledge we should be as guilty of a criminal act as the man who robbed another's house, for we should have robbed the people of their votes. When the electors saw fit to return the Conservative party to power no course was open but to carry out the plank in reference to Prohibition and obey the mandate of the people. A Bill has been prepared, which, going as far as possible, will at the same time keep within the powers of the Province and not run the danger of being set aside. The task required ability and judgment. As Attorney-General I have considered the Bill, clause by clause, with Mr. Aikins, and I now come before the House asking that it be made law.[11]

The provisions of the Macdonald bill, which was passed in July 1900, included:

1. All places where liquor was sold were to be closed.
2. Only drugstores were to be permitted to sell alcohol and only under prescription.

3. No compensation was to be paid liquor dealers for their losses sustained by being put out of business.
4. Private persons could still import liquor from outside the province for consumption in their own homes. (A loophole made necessary by the constitution.)
5. The law was not to come into force until June 1, 1901, when all existing licences would have run out.

Alas for Macdonald's brave words, his Prohibition act was to come to nothing. The assent of the lieutenant-governor was barely affixed to the act before a federal election campaign erupted and Macdonald was persuaded to resign as premier of Manitoba to run against Clifford Sifton in the Brandon constituency. Sifton had joined the Laurier cabinet in 1896 as Minister of the Interior, a portfolio which gave him control of all the natural resources of the northwest and made him the prime dispenser of federal patronage. He had, moreover, turned his Brandon constituency into a personal fiefdom. He was not only a second-generation stalwart of the Temperance cause, he was a practising teetotaller and a devout Methodist. And he was almost a native son of the city, for he had started his law practice there.

The Conservative party, so fresh from its unseating of the Liberals in Manitoba, was eager to put the blocks to Sifton as a first essential to taking the province into the federal Conservative column. But to unseat such an incumbent would require a Herculean effort and a superb candidate. They thought they had such a man in Hugh John Macdonald. As a candidate he was everything Sifton was not. He was friendly, outgoing, cheerful, and entertaining, while Sifton was the icy logician, combative and arrogant. How Macdonald was ever persuaded to enter such a contest will forever remain a mystery. He had only recently settled comfortably into the office of premier of Manitoba. He could look forward to a reasonable tenure and a life full of satisfaction as his province's leader. But the son and heir of Sir John A. could not resist the blandishments of the national leaders of his party. His decision to contest Brandon was as ill-advised as it was doomed.

At first glance, Macdonald's own Temperance stance and his record on the liquor question should have endeared him to Temperance-dominated Brandon, and strategists tried to turn it to his advantage. Sifton was held up to ridicule as a member of the Laurier cabinet which had refused to enact national Prohibition after the 1898 referendum. Sifton was a traitor to the cause of Temperance! But Sifton had his own record on the Manitoba Schools Question to talk about to Orange and Protestant Brandon, and his long leadership of the Brandon Drys helped counter the effect of the traitor charge. He won the seat rather handily with a majority of 747 votes.

While Macdonald was off fighting the battle of Brandon, R. P. Roblin, who had not even been a member of the Macdonald cabinet, "neatly annexed" (in the phrase of J. W. Dafoe) the premiership of Manitoba. He gave his immediate attention to scuttling the Macdonald act. The liquor interests charged that the law was *ultra vires* because it infringed certain rights granted the Hudson's Bay Company under the Northwest Territories Agreement. Instead of enforcing the Macdonald law, Roblin had it referred to the courts. The Manitoba court held it was *ultra vires* in several particulars because it affected trade and commerce, which were under federal jurisdiction. An appeal was carried to the Privy Council, which reversed the Manitoba court and ruled that the act was within the power of Manitoba to enact.

Once again the cheers went up from the Prohibitionists. This, they told each other, had to be the happy ending at last to all their struggles. Not quite, said Premier Roblin. On January 15, 1902, he announced that another plebiscite would have to be taken to make sure Manitobans had not changed their minds since they had last voted four years before. And not only that, he announced that the plebiscite would have to be carried by a two-thirds majority to become law.

To many of the Dry leaders, the Roblin plebiscite was a dodge so transparently fraudulent that they wanted no part of it. In the Dominion plebiscite, the Dominion election list had been used. There would, however, be no voters list for the Roblin plebiscite. Anybody who turned up at a polling booth could vote after completing minor formalities. It was, the Temperance people said, an open invitation to corruption, and coming as it did so soon after the Manitoba election and the federal plebiscite it was palpably unnecessary.

By this time the leaders of the 1883 drive for Temperance were gone and in their place had come new leaders who lacked nothing in either vigour or conviction. They organized a mass protest in Winni-

peg and when spokesmen for the Roblin government tried to explain
the government's position they were howled down. But when the
Prohibitionists themselves held a rally to make plans to marshal the
Prohibitionist vote to the polls once again, it also broke up in dis-
order. One faction demanded that the Dry forces boycott the Roblin
referendum, the other wanted to get out the vote. When they tried
again to reconcile their differences, they only succeeded in intensify-
ing them.[12]   The split divided all the denominations down the
middle rather than one from the other. Thus Principal Patrick of the
Brandon Presbyterian Theological Seminary was opposed by the
Rev. E. A. Henry, one of the most prominent Presbyterian preachers. For the Methodists, the Rev. R. P. Bowles favoured getting out
the vote and Principal Sparling of Wesley College, perhaps the most
respected Methodist in Manitoba, strongly advocated boycotting the
referendum.

With the Temperance legions so badly divided, the test might well
have been lost in an honest election. As it was, Prohibition was
snowed under, 22,464 to 15,607, in what the Drys described as a
howling farce. Voting irregularities were charged at almost every
poll, and the peak was reached in St. Boniface where twice as many
votes were cast against Prohibition as there were certifiable voters in
the constituency.

With the results of the referendum in his pocket, Premier Roblin
could afford to be magnanimous toward the embattled clergymen.
He loosened regulations governing voting under local option which
permitted individual municipalities to opt for Prohibition. He tightened regulations of Winnipeg hotels and was able to boast, because
of the manner in which the saloons were concentrated in the Main
Street area, that he had freed ninety-eight per cent of Winnipeg from
contact with the liquor problem.

The Roblin referendum almost totally destroyed the Manitoba
Temperance movement. It took nearly a decade for the differences
to settle and for the Drys again to come together in a cohesive
movement with a clearly defined objective. Some of the leaders
leaned toward the organization of their own political movement.
Nothing came of any of this agitation and the Roblin government
was able to ignore the prohibitionists. It always had the plebiscite
vote as justification for doing nothing. In the decade after the Roblin

plebiscite, the main interest of the Temperance forces returned to the local option areas as they sought to dry up the province piecemeal. During the next five years the Drys put on a succession of locally generated local option drives. As a result the number of Dry municipalities rose steadily from twelve in 1900 to a total of over thirty, with the result that the sale of liquor was illegal over most of southwestern Manitoba. [13]

Beyond the Manitoba border the struggle against the demon rum did not become serious until the Territories attained provincial status in 1905. Until then agitation for home rule and mundane issues such as inadequate coal supplies, poor rail connections, and all the vexing trivialities of small-town life more than kept the people occupied.

Nevertheless, a sort of "x" factor seemed to come into play whenever a town reached 1,000 in population. Drunkenness got out of hand, the streets tended to become disorderly, and the need for better control of the liquor problem got talked about.

In Saskatchewan the first provincial administration, under Premier Walter Scott, was not yet settled in office when a large delegation appeared on January 17, 1906, urging it to crack down severely on the liquor traffic. But the Liberal government, along with the connivance of small-town politicians allied with the liquor interests, frustrated the efforts of the Prohibitionists. Premier Scott was not unsympathetic to their cause. He was quite prepared to submit the matter to a referendum, but the Drys balked at his conditions, which entailed getting a clear majority of 50,000 votes in favour of Prohibition.

When the Temperance legions got nowhere with the Saskatchewan government they sent E. B. Keenleyside, a particularly dedicated disciple of total abstinence, out into the hinterlands to organize local option votes in the province's one hundred and fifty municipalities. He was greeted enthusiastically, except when he tried to get the co-operation of the municipal officials who seemed to have a built-in bias for the booze trade. The provincial law required the municipalities to hold a plebiscite when a petition containing a stipulated number of electors was received. Many officials ignored the petitions. One municipal clerk disappeared from his office until it was too late to act on the petition. Another called the council meeting two days too late to read the by-law. At one meeting a councillor left the meeting when the motion to submit the plebiscite came up and the council lacked a quorum. A number of councils rejected petitions when lawyers for the liquor interests intervened. There were no voters lists, so anybody could enter a polling booth and demand and get a ballot.

Despite all such skulduggery the Drys managed to carry forty-odd municipalities. Then the opposition took to the courts with arms filled with technicalities. One vote was quashed because a returning officer went to lunch, another because the lawyer hired to draft the by-law bungled the job, another because it was proved that some illegal votes were cast. Of the more than a dozen cases that were challenged in court, only two of the Dry votes were confirmed. At the end of five years the Saskatchewan Drys were almost prepared to write off the local option route as highly unlikely ever to lead to an advance of Temperance.

While all this was happening in the rural areas, the regulations were being loosened and bent in the cities of Manitoba and Saskatchewan. The bar hours were extended. The privilege of selling liquor was extended to clubs, and in Manitoba the Roblin government consistently issued licences to bars even after local option votes in that area had gone in favour of Prohibition.

Alberta, after the licence system was adopted in 1891, seemed to live much more comfortably with its whisky than either Saskatchewan or Manitoba. Why this should have been so is difficult to understand. One reason may be that it was the last province settled and the vocal opposition to the abuse of alcohol which arose in Manitoba in 1880 did not reach important volume in Alberta until after it reached provincial status. Certainly in the Laurier referendum the vote in Alberta was much closer — 1,708 for Prohibition to 1,331 against, out of an eligible electorate of 9,522. When the Rev. W. G. Fortune became the organizer of the Temperance and Moral Reform Society in 1907, his early interest seemed to have been in combating treating, and getting locals of the Anti-Treating League started.

As the big waves of the immigration flood from the Sifton drive for settlers hit the prairie provinces, the struggle between the reformers and the politicians was no better than a stand-off. On one hand the reformers had clearly made a great deal of progress with what Premier Roblin called moral suasion in expanding public support for Prohibition. But they had not yet devised a method of convincing political parties that theirs was a movement to be feared and courted. The same Conservative party of Manitoba which had gone along with Hugh John Macdonald's Prohibition plank and had voted it onto the statute books went along quite as willingly with Roblin's repudiation of everything that Macdonald had stood for. Roblin not only rejected the appeals of the Temperance zealots, but heaped scorn upon them. He ridiculed the idea that there was something inherently improper in one man's buying another man a shot of booze.

> Now what is the treating custom? The treating custom is simply the manifestation of the social and the intellectual qualities of man as contra-distinguished from the ordinary brute creature. If you take away the social qualities of a man, you have something very little better than a brute. Here is a declared intention to curb, restrain, destroy if possible, that social side of life. In the first place, I think it is absolutely wrong to make any such attempt. Secondly, I know it is absolutely impossible without exterminating the race, and therefore I refuse to acknowledge the desirability of any such action. [14]

Roblin did not need the Prohibition vote to get elected because the electors of Manitoba did not differentiate between Grits and Tories when it came to whisky. They voted Conservative or Liberal for other reasons and did not change, in any important numbers, because of a candidate's or a party's rejection or support of Prohibition. Roblin had certainly demonstrated that by increasing his majority in the 1903 provincial elections which followed the Roblin plebiscite fiasco. He repeated his success in 1907 and 1910.

In Saskatchewan, Premier Scott noted sadly that his early support of a number of Temperance proposals had paid no political dividends at the polling stations. Later he had held to his position on the referendum question without suffering politically for defying the Temperance forces.

The million immigrants who descended upon western Canada in the decade following the Roblin plebiscite, however, provided a

potent new ingredient to add to the Temperance brew. What could
not be done by the combination of deeply held religious conviction
and economic self-interest would be done when social consciousness
developed to a point where it became a social gospel, which not even
rascality and dishonesty in politicians could neutralize.

The slogan
that won the west

For thirty years, no matter what they tried or how hard they tried, nothing seemed to work for the Temperance movement on the prairies. Then, about midway through the first decade of the twentieth century, everything started to work, and the movement began to pick up both speed and strength from all directions. Many factors contributed to the change, of which three were paramount:

1. The mass influx of new immigrants caused the population of the cities and towns to explode upward.

2. The adoption of the "Banish-the-Bar" slogan.
3. The adoption by Saskatchewan and Alberta of direct legislation
acts under which, if a certain specified percentage of the electors
petitioned for any legislation, the government was required to
hold a plebiscite on the question and, if the electors voted in
favour, to enact the legislation.

Most of the more than one million people who descended upon
the prairies in the decade before the First World War settled on the
land. But tens of thousands were artisans, tradesmen, and clerks who
reached the cities and towns and went no farther. As a result, scores
of instant towns sprang into existence between Winnipeg and the
Rockies. And it was these men, crowding pell-mell on top of each
other into the cities, who created housing congestion beyond anything experienced before or since.[1] They were, moreover, predominantly young, predominantly single, and predominantly full of vim
and vigour. The seemingly endless stream in which they came provided all the major cities with their own horror stories about filthy
and unsanitary overcrowding in rooming houses, flophouses, cheap
hotels, and squatters' tents. The only recreational facilities available
for the unattached males were the bars and brothels, and they
stormed into both in ever-increasing numbers.[2] Drunkenness became endemic in the whisky strips of the cities, and with the skyrocketing of drunkenness crime of all kinds kept pace.

The following tabulations are illustrative of conditions in the
three provinces:[3]

CONVICTIONS

YEAR	FOR DRUNKENNESS			FOR ALL OFFENCES		
	Man.	*Sask.*	*Alta.*	*Man.*	*Sask.*	*Alta.*
1907	4,602	1,741	1,459	9,255	5,319	4,473
1908	3,639	1,318	1,990	8,626	5,199	6,121
1909	3,590	1,334	2,214	9,093	5,120	6,878
1910	4,289	1,885	3,543	10,026	7,248	9,515
1911	5,832	2,359	4,041	13,413	8,294	10,269
1912	6,925	2,462	6,657	15,287	10,404	16,775
1913	7,493	2,970	7,283	18,095	13,328	19,426
1914	6,193	2,142	5,710	16,334	13,782	19,043

It might well have been that no causal relationship could be proved in the striking correlation between the growth of drunkenness and the growth of crime of all kinds. It might be argued that both were the result of the massive influx of population into an area that was utterly unprepared to provide even minimal services for the people. Certainly the sudden mixing of large numbers of people with a diversity of national, racial, religious, and economic backgrounds, in an economic climate subject to rapid change and sudden storms, was bound to create social chaos. Most of this congestion and racial mixing took place within the poorest sections of the cities, which were in turn closest to the downtown bars.

It could well have been, as Premier Roblin insisted, that the concentration of boozeries on the Main Street strip of Winnipeg had isolated most of the city from the worst manifestations of the liquor problem. But there was one factor which kept bringing the problem home to most of the working population regardless of where they lived. That was the universal custom, not only in Winnipeg but throughout the entire country, of cashing monthly pay cheques in the bars and "standing a round" with the proceeds.

In good times and bad, the working class of the western cities lived from payday to payday. In the period before the First World War, one of the longest-standing grievances had to do with the distance between paydays. Many, if not most, industries paid their workers once a month; some paid every fortnight. Payment by the week was rare. In 1912, for example, the House of Commons passed an amendment to the railway act which would have forced payment of railway workers' wages every two weeks. It was defeated in the Senate. Intermittently for twenty years, resolutions calling for weekly or bi-weekly wages were approved by Trades and Labor Congress conventions.[4]

A second persistent demand was for payment in cash instead of by cheque. The normal banking hours of the country were from 10 a.m. to 3 p.m., which meant that the banks were closed long before the workers got off work at 6 or 7 at night. Most families ran monthly bills at neighbourhood grocery and butcher shops, where cheques might have been cashed. These establishments, however, were controlled by early-closing by-laws. The one place that was always open and always had cash on hand to accommodate the workers was the boozery, and there was always a handy saloon en route home from work.

The Stock Exchange Hotel in Winnipeg was located on the southeast corner of Logan Avenue and Arlington Street, where the southbound Arlington streetcars connected with the east-bound Logan Avenue streetcars. It was a transfer point for the several thousand C.P.R. shop-workers going south. It was handy for the workers employed in the packing plants and in the Dominion Bridge steel plant. On payday nights the C.P.R. employees would hit the street at that corner at a dead run before their streetcar stopped and race to get to the head of the cheque-cashing line-up in the Stock Exchange bar.[5] Ten miles away, at the foot of Marion Street in St. Boniface, the workers from the new union stockyards raced each other to the Stockyards Hotel with the same objective. Other workers, realizing that the congestion at these bars would be impenetrable, elected to take the streetcar to a transfer point on Main Street and work their way down the block until they found a place where they could get within fighting distance of the bar.

Elsewhere in the western cities the problem did not become as acute as it was in Winnipeg. The Manitoba capital had a twenty-year jump on the others in industrial and commercial development. In 1911 its population exceeded that of Calgary, Edmonton, Regina, Moose Jaw, Saskatoon, and Brandon combined. And so, in all probability, did its consumption of booze.

Cashing pay-cheques put a heavy strain upon the resources of the bar owners. Even in the days when carpenters and plumbers earned twenty dollars a week, upwards of five thousand dollars in cash might be needed by the Stock Exchange or the Stockyards hotels. Few of the hotel owners were financially able to keep five or ten thousand dollars in spare cash lying around to accommodate their drinking customers. Mostly they signed one-day notes at the bank for the currency and returned the following morning with the pay-cheques. While the cheque-cashing operation was one that all bars performed as an essential business practice, it was not done without feelings of unease. George Vivian, for example, had a mile walk from the bank to the Stockyards Hotel with his payday package of five thousand dollars. He was a clay pigeon for any hold-up man who wanted to victimize him, but he survived both the hotel business and cheque-cashing for three decades without ever losing a dollar.[6]

Only slightly less popular than the bars for cheque-cashing were the "wholesale" liquor stores which took up most of the space not occupied by hotels and poolrooms on Main Street and the intersecting avenues. The stores were called "wholesale" not because they supplied the bars and retailers with booze but because they sold it to consumers in quantity.

Most of the wholesalers imported their booze in barrels and did their own reducing and bottling, frequently under their own special brand names. It was standard practice to permit the customers to sample their wares and choose their purchases by taste. This custom led to the development of steady customers as the drinkers came to swear by the booze they bought from one store, and to swear at the elixir supplied by others. The cannier drinkers much preferred the stores to the bars, for they could obtain a case of potable Scotch from a wholesaler for ten dollars, compared with the thirty dollars the same quantity would cost at two bits a slug in a bar.

For the majority of the workers, payday tarrying in the bar was a sort of ritual they went through without ill effects. They would cash their cheques, slap a bill on the counter, and buy a round for the group they were with, usually four or five drinks. Then they could knock back their return treats and leave with most of their pay still intact. But there was a large enough minority which left most of the month's pay behind to create serious social problems that screamed for attention. The Protestant clergy heard the echoes of the screams.

Ontario, in 1910, sought to solve the problem by passing a law to prohibit the cashing of pay-cheques in bars. It worked about as well as any law affecting booze, yet there were angry protests from the industrial workers of the province. What was the good of a payday if they couldn't cash their cheques and have a friendly drink with their mates? Clearly another law was needed — either to force the banks to stay open late enough to cash the cheques on paydays, or to force the employers to pay cash. The labour unions of Ontario opted for the latter and passed resolutions, year after year, demanding a law to enforce cash payment of wages.[7] The agitation over how and when wages should be paid extended from before the turn of the century to well into the First World War before unions became strong enough to take care of the matter in their contract negotiations.

There is no suggestion, of course, that the payday stampedes for the bars drew the participation of the entire working force. Within

society generally, it was probable that nearly half the male population and ninety-six per cent of the female were of temperate habits,
even total abstainers. Nor is there any doubt that as one consequence
of the collapse of the real estate boom in 1912, patronage in the bars
everywhere dropped off, as drinking has always fallen off during
economic depression. When all the concessions to reasonableness are
made, however, the fact remains that the large floating single population of the era before the First World War turned the downtown
drinking strips of the cities into rowdy and roistering neighbour-
hoods into which ordinary citizens hesitated to wander.

When payday came on Saturday even the more temperately
inclined tended to join the general debauch. After three or four
drinks the will to resist the urge to stay for "one more round" was
undercut by this clincher — there was no need to get up for work in
the morning. This was a doubly persuasive argument in the instant
towns and at the sites of the large construction projects. The Saturday spree was something to look forward to during the dawn-to-dusk
work-days in the dirt and sweat of labour gangs; and sleeping off a
Saturday binge was as good a way as any to get through the strict
Presbyterian Sunday the Sabbatarians had imposed upon town and
city alike.

When the Canadian Pacific Railway embarked on the construction of its huge Bassano irrigation dam in southeastern Alberta in
1909, the first result was a real estate boom that would have done
Winnipeg proud. An unimproved lot on the unimproved main street
of the town sold for $17,500, a franchise was let to the promoters of
a streetcar line, and the town soon boasted four hotels with bars
catering to the one thousand teamsters and navvies who were employed on the construction of the earth-filled dam.[8] On Saturday
night they invaded the town en masse and circulated from bar to bar
until their appetites were sated and their kidneys floating. As Len
Nesbitt, the pioneer journalist and founder of the *Brooks Bulletin,*
once observed, "Bassano was the one town where you could *hear* the
drinking long before you caught sight of the drinkers." In Lethbridge, payday in the mines frequently triggered a three-day
bacchanal even when it came in the middle of the week.

The Saturday drinking habit extended even to the small towns,
where Saturday shopping was the long-established custom of the
farm population. The farmers generally drank far less than their
urban brothers and the farm areas were always the strongholds of the

Prohibitionist movements. Among those who did imbibe, mere distance helped to keep their drinking from getting out of hand. Unlike the city drinkers, most of whom were seldom more than ten minutes' walk from the nearest bar, the farmers were often up to fifteen miles from town, with little chance of slipping away for a quick hair from the dog that bit them. On Saturdays it was different. With families dispersed into the country stores to shop, visit friends, and exchange gossip, the farmers had the opportunity if they had the urge. Farmers, however, had one barrier against over-drinking that the workers lacked. They lived on credit from crop to crop. Acquiring a reputation for boozing was certain to impair any farmer's credit rating. In addition, few boozeries, city or country, gave credit at the bars.[9]

Inspector George Logan was a rookie patrolman on the Regina police force at the outbreak of the First World War. His beat extended eastward from the C.P.R. station into Germantown, where the bulk of the immigrant population was served by several hotels. Logan was almost six feet tall, and a Scottish childhood diet of oatcakes and porridge had given him a well-muscled frame and the strength of a young ox.

"We never had much trouble handling the drunks physically," he said, "but they were an infernal nuisance, particularly on Friday and Saturday nights and paydays. You know, if you couldn't get them to go home and they got fighting drunk or disorderly you had to take them to the station. Well, you didn't really want to arrest them, d'ye see. But you had to keep order on the streets. And you had to do it mostly on your own because they couldn't have you forever calling for the wagon just to haul drunks to the station.

"The main trouble was their friends. If you decided you'd have to take one of them in there'd be all kinds of crazy business, like a friend grabbing hold of the prisoner and pulling him one way while you pulled the other.

"But come to think of it, that wasn't the worst. The worst was the drunks who passed out on you. Sometimes, if it was late in a summer night you could kind of look the other way and just leave 'em lie. Most of the time, you were for it. You had to take them in. Well, I had a friend on the beat and he used to lend me his wheelbarrow. Many's the night I've loaded drunk after drunk onto the barrow and wheeled them off to the station."[10]

In Winnipeg, there is a legend that the city had an informal arrangement with Ginger Snooks, its most famous scavenger, to make a midnight sweep of the alleys behind the Main Street hotels with his horse and wagon during the late fall and winter, and to cart the passed-out drunks to the police station. His fee was one dollar per body delivered. No trace of a minute approving the arrangement has been located but it was just the kind of a deal that would have made sense in Winnipeg.

Across the river in St. Boniface a somewhat similar arrangement was in operation until 1928. The police department had an arrange-ment with a livery stable next to the St. Boniface Hotel at the foot of Provencher Avenue. Whenever a policeman on a beat came upon a passed-out drunk he was required to send for a dray from the stable. The stable owners charged one dollar to transport the drunk to jail. It was a substantial money-maker for the city, for a ten-dollar fine, extracted from the drunk the following morning, would leave it with a nine-dollar-per-drunk net profit. [11]

Aside from their usefulness in cheque-cashing, the bars had noth-ing whatever to recommend them. An American writer, describing an American saloon, might well have been talking about ninety-five per cent of the bars in western Canada when he wrote:

> It was a mysterious maleficent, awesome institution, almost flamboyantly wicked. . . . The most notable thing about a saloon was its stink. It was a flusty, musty odor, damp and clammy, an odor compounded of sawdust, tobacco juice, malt, metal polish and whisky. [12]

The bars on the prairie were made more odoriferously offensive by an assortment of smells all their own. In all the cities, though in Winnipeg less than in the others, there were livery stables hard by the hotels. The aroma of the stables was wafted bar-ward on the evening breezes that came behind a rain. It was mixed with the trade smells that stuck to the clothing of the workers. Thus a bar patronized by the railway shop-workers would smell of cinders and machine oils; the saloons favoured by the employees from the slaughter-houses had slaughter-house odours; and those patronized by clerks and bookkeepers around the city halls smelled of the recently patronized or adjacent barber shop.

The bars were deplored by the moral reformers because they were deplorable places. Yet they resisted their every attempt to get rid of them until the reformers invented the Banish-the-Bar slogan. The theological arguments over Temperance were submerged. A person did not have to be for liquor or against it. He only had to be against the bars. The sheer simplicity of the slogan made it an inspired stroke of genius for the anti-whisky crusade. In such low esteem were the bars held by everybody but the saloon-keepers and bartenders that nobody came openly to their defence.

The Banish-the-Bar campaign, however, was far from being just another Prohibitionist's brain-storm. The awakening social consciousness was being manifested in a dozen ways on the prairies soon after the turn of the century. There were drives for the construction of hospitals where the indigent sick might be cared for. There were campaigns for such things as workmen's compensation in case of accidents on the job. Crippling industrial accidents were pauperizing hundreds of families of industrial workers. There was a growing clamour for a compulsory school attendance act and for factory acts to abolish child labour. Humanitarians wanted the protection of the law extended to women, children, and lunatics. The women were hell-bent on obtaining the right to vote. Juvenile courts were needed for children who ran afoul of the law.

The Women's Christian Temperance Union, which had begun with the simple objective of combating the whisky evil, had by this time raised its sights substantially. It became a sort of catch-all for all the causes which agitated Canadian womanhood all across western Canada. Thus it established a rescue home for unwed mothers, did some family liaison work, campaigned for woman suffrage, passed resolutions against sending cigarettes to China and against Sunday golf-playing and gambling, and a resolution for a law to prevent girls under sixteen marrying boys under eighteen.

Another plus for the Prohibitionists in addition to the awakening social consciousness was the rapidly moving drive toward church unity with the Methodist, Presbyterian, and Congregationalist churches. As the church leaders became better acquainted with each other during their efforts to sweep doctrinal differences aside, it became much easier for them to join in advancing what came to be called "the social gospel".

The simplest measures of social welfare, which would be taken for granted fifty years hence, were still being fought for and bitterly opposed in 1907. On November 15, 1907, the Rev. S. D. Chown, secretary of the newly organized Moral and Social Reform Society of the Methodist Church, and the Rev. J. G. Shearer, of the Temperance and Moral Reform Society of the Presbyterian Church, came to Winnipeg for the conference. It was a large assembly at which all the main religious groups had delegates in attendance, including not only the main Protestant groups but the Anglicans, the Roman Catholics, Greek Catholics, Salvation Army, and Unitarians. It also attracted the support of the United Grain Growers, the Trades and Labor Council, and an assortment of business groups. The Banish-the-Bar slogan came out of that meeting and it quickly became the rallying cry of the Manitoba Prohibitionists.

From a movement that had been decimated by the "Roblin riffy-rum-dum" of 1902, the Prohibitionist forces were reunited and revitalized to the point where, in 1909, a mass following of over a thousand supporters accompanied the leaders to the legislature when a new Prohibitionist petition was presented. The Roblin government continued to flout the demands with seeming impunity, but it clearly underestimated the ground swell of support that was building outside the bounds of the church-orientated populace. The great waves of immigrants washing over the west intensified all the social problems — environmental, economic, medical, cultural, and racial. The pristine simplicity of the Banish-the-Bar crusade made it child's play for the Prohibitionists to trace the roots of all the social problems to the whisky trade. That technique brought new recruits flowing to the cause from the socialist labour movement, the suffragettes, the single taxers, and the agrarian free-traders.

There were losses as well as gains for the Drys in the years following the organization of the Social and Moral Reform Council. The high hopes that a common Catholic-Protestant front against the bars could be established were quickly dashed. By selecting the boozeries as their primary target, the militant Orangemen who led the Banish-the-Bar movement backed not an inch away from their traditionally militant anti-Catholic stance. They kept a hawk-like watch on the educational system for any signs of concession to the Manitoba Catholics. In Saskatchewan the existence of a handful of Catholic and French school districts kept the fires of religious conflict burning brightly.

In addition to their periodical general assaults on the Catholics, the Protestants frequently combined damning the bars with damning the separate schools systems and the French-language schools as well. Thus the Methodist Church at its Brandon convention resolved "that there could never be a compromise between the Christian Church and the Liquor traffic, and that bilingual schools were a menace to the welfare of the nation and must be discontinued."[13] Nellie McClung, the novelist-turned-Banish-the-Bar-evangelist, could seldom resist the temptation to pay her disrespects to the Catholic Church during her oratorical forays into the countryside. In the Manitoba election of 1914, there were so many Protestant clergymen supporting the Liberals that Premier Roblin angrily lashed back at them as "Prohibitionist cranks and clerical politicians".

The war of bandied words between Catholics and Protestants reached its peak in that election. By the opening of the campaign the Banish-the-Bar crusade had reached a point where no politician could any longer ignore it. The Liberal party under T. C. Norris, in opposition now for fifteen years, became the party of social reform. Not only did the Liberals promise a Prohibition plebiscite, they promised woman suffrage as well, and came out strongly for a compulsory school-attendance act, which the Roblin Conservatives had steadfastly refused, and for the establishment of direct legislation by initiative and referendum. In short, the Liberal platform might well have been written by the Social Service Council which had succeeded the Social and Moral Reform Council.

As it had been in all Manitoba elections for twenty years, the still-festering sore of the bilingual-school issue was jabbed into open suppuration. This time it was the Francophone Archbishop Langevin of St. Boniface who started the ruckus. In a statement on the educational system Archbishop Langevin, in an almost casual aside, said that it was best for the church to stay out of politics, that by doing so the church had been able to obtain concessions from one party in Saskatchewan and from a different one in Manitoba. The Orange Lodge leaped into the fray. The Rev. F. B. DuVal, celebrating his twenty-fifth anniversary as minister at Knox Presbyterian Church in Winnipeg, let fly with both barrels at the archbishop.

> What can the righteous do when men have so little honor
> as to cling to the party stealing the pig so long as they are
> given a piece of the pork. It makes one feel a righteous

resentment to hear an Archbishop talk of receiving favors
from one party in Saskatchewan and another in Manitoba.
If past history has not shown the necessity of separating
church and state, in God's name what can show it? [14]

The *Orange Sentinel,* published in Toronto, warned all Orangemen against voting for the Conservatives:

> No Orangeman can vote for a Roblin candidate without
> voting for the maintenance of Papal schools, multiplica-
> tion of languages in their educational system, encourage-
> ment of parents who deprive their children of their right
> to education, and cutting the head off the Orange dragon.
> The rank and file will disappoint the Archbishop Lange-
> vin's hope that the Orange Order will commit suicide by
> voting for a party he controls. . . . They will co-operate
> with all patriotic, moral and progressive forces in encom-
> passing the downfall of one of the most depraved minis-
> tries that ever debauched a Canadian province. . . . [15]

But not quite.

Despite the vigour with which the Prohibitionists supported the
Liberals, the Roblin Conservatives were returned by a small majority. It was a Pyrrhic victory of the doomed and the damned. Within
months they were driven from office in disgrace with the breaking
open of the two-million-dollar Legislative Building construction
scandals. The Liberals, again with the Banish-the-Bar movement in
full support, won in a landslide in 1915 and within a matter of
months ordered a plebiscite on Prohibition.

It was in Saskatchewan, however, where the Banish-the-Bar movement was to draw first blood. In the fall of 1913, with the Rev.
George Lloyd, the Anglican Bishop of Prince Albert, at the helm, a
massive campaign was launched to get petitions for a plebiscite. The
Licensed Victualers Association got a slush fund together and hired
Frank Brunner, a Regina hotelman, at a salary of $250 a month to
organize a counter-attack that would destroy the Liberal government. All they destroyed, in the end, was the reputation of a couple
of Liberal members of the legislature who were found guilty by a
royal commission of accepting bribes from the Brunner group. [16]

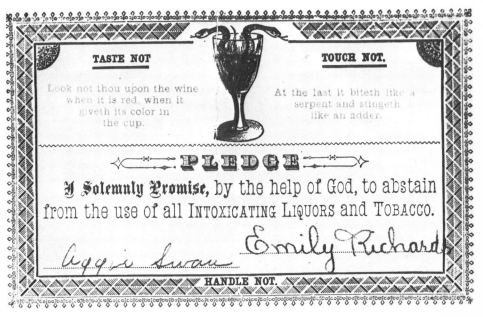

TASTE NOT

TOUCH NOT.

Look not thou upon the wine
when it is red, when it
giveth its color in
the cup.

At the last it biteth like a
serpent and stingeth
like an adder.

PLEDGE

I Solemnly Promise, by the help of God, to abstain
from the use of all INTOXICATING LIQUORS and TOBACCO.

Aggie Swan *Emily Richards*

HANDLE NOT.

1.   The most popular phrase to come out of the Temperance and Prohibition movement was "signing the pledge". The cards were pocketbook size and, in theory and often in fact, were carried as a constant reminder of the promises made.

(*overleaf*) 2.   The Headquarters Saloon, somewhere in the prairie west about 1885. Whisky aplenty — as well as the cigars and musical instruments — indicates a celebration, but there isn't a smiling face to be seen.

(top) 3.   The executive of the Woman's Christian Temperance Union that met
in convention in Regina in 1908. In the back row on the right is Mrs. L. C.
McKinney, the first woman member of a prairie legislature and a prohibitionist
leader in Alberta for more than twenty-five years. She was also one of the most
eloquent and effective of the suffragette speakers on the prairie hustings.

(lower) 4.   Nellie McClung was the most famous and most active woman orator in the west. She was active in the temperance movement and women's rights
crusades for over thirty years. A well-known writer and novelist, she com-
manded fees of up to $200 a week to speak at temperance gatherings in rural
areas all across the prairies.

5.   Calgary House, the city's first hotel, in 1883. Built during the construction of the C.P.R., it is typical of, though a good deal larger than, the hotels that were thrown up in the instant cities that sprang up along the main line.

6.   The famous bar of the Alberta Hotel in Calgary, about 1900. Here Bob Edwards and Paddy Nolan shared rounds with such lengendary western cattle barons as Pat Burns, George Lane, Roper Hull, and Dan Riley.

7

8

9

(*overleaf*) 11.   The well-stocked Weston Liquor House at the corner of King Street and Logan Avenue in Winnipeg, about 1915, complete with liquor advertisements, Gibson girl calendars, and a substantial safe.

(*left*) 7,8,9.   High River, Alberta, was well supplied with hotel bars. Shown are the Oxford Hotel, the Astoria Hotel, and the Alberta Hotel.

10.   The bar of the Alberta Hotel, Crossfield, Alberta, *circa* 1911.

12.   The bar of the Windsor Hotel, Saskatoon, in 1903. The gentlemen at the bar are drinking beer, a practice not encouraged by the bars, which preferred the higher profits of hard liquor.

13.   A combined pool hall and bowling alley in Estevan, Saskatchewan, about 1904, with a small bar behind the cast iron heater.

14.   "Positively No Credit Given at This Bar" — and at most others in the west. Other than the sign over the cash register that says "Zimmerman Hotel", the location of this bar is unknown, but it is well stocked with bottles, a brass rail, and spittoons, as well as towel hangers — but no towels. The decor includes the traditional nudes, advertisements for Saskatoon and Drewry's beer, and portraits of King Edward VII and Queen Alexandra.

(*above*) 15.　The front desk at the Wainwright Hotel, about 1910. The newspaper the bearded gentleman is reading is a special booster edition of the *Edmonton Bulletin,* with a bold headline "Don't Knock the Best City on Earth — You're Living in it!"

(*top right*) 16.　The very elegant bar of the Edmonton Hotel with a background of intricately designed pressed-metal wall covering, deer heads, stuffed birds, and miniature palms.

(*lower right*) 17.　The bars in small centres were less elegant and rather more cluttered. This is the bar of the Imperial Hotel in Lagenburg, Saskatchewan, about 1911.

18.	Most communities had a local
W.C.T.U. group. This photograph
was taken at a convention of the
Alberta Association at Tofield,
Alberta, in May 1916. The lone
man is the Reverend W. G.
Fortune of the Social and Moral
Reform League, and no doubt
the inspired guest speaker at the
gathering.

19.	A parade float with the children of the Hillhurst Presbyterian Sunday
School, Calgary, during the crusade for prohibition. The sign reads "Vote to
Protect Us — Banish the Bar".

20.   Harry and Sam Bronfman, *circa* 1935.

21.   Two members of the R.C.M.P. with a seized still in the 1930s.

22.   A relatively sophisticated small still seized near Edmonton in 1919. Such a still would probably produce about two hundred gallons of whisky a week.

The counter-attack failed miserably, but the drive for a plebiscite was stalled in a bitter argument between Premier Walter Scott and the Drys over the number of votes it would take to bring the prohibitory law into effect.

To demonstrate conclusively that the people wanted Prohibition, Scott insisted that a minimum of fifty thousand votes would have to be cast in favour. The Temperance people were unwilling to concede that this was a fair figure, contending that a thirty-thousand vote would be sufficient. Scott, seemingly in a huff, withdrew his plebiscite legislation. Then, in March 1915, in a speech at Oxbow that took everybody by surprise, he announced that all the bars in Saskatchewan would be closed on July 1, 1915.

Liquor would still be for sale under the new law but it would only be sold in government stores and in these only if they were not rejected under local option votes. The government would take over all stocks of liquor in the province when the bars were closed and would pay for them, but there would be no compensation for either the liquor dealers or the bars which were put out of business. He also promised a plebiscite would be held later on to see whether the citizens wanted the government to remain in the liquor business. The reaction to the Scott speech was instantaneous and laudatory. The Saskatoon Labor Council wired its unanimous approval. The churches of the province organized thanksgiving services. The newspapers with one voice applauded the move with only a mild quibble because Scott had not gone for total Prohibition. The Boards of Trade of the major cities passed congratulatory resolutions.

When the July 1 deadline arrived the government closed 406 bars, 38 wholesale liquor dealers, and 12 clubs, and replaced them with 23 dispensaries. It was estimated that the closing of the bars cut liquor consumption in the province by ninety per cent. The Rev. J. A. Dagle, the Methodist superintendent of missions, said that 20 bars and 4 wholesales in Saskatoon had been replaced by a single store. In the summer the former had averaged at least two hundred dollars each a day in business. That was about the business the government dispensary was doing.[17] Yet even this was not enough. Seven districts opted for a vote on the dispensaries and on December 13, 1915, all seven voted the liquor stores out by whopping majorities, even, to the surprise of all the pundits, in the predominantly foreign districts.

Scott's action in closing the bars in Saskatchewan provided a quick demonstration of the domino theory in action. The Government of Alberta was nudged into calling a plebiscite for July 21, 1915. The Alberta campaign was the culmination of one of the shortest and sharpest Prohibitionist efforts in Canada. It began with the establishment of the Temperance and Moral Reform Society in 1907, with the Rev. W. G. W. Fortune as general organizer. At first progress was slow. Fortune took to the glory trail and was soon a familiar figure wherever there was a Protestant church in Alberta. He made speeches, hounding his listeners into signing total abstinence pledges, and, when he encountered resistance, was prepared to settle for signatures on anti-treating pledge cards which the holders could use in bars to dodge the "I-buy-you-one; you-buy-me-one" trapdoor to drunkenness. In Alberta the cause was advanced tremendously once it got the overwhelming support of the United Farmers of Alberta. Most of the farm leaders of the time, from Henry Wise Wood on down, were dedicated foes of the liquor traffic and many of them were lay preachers into the bargain.

The U.F.A. was the most disenchanted of all groups with the way political parties operated in Canada. It pushed with the utmost vigour for direct legislation by public petition followed by plebiscites, and finally, in 1913, the Liberal government passed the necessary measures to bring it into operation. Once the legislation was on the books, the Temperance and Moral Reform League and the W.C.T.U. united with the U.F.A. in a frenzy of petition-circulating to bring the Prohibition question to a plebiscite. The law required, for the petition to be valid, that it contain eight per cent of the names of the registered electors in eighty-five per cent of the province's constituencies.

In the summer of 1914 over five hundred canvassers descended upon the electorate. The enthusiasm with which electors signed the petition was an augury of what was to come. The canvassers got thousands more names than the regulations required. The government prepared legislation along the same lines as the Macdonald Act of Manitoba and called the plebiscite for 1915.

Everybody then got into the act, from the smallest schoolchildren, who paraded in their Sunday-best white dresses, to the aged and the infirm. At its 1914 convention, the U.F.A. passed a supporting resolution by the unanimous vote of the six hundred delegates on the floor. The United Grain Growers of Alberta added their voice to the cause. Even the Alberta Medical Association, at its Edmonton convention, gave its overwhelming endorsement to Prohibition. [18]

Unlike the other provinces, Alberta's major newspapers did not join the Dry campaign. The *Edmonton Journal* and the *Calgary Herald* enthusiastically attacked the proposed legislation. Both newspapers largely boycotted the mass meetings being staged by the Drys, and the *Journal*'s editorial page in the latter days of the campaign was given over largely to attacking the Drys. It closed its letters column to communications from either Drys or Wets, while the *Herald*, on the other hand, opened its column wide to the pro-bono-publicos attacking the Prohibition law. *Journal* reporters, who did cover some of the small-town meetings, filed reports which had little resemblance to those written by the *Edmonton Bulletin*, *Calgary News-Telegram*, or *Calgary Albertan* reporters. The *Edmonton Bulletin* gave columns of space to Temperance meetings which the *Journal* ignored, and the *Journal* gave generously of its space to opposition meetings the *Bulletin* ignored.

The most shattering journalistic surprise of the campaign was the embracement of the Prohibitionist cause by Bob Edwards, the notoriously well-lubricated editor of the Calgary *Eye-opener*. To his wide circle of drinking companions, it was an "et tu Brute" betrayal that passed all understanding. Yet Edwards was far from alone among alcoholics who worked on the side of Prohibition. A *News-Telegram* reporter, in a survey of the town of Brooks, noted that the town drunks were all working hard with the Prohibitionists. They too were convinced that if the temptation were far enough removed their troubles with the Devil's brew would vanish. [19]

Aside from the newspapers, the only other dissenting voices were those of the organized hotel owners in the Licensed Victualers Association, the Bartenders' Union, and the Alberta Federation of Labor. The Wets imported Dr. A. C. Windle, a Chicago editor of moderate renown who, unhappily for them, had been running pro-German articles in his magazine. He collided head on with the Rev. J. H. Patterson, a string-thin Baptist minister who held all provincial records for tireless oratory.

Patterson was everywhere, often speaking at half a dozen meetings a day. When the Drys discovered what the Wets were up to with their imported Demosthenes, they almost ran Windle into the ground. Wherever he stopped, he would be confronted with a Prohibitionist, as likely as not the Rev. Mr. Patterson, or the Rev. Ben Spence from Toronto. There were always enough Temperance supporters in any audience, particulárly in the country points, to assure that Windle's speeches never went unanswered. Indeed there were many times when the American discovered that the Prohibitionists had completely taken over his meeting. In addition to the heckling at meetings he was subject to a stream of personal abuse in the Prohibition-supporting newspapers. The *Edmonton Bulletin* noted that

> Herr Windle of Chicago has suspended his efforts to help Germany beat the Allies long enough to come to Alberta and try to beat Prohibition.[20]

It was a forlorn hope. On the night before the plebiscite, in one of the longest parades in Calgary's history, ten thousand marchers braved a soaking in a sudden thunderstorm to whip up the last-minute fervour of the urban populace. A demonstration of equal size was staged in Edmonton.

Of the province's 140,000 registered electors, 97,000, or a truly remarkable seventy per cent, went to the polls and voted in Prohibition by 58,295 to 37,509. The drive had been spearheaded by the farm organizations, but one of the remarkable aspects of the results was the margin of victory of the Drys in the cities. Of Alberta's six metropolitan areas only Lethbridge voted wet. Calgary was dry by 7,600 to 4,750 and Edmonton was slightly drier at 7,400 to 4,200.

With the bars shut in Saskatchewan and Prohibition on the way in Alberta, Manitoba's course was set when the Liberals in the 1915 election all but destroyed the Conservative party. A plebiscite was called for March 13, 1916, on the question of adopting the Macdonald Act, which had been in limbo for sixteen years.

The vote set off an emotional orgy that outstripped even the 1914 election. The country had been at war for a year and a half, during which nothing had gone well. The early expectation of a quick victory had been shattered. The awesome submarine campaign was sinking a ship a day on the approaches to England. The Canadian troops had undergone the dreadful gassing at Ypres and were bogged in the mud of Flanders. Zeppelin raids on London had given the world a foretaste of the holocaust to come. At home shortages were beginning to appear and the cost of living was rising. At the very least, the Prohibition plebiscite of 1916 gave the people a chance to get their minds off the war. They made the most of it.

Going to meetings, indoor and out, was a favoured Manitoba pastime from the days of Louis Riel. As the campaign developed, every publicity dodge yet devised was put to work for the Prohibitionist cause. W.C.T.U. leaflets — dodgers they were called for a reason that is obscure — stuffed the mail boxes. Signboards blossomed with illustrations that identified the demon rum with Kaiserism. Every newspaper in the province save two joined the crusade with all editorial guns blazing. The exceptions were the French language *La Patrie*, published in St. Boniface, and the *Northwest Review*, a house organ of the Irish Catholics in Winnipeg.

The near-unanimity of the support for the Dry cause was beyond belief. A convention of the United Grain Growers passed a resolution unanimously supporting it. The Retail Merchants Association gave it its endorsement. All the agricultural papers and all the financial papers and all but a handful of country weeklies supported it. It was officially endorsed by both the Liberal and the Conservative parties. In Winnipeg itself, the wealthiest and most prestigious tycoons of the town clamoured for places on the bandwagon and on the public platforms. Among them were Isaac Pitblado and Sir J. A. M. Aikins, the most honoured names in law; George Ryan, the boot-and-shoe millionaire; Arthur Congdon and E. D. Martin, the wholesale district's biggest names; and George Jackson, a construction industry leader. They were joined by every Protestant minister in the province.

Such overwhelming support gives rise to the question of who the enemy was. Who was standing up in defence of embattled John Barleycorn? Nobody, really, but the Bartenders' Union.

The Trades and Labor Council ducked the issue, probably because a thousand-odd members of the Bartenders' Union were fighting for their economic lives. The bartenders brought in Clarence Darrow from the United States to try to stem the tide in the last week of the campaign. Darrow was then at the peak of his fame as a defender of the McNamara brothers in the *Los Angeles Times* dynamiting case. He comfortably filled the Pantages Theatre for two meetings in which he attacked Prohibition as an infringement of personal freedom and blamed the rising incidence of crime on poverty and not on booze.[21]

Whether Darrow was much of an asset to the Wet cause is doubtful. With the war going badly, and with the Americans standing on the sidelines and giving voice occasionally to pro-German sentiments, importing an American orator was an error in judgment, though hardly as egregious as the one the Wets had committed in Alberta by bringing in A. C. Windle. The Wets, as the Drys were doing, made what yardage they could by appeals to patriotism. One of the Wet slogans was "Be British! Stand by the License System! Vote No!"

The Darrow theme, while it was one which obviously appealed to the union members, did not convince all labour sympathizers. Fred Dixon, Winnipeg's most respected labour politician, joined such socially conscious preachers as Salem Bland, C. W. Gordon, F. B. DuVal and J. H. Hughson in both church services and public rallies.

On the eve of the plebiscite there were day-long church services throughout the city with speakers moving in batteries from one to the other. Included in the speaking corps were F. S. Spence of Toronto, the most dedicated Prohibitionist Canada ever produced, Nellie McClung, and Percy Hagel, the Winnipeg lawyer, who had been disbarred for his part in the escape of the convicted murderer Jack Krafchenko. Hagel, blaming his disgrace on drunkenness, was a prime attraction on the lecture circuit, even though somewhat unreliable in his attendance at scheduled meetings.[22]

The result was clear. Out of forty-six constituencies only three voted Wet. The total vote was 50,484 to 26,502 in favour of Prohibition. If the women had been able to vote, the majority would have at least doubled. North Winnipeg and St. Boniface were both moderately Wet. Whether the electors in polyglot North Winnipeg and French St. Boniface were voting for whisky or against the anti-Catholic stance of the Protestant Prohibitionists was at least arguable.

Saskatchewan quickly became restive with its liquor dispensaries ladling out booze while its sister provinces had voted dry. The pressure from the Banish-the-Bar zealots became irresistible and a plebiscite was called for December 11, 1916, to decide whether to maintain the stores or go for Prohibition. It was a campaign that exhibited none of the bread-and-circuses aspects of those in Alberta and Manitoba. The people of the province had lived for almost eighteen months under a system which severely restricted liquor outlets but nevertheless did provide the thirstier citizens with a legal libation.

The Saskatchewan system had another thing going for it — decent booze. For the first time within the memory of man on the prairies, there was at least a modicum of quality control of the booze supply. When the government had taken over the liquor in the hands of the dealers the previous July, it ran samples through analyses to test the quality. It found that on the average it was sixty per cent water, and contained all manner of poisonous ingredients, albeit in less than lethal quantities, including wood alcohol, a poison that could bring on blindness.

Despite the great change for the better, the electors of Saskatchewan left no doubt of their desires. They voted out the dispensaries and opted for complete Prohibition by a vote of 95,249 to 23,666. There was little discernible difference in the vote between the cities, towns, and rural areas. The cities voted dry by 13,744 to 1,963, the towns by 11,736 to 1,281, and the rural municipalities by 54,946 to 17,996. Saskatoon went Dry by ten to one, Regina, with its large German population, managed only five to one.

If the intention of the Banish-the-Bar crusade was to reduce the social consequence of unbridled boozing to a minimum, then that objective had been achieved by the middle of 1916. The Manitoba Temperance Act came into force on June 1, 1916, the Alberta act a month later; Saskatchewan had substituted the dispensaries for the bars and would move to complete Prohibition on May 1, 1917.

If the intention had been, however, to turn the prairie provinces into an area in which the consumption of beverage alcohol was to be completely done away with, the effort was in vain. Even with adequate enforcement, which was totally lacking, there were enough loopholes left to enable a determined drunk to drink almost without pause. Each of the provinces sported seven or eight breweries which operated under federal charter. They continued to run unhindered. Despite the weight of medical evidence to the contrary, the notion that there was medicinal value in alcohol was still widely held. So there were provisions in the provincial acts for the prescribing of liquor by the medicos and for its sale by drugstores. Because the movement of booze in interprovincial jurisdiction was a federal matter, the provinces were restrained from interfering with imports and exports, particularly imports for export.

The hotels, better than 1,300 in the three provinces, had been deprived of a most important source of income. The owners being businessmen, they were hardly prepared to be driven into bankruptcy, if that was to be their fate, without making an effort to survive. In Saskatchewan the government adopted a system of subsidizing the country hotels. All provinces permitted them to sell Temperance beer of not more than two per cent alcoholic content.

It was only a matter of hours before the more enterprising merchandisers discovered the loopholes in the law. The town of Kenora, Ontario, blossomed overnight with export liquor stores to serve thirsty Winnipeggers, and many a former bartender got a job soliciting orders in Winnipeg for booze to be shipped in from Kenora. Beverage alcohol was outlawed, but advertising its virtues was not. Winnipeg newspapers carried a substantial volume of beer and whisky advertising. One agency, getting a step on its competitors, advertised in the Winnipeg papers that its customers could save freight charges by ordering from Kenora and taking delivery directly from a Winnipeg brewery as soon as the order was mailed to it from Kenora. Manitoba blocked that hole, but others developed.

The breweries continued to brew regular beer and to ship it from the brewery to customers in other provinces. In the Manitoba, Saskatchewan, Alberta across-the-borders shipping, it was usually billed as Temperance beer. It was up to the agents of the shippers to sort strong beer from weak beer for hotels which were doing the importing. If the hotels also decided to sell whisky along with the strong beer, it could also be imported from a neighbouring province.

The final outlawing of beverage alcohol came as a result of the war and the action of the federal government in shutting off supplies. Under the War Measures Act it passed an order-in-council forbidding the shipment after May 1, 1918, of liquor into any province where the purchase was forbidden by a provincial law. The ukase was to run until one year after the end of the war. That order, and stringent restriction of the use of grain in distilling and brewing, effectively brought John Barleycorn as close to his deathbed on the prairies as possible, lacking the total abolition of the manufacture, sale, and possession of beverage alcohol.

Prohibition:
where it worked,
where it didn't

The Prohibition era of the prairie provinces is difficult to define precisely because neither the starting nor the ending dates in the three provinces coincide exactly. Because it is convenient to count years in multiples of ten, it can be said with a fair degree of accuracy that the Prohibition decade ran roughly from 1914, when there was a modest expansion in the number of local option areas that went dry in Manitoba and Saskatchewan, to 1924, when public procurement of distilled damnation again became legal for residents of two of the prairie provinces.

The change which that decade wrought in the life-style of the population was greater than in any other ten-year period in western Canadian history. With the pauperizing effect of unrestrained boozing removed, a new tranquillity came to family life in the cities and towns. As drunkenness disappeared from the streets crime of all kinds declined sharply. That there is a relationship between liquor and crime can be proved statistically and is graphically demonstrated in such works as that of Robert E. Popham and Wolfgang Schmidt for the Alcoholism Research Foundation.[1]

The spectacular statistical correlation of drunkenness and crime, which is so apparent for the prairie provinces, applies to all other sections of Canada as well. Drunkenness peaked on the prairies with the great immigration and construction boom of 1913. Then the picture improved greatly in 1914 for three reasons, two of which were unconnected with liquor. The outbreak of the First World War brought about the absorption of thousands of single men into the Canadian army. The severity of the economic depression which followed the collapse of the real estate and construction booms drastically reduced the available income which could be spent in the bars. Despite the unhappiness of the Banish-the-Bar leaders, the various prohibitory measures which came with the local option plebiscites were beginning to bite into the whisky trade. With the onset of Prohibition and the closing of all the bars, the convictions for drunkenness dropped to minor fractions of the totals for 1913.

In Manitoba there were 7,493 convictions for drunkenness in 1913, a drop to 3,114 in 1916 and to 1,085 in 1917. With the end of the war and the return of the army, drunkenness convictions rose to 1,570 in 1919 and to 2,330 in 1920, during the hiatus when the flood-gates were opened for cross-border liquor shipments. The 1920 peak for drunkenness convictions was not touched again in Manitoba until well after the end of the Second World War.

Exactly the same trends are seen in Saskatchewan: a peak of 2,970 cases in 1913, a drop to 1,062 in 1916, a low of 434 in 1918, and a jump to 919 in 1920.

In Alberta the decline was from 7,283 cases of drunkenness in 1913 to 391 in 1917 and a rise to 1,536 in 1920. It should be noted in connection with all the numbers that the figures, striking as they are, may distort the picture unfavourably for the Prohibition era. During the pre-Prohibition years, as it has been previously noted in passing, drunkenness *per se* was seldom cause for arrest. It was only when the drunks became unreasonably obstreperous or belligerent that they became subject to police action. During Prohibition a reeling drunk would probably be carrying a bottle somewhere on his person and hence, being illegally in possession of liquor, was subject to arrest on sight.

The statistics for convictions for crime of all kinds parallel those for drunkenness. In Manitoba the peak was reached in 1913 when there were 18,095 convictions. There was a steady drop to 8,155 in 1917 and a jump to 12,516 in 1920. The Saskatchewan figures were: a peak of 13,782 in 1914 instead of 1913, a drop to 7,072 in 1917, and a rise to 7,991 in 1920. In Alberta the figures were 19,426 in 1913, 6,627 in 1917, and 8,459 in 1920.

The statistics which backstop the law-and-order aspect of the social revolution are thus available, but there are no statistics for the equally striking changes in the lives of the people. And for good and sufficient reason. This was the age before the gathering of statistics had become an international mania. No teams of census takers knocked on the doors of the former patrons of the now-outlawed bars to inquire into their welfare and new way of life. No doctors of sociology and assorted resource persons poked and probed to assess the make-up of the urban welfare rolls. And again for good reason. There were no welfare departments in any prairie city, even for the wives and families of the soldiers off in France fighting for King and Country.[2] There were neither welfare workers nor sociologists. There were only "relief" offices, where the destitute might beg temporary sustenance from miserly administrations.

Nevertheless there is evidence of the vast social changes in progress. It comes by way of random one-paragraph stories in newspapers, in afterthought comments in police reports, in the plaintive yearnings in print of bored police reporters for the excitement that was theirs on the police beat before the war.

There is evidence, of a sort, in the non-news that replaced the crime news in the daily papers. It was probably a reaction to this non-news, this day after day of nothing happening worth reporting or publishing, that led to an overplay of crime when it did occur, if the crime was related to booze. Thus when the provincial police raided a Temperance hotel and seized a truck full of strong beer, or caught a Ruthenian farmer brewing a modest supply of vodka from his potato peelings and vegetable waste, it was big news. So was the arrest of a rum-runner, or a small-town bootlegger, or a roundup of celebrants at a Ukrainian wedding. But if all the liquor involved in all the lawbreaking reported in a month was gathered in one spot it would hardly have equalled the booze sold by a single city bar on a single payday in the pre-Prohibition decade.

The reports of social gains began to trickle into print very quickly after the general prohibitory laws went into effect. The *Winnipeg Tribune*, in a dispatch from Seattle, Washington, on March 8, 1916, reported that during the first seventeen days after that state went dry, the merchants sold more meat, eggs, and provisions than they had sold in the previous three months. On August 2, 1916, the *Edmonton Bulletin* reported that during the first month of Prohibition in Alberta savings accounts rose by one hundred per cent. In his annual report for 1917, Chief of Police Alfred Cuddy of Calgary emphasized that Prohibition had acted as a preventive for every type of crime. Arrests for drunkenness had dropped in Calgary from 1,743 in 1914 to 183 in 1917. The police force that once had sixty-three constables patrolling the streets was down to twenty-eight constables, and one of its previous four district stations had been closed.[3]

In 1918, the military authorities in Calgary opened negotiations with the civic authorities to rent a stock of iron bars and cell doors from its abandoned regional police station. The cells had been removed from the building, which was put to other use, and stored at the exhibition grounds.[4]

A striking testimonial came from Mr. Justice T. G. Mather of the Manitoba Court of King's Bench in 1918:

> While liquor was freely sold in the bar rooms and through-
> out the Province, a very large proportion of the criminal
> cases that came before the courts were for the affliction of
> personal injury, such as wounding, stabbing and murder,
> committed during a drunken brawl or while under the
> influence of intoxicating liquor. Since the introduction of
> Prohibition there has been a very large diminution in the
> number of wounding cases. One further result is that with-
> in the last six months the gaols at Morden and Minnedosa
> have been closed because there was no longer any neces-
> sity to keep them open.[5]

In his report for 1916, Inspector Spalding of the Moose Jaw detachment of the R.C.M.P. credited Prohibition with being responsible for the reduction in both crime and poverty. Crime, he said, was down by seventy-five per cent, and during the whole year only three or four cases of destitution were reported, a marked contrast from previous years when much of the responsibility for handling numerous cases of destitution fell to the police.[6]

When the Prohibition campaigns were on there was a loud cry from the country hotel owners that closing the bars would bankrupt them. Many of the arguments advanced were most cogent. Over long stretches of winter weather the hotels stayed empty while the fuel bills skyrocketed. Gleichen, Alberta, was a town of seven hundred and had two hotels. S. D. Curran, the owner of the larger of the two, said that he lost between $800 and $900 a month on the rooms-and-meals side of his operation on a year-round basis. Only the profits from his bar enabled him to stay in business.[7]

With the closing of the bars, many hotels in the small towns did close their doors. But things eventually sorted themselves out, the hotels reopened, and Inspector Spalding was only one of many observers who mentioned the reopening of accommodation in all the towns where it was needed. He noted as well that the opinion was unanimous among the businessmen, doctors, storekeepers, and farmers that closing the bars was a step long overdue.

Similar conditions were noted by Inspector West of the Battleford division of the R.C.M.P. He reported that there had been a very marked change in the different towns in his jurisdiction. The farmers were now coming in from the country, doing their business, and leaving for home. Loafers had disappeared from the streets of the towns, drunkenness was almost unknown, and the municipal offices noted an increase of ninety-five per cent in tax payments.[8]

The *Saskatoon Phoenix,*[9] in a general survey of northern Saskatchewan, noted that all towns but one reported general improvement in public morals. Cases of drunkenness on the streets had become so rare that when a drunk did appear he created a mild sensation. Before Prohibition drunks were so numerous that nobody paid any attention to them. One of the most notable changes was apparent on the trains, which had once been notorious for the drunken behaviour of the smoking-room crowds. Now a tomb-like silence pervaded the sleeping cars and day coaches.

The Northwest Commercial Travellers Association did a survey of its members and concluded that hotel accommodation had improved with Prohibition. The hotelkeepers were now faced with the necessity of living off the incomes from their rooms and dining rooms and were paying much closer attention than before to the welfare of their guests.

Fred Dixon, the Manitoba labour leader, noted that before Prohibition, whenever he had come home to Winnipeg, he was always shocked by the number of drunken men and sometimes women he encountered on Main Street. He had been ashamed that his city and province could maintain institutions which were so degrading to humanity. "Now", he said, "I can walk the streets without meeting a single drunk and naturally feel more proud of the city to which I belong and the province in which I live." [10]

W.R. Motherwell, the Minister of Agriculture of Saskatchewan, wrote:

> So far as the working out of prohibition is concerned, it is past debating, we wouldn't return to the old order of things if we were paid to do so. The first six months or a year after the licensed bars were abolished we kept track of the crimes and convictions under the old order compared with the new. The reports were so favourable in this respect to the new order that we have ceased making comparisons. [11]

Charles Tutt was a Salvation Army adjutant at Brandon during and just after the First World War and then moved to Regina. He recalled:

> As a member of the Regina Relief Board, I was present at all the meetings during the past winter and I can state that there was no case mentioned in which it was possible to suspect drinking as a cause, or as one of several contributing causes. . . . Poverty is not now caused by drinking as in the days past when a large proportion of the cases coming to our notice were the result of drinking.
>
> During the year 1920-21 I was official relief officer for the city of Brandon and in that year under Prohibition not

a case of poverty through drink came to my attention and I was acquainted with every case relieved. Anyone who knew the conditions prevailing before Prohibition came into force knows that this is remarkable proof of its efficiency and value, for cases of poverty abounded as a result of drinking husbands and fathers. . . .[12]

Little in the way of statistical information was ever compiled in western Canada on the effect of boozing on industrial efficiency, perhaps because there was so little industry. The behaviour patterns on the prairies, however, were so similar to those of drinkers everywhere that the probabilities are strong that the packing plants, railway shops, steel fabricators, and wholesalers all experienced the same problem of Monday morning blues that afflicted eastern Canadian and United States employers. A good summary of the general American situation was contained in the statement of Henry M. Leland, then president of Cadillac Motor Company of Detroit. He said: "For years previous to the passage of this [Eighteenth] Amendment, on each Monday morning there were from 300 to 500 men absent trying to sober up from the effects of the Saturday night and Sunday drinking. Immediately after it went into effect, this Monday morning delinquency was entirely eliminated. Monday morning became like any other morning — the men all at work."

E. J. Buffington, president of the Illinois Steel Company, added this comment:

The men, because of prohibition, are more contented, and homelife is improved. The women tell us that they receive more money for the home and for clothing and for other domestic uses, and everybody seems to be happy — Our opinion of the influence of prohibition upon our employes is that the employes report for work with greater regularity, resulting in a decrease in the percentage of labor turnover; that the average efficiency of employes has increased; that personal injuries, due to accidents at the mills, have decreased, and the average economical condition of employes' families is improved. [13]

When the Toronto Board of Trade conducted a survey of its members it found them strongly in favour of Prohibition for many of the same reasons. They reported that lost time was down by eighty per cent, there was a sharp drop in accidents, and retail grocers were collecting their accounts quicker than ever before. Monday morning absenteeism was a thing of the past. One bailiff reported his business was off sixty per cent and said it was very rare indeed when he was called upon to make seizures in workers' homes for non-payment of rent.[14]

Most of all, the reports emphasized the improvement in business that followed Prohibition. It was all-encompassing. The Mason and Risch Piano Company noted enthusiastically that even the piano business was benefiting. A Yonge Street merchant in Toronto said: "The money which used to be spent on liquor is now diverted to other channels and mostly spent for comforts and small luxuries for the family, or the improvement of homes, by which every merchant along the street is now benefitting." In the United States, a survey was taken of the retail trade. It was discovered that the business done by the ten-cent stores scored the greatest increases of any and this was the branch of merchandising which depended almost exclusively on working-class patronage.

North American railways all had a rule against employees' drinking on the job, or going on a shift while under the influence of liquor. For the running trades, the office clerk who booked the running crews onto their trains was charged with enforcement of Rule "G". If any employee showed signs of a hang-over he could not be assigned a train until he had sobered up. That the rule was frequently ignored is attested to by a dozen old-time railroaders, and the occasional newspaper story. On February 15, 1916, a Canadian Pacific Railway train pulled into the station at Neville, Saskatchewan, and the crew was so drunk they could not get the train started again. The passengers had to wait until another crew could be brought in from Swift Current to replace them.[15]

The extent to which alcohol contributed to the frightful annual accident toll of the railways is beyond determination, but it must have played a not inconsiderable role. In 1913, the casualty toll on Canadian railways was 653 killed and 2,235 injured. Included in the fatality toll were 250 who were killed while walking on the tracks, and 1,825 of the injured were railway employees. Certainly in most of the comments of the industrial leaders on the drinking problem, it was noted that accidents dropped sharply after Prohibition.

Here and there a poignant insight into the change Prohibition made in the lives of the least privileged classes of society is provided by personal recollection:

> A somewhat humorous result of the success [of prohibition] came out at a subsequent W.C.T.U. meeting when it was found that a number of women had lost their washerwomen. These women did not have to go out to work any more and the members had to do their own washing. I remember a woman (who had recently given birth to a new baby) that mother had helping her; she had a "big girl" four years old who looked after the baby while the mother worked. After the bars were closed, she stopped work because she said "her man came home [from work]. He liked a bottle but it was too dear."
>
> My sister went in training as a nurse in 1919 and during her three years an alcoholic patient was a rarity. There were a few after Christmas and New Year's festivities and if a girl didn't happen to be on the men's ward at that time of year she could get through her entire training without ever seeing a case of D.T.'s. [16]

It is important to note, in connection with this catalogue of testimonials, that the era to which they referred covered only a small segment of the Prohibition Decade, mainly 1917 to 1919, the period in which the closest approach was made to complete Prohibition. Even in this short span, there were loopholes through which booze continued to flow for the determined thirsters after the forbidden juice. This fact in turn points up two blind spots in the Prohibitionist mind. The first might be described as an all-encompassing naïveté. The second was lack of insistence on *total* Prohibition, which led to an under-estimation of the time-bombs that were built into the loop-holes that were permitted.

It seemed an integral part of the Prohibitionist faith that by banning the bars they would outlaw the thirst for booze; that by removing the temptation that lurked on every downtown street corner, mankind's attention would be permanently diverted from the ingestion of alcohol. It was an illusion which, strangely enough, had some basis in reality. In every Temperance movement there were representatives of the drinking population who were desperates for crutches on which to lean. Their remorseful seizures could keep them sober for weeks. But the bars represented an ever-present temptation and the hymnists might well have had this group in mind during the composition of their supplication for guidance from temptation.

The demonstrable fact was, of course, that for the mild tipplers and the town drunks alike, Prohibition, even in its most attenuated form, in the early years did reduce liquor consumption by at least eighty per cent. And in all probability it also reduced the numbers of drinking people by eighty per cent. The possibility that a twenty-per-cent minority would develop seems never to have occurred to the Banish-the-Bar crusaders. It was this thirsty one-fifth or so of the drinking force, which was prepared to go to endless trouble to search out sources of gratification, that, indirectly, eventually brought the prohibitory structure crashing down in ruins.

The utter naïveté of the Dry forces can best be illustrated by the developments in Saskatchewan. When the bars were closed in 1915 no law enforcement agency was set up to keep them closed. Instead the government decided to appoint a handful of regional observers, usually clergymen, to keep an eye on things to make sure that the law was respected.

In the event that any violation of the liquor law was discovered, the regional overseers would notify the R.C.M.P., who would take the matter in hand. But why should the Saskatchewan government expect any difficulty? When it closed down 403 bars in hotels across the province in 1915 it also opened 20 liquor stores where the citizens could get their booze if they wanted it. Unhappily for this rationale the thirsters were spread unevenly around the province and many lived at inconvenient distances from the liquor stores. This fact in turn led to the flow of booze into the province from mail-order houses in Alberta and Manitoba. And for those who could not afford the mail-order price, or who could not abide the long wait between sending an order and receiving the bottle, there was the nearest drugstore.

The delusion that there was even a trace of medicinal value in alcohol died hard, and it was not even sick at the time Prohibition went into effect. Doctors were empowered to prescribe booze for

their patients and druggists were allowed to keep a stock of un-
bottled whisky on hand in kegs; others carried regularly bottled
brands. There was no limit on the quantity doctors could prescribe.
Again the 80/20 majority-minority ratio became a factor in assuaging even mild thirsts. There is little doubt that at least eighty per cent
of the doctors and a like proportion of druggists were against the
prescription system. But the twenty per cent worked it for all it was
worth. In one prosecution in Calgary, witnesses reported they had
walked into the office of a rather notorious prescription writer and
told him that they were bound for Banff on a fishing trip and were
fearful lest they catch a chill while fishing. He prescribed a quart of
Scotch as a chill preventative. Ultimately the publication of such
cases moved the medical societies to urge some restraint among their
members and they emphasized their concern by suspending the
licences of the non-compliers.[17]

In all the provinces, in the beginning, prescriptions were filled
without limitation as to quantity, except that practice seemed to
dictate that a maximum of one imperial quart would be about right
for patients who could afford it or had an imperial thirst. Those who
could not afford a full quart could get a twenty-six-ounce bottle or a
twelve-ounce flask. In Saskatchewan, it was not until 1919 that a
newly appointed liquor commission discovered that there was no
regulation which required doctors to keep track of the prescriptions
issued. There was, however, a record of sorts kept by the vendors
who supplied the druggists. As regulations were made limiting the
amount of liquor which could be prescribed, the importance of the
drug outlets in maintaining the addiction of the thirsty minority
dropped sharply. Saskatchewan druggists in January 1917 filled
29,640 prescriptions for twelve-and twenty-six-ounce bottles. In the
same month five years later they handled only 7,126 bottles of eight
ounces each.[18]

More important than the druggists, however, in maintaining the
flow of throat lubricants were the breweries. The druggists did not
go after business, the brewers did. Operating as they did under
federal licence, it was beyond the constitutional power of the provinces to close the breweries down. The same ambivalent Prohibitionist attitude that permitted the doctor-druggist outlets to survive
also permitted the hotels to sell so-called Temperance beer. Thus a
score of breweries scattered across the prairies worked full time

during the early years of Prohibition making what was ostensibly Temperance beer, but a substantial quantity of which was more likely than not strong beer.

The importance of beer as a bootleg stock in trade was that it could be shipped interprovincially — as Temperance beer, of course — even when the ban was up against whisky. Within the carloads of Temperance beer that were shipped from Winnipeg to Saskatoon, and from Saskatoon to Winnipeg, there were barrels of strong beer, specially marked to prevent their detection by liquor inspectors.[19] The city hotels were encouraged to keep their bars open for the sale of weak beer, which could disguise the fact that the hotel also had strong beer and whisky available for its known customers.

The hopes of the city hotels that they would be able to survive on Temperance beer with bootlegged strong stuff on the side were quickly blighted. A generation of drinkers accustomed to the bite and sharp kick of pre-Prohibition rot-gut became waterlogged before they became intoxicated. For another thing, the once boisterous atmosphere of the bars was replaced by a shushed quiet as the bartenders strove to attract as little attention as possible from the gendarmery. Prohibition broke the after-work, Saturday-night, payday drinking pattern of the working class and the drift away from the bars became almost a stampede. The boisterous treating and singing and horseplay was replaced by a funereal silence. Getting drunk wasn't fun any more.

The hotel business had over-expanded outrageously during the pre-war boom. Winnipeg had ninety-six hotels in 1914, three-quarters of them within a mile of the C.P.R. station, and the other cities were in proportion. It was inevitable that the business was headed for a shake-down even without Prohibition. Prohibition brought many of the hotels to the verge of bankruptcy. To assist them, and to encourage them to keep their bars going, the breweries adopted the practice of lending their customers money with which to pay their fines when they were caught bootlegging. By the end of Prohibition many of the hotels had been taken over by the breweries for their debts.

That, however, could not be attributed to the vigour with which the provinces enforced their liquor laws. Whether that responsibility evolved into the bailiwick of the R.C.M.P., the provincial police, or the Liquor Commission inspectors, an enforcement vacuum of sorts developed in the cities. The provincial operatives were confined mainly to the rural areas and city enforcement was left largely to city police. They had little stomach as individuals for snooping into dusty basements in search of booze or strong beer. Nor were they overly encouraged to do so by the various civic governments.

By 1916, the cities of the west were engaged in a desperate struggle to maintain even admittedly inadequate services for their people. The collapse of the pre-war real estate boom had left them with millions of dollars' worth of uncollected and, as it would turn out, uncollectable taxes on their rolls. By the end of the war great stretches of vacant real estate for which the cities had gone into debt to provide miles of sewer and water mains were given over to the cities for taxes. To avoid bankruptcy, the cities cut services to an irreducible minimum and among the services cut hardest were the police departments.[20] In such circumstances, law enforcement activities tended to be concentrated in areas that mattered most — rounding up aliens, enforcing the wartime law against being unemployed, keeping a sharp watch for violent crime.

Despite less than enthusiastic participation of the police in the enforcement of Prohibition, it actually took several years for the illegal drinking to get substantially out of hand. In Winnipeg, during the general strike of 1918, the leaders were unanimously of the opinion that Prohibition had been an important factor in the complete absence of violence. Similarly, the famous general strike of 1919, which lasted for over a month and involved most of the city's working force, was notable for the lack of violence. It was only toward the end, when tempers on all sides were frazzled beyond endurance, that a riot broke out. It too was featured by the sobriety of both the strikers and their opponents.

This lack of vigorous enforcement served to encourage the bootleggers, and by late 1919 there was enough drunkenness around Winnipeg to attract the attention of the Social Service Council, which sent a delegation to city hall to urge the city to ginger up its enforcement. The request was rejected out of hand by the chairman of the finance committee, who told the delegates they were talking to the wrong people. The provincial government, which got all the money from fines levied on the bootleggers, was the one that should pay the cost of enforcement.[21]

For their part, the provincial governments had grievances of their

own. Their officers periodically raided the breweries and hauled
away great quantities of strong beer and beverage alcohol. In Manitoba one raid alone yielded up eighty barrels of illicit booze. Under
federal licence law, breweries with three convictions could have their
permits cancelled. Manitoba had one brewery with thirteen violations still running at top capacity while Ottawa turned its back. [22]

Enforcement of the law against the breweries was difficult in the
extreme. The authorities had to prove that the strong beer was in
fact being shipped to Manitoba destinations for sale in Manitoba. It
was a simple matter to ship a carload into Saskatchewan and then
return it clandestinely. Most often it was simply loaded onto the
brewery trucks and delivered direct to the hotels. As the trucks
moved through the city streets they were ignored by the city police.
Whether the trucks were loaded with strong beer or weak beer was
no concern of theirs, and few, if any, avenues of communication
existed between the various police forces.

A classic example of the lack of co-operation that existed occurred in 1922. The Manitoba Provincial Police, acting on a tip that a
bank was going to be robbed in western Manitoba, set up an ambush
and were well prepared to gun down the robbers if they failed to
surrender. The robbers nevertheless broke through the ambush and
got away. The Provincial Police had not notified the R.C.M.P., who
were also patrolling the area for bank robbers, that an ambush was
being set up. [23]

It was not long before the lack of any genuine interest in enforcing
Prohibition began to be reflected in the magistrates' courts. Enforcing the law might have proved difficult, though far from impossible,
for an efficient and dedicated staff. In the face of the very tight
labour market that prevailed, recruiting such a staff was impossible.
There were many better ways of making a living than being a liquor
spotter. As a result, those who would take the jobs were often men
of less than exemplary character. And, because in the beginning in
each province it was necessary to prove sale to obtain a conviction,
the enforcers actually participated in violation of the law as they
exchanged their marked money for booze. It was to overcome that
problem that the Alberta government, on July 1, 1917, made it
illegal for any resident of the province to be in possession of more
than one quart of whisky.

Whether the offence was possession or sale, magistrates refused to convict on the word of a single spotter that he had bought the liquor offered in evidence from the prisoner in the dock. It was "one man's word against another's", and the word of a bootlegger seemed as believable as that of a liquor spotter. Though the magistrates voted for Prohibition, and sometimes joined in the clamour for more stringent enforcement, they shared the wide public prejudice against the people who were responsible for enforcing the law they helped to enact. To overcome this prejudice and obtain convictions, the liquor inspectors had to work in pairs, which made enforcement almost impossible against small-town bootlegging.

Unlike Don Quixote in his windmill-tilting campaign, the Temperance law enforcers seldom went searching for offenders on their own. Usually they acted on complaints which poured into the liquor commissions' or attorney-generals' offices from helpful citizens. As an example, a woman in the town of Barons, Alberta, complained that the druggist was selling whisky to the town drunk, and, worse still, was seen abroad in a dazed condition himself.[24] Following regular procedure, two liquor inspectors were dispatched to the town to investigate. As a normal thing, it would be scarcely half an hour after the arrival of any such strangers in town before the whole town knew that they were "liquor spotters". Such was the temper of the times that they would have been able to count on the assistance of ninety per cent of the inhabitants. Within the other ten per cent there would be several who would set out enthusiastically to warn the bootlegging suspect of their arrival.

It was possible, of course, for the officers to remain incognito, if they were comparatively new to the force, hung around town for a week under one pretext or another, and assembled enough evidence to justify a raid on a person suspected of having a large cache of illegal liquor on hand. But in most cases an actual sale had to be proved, and only a hungry bootlegger or a village idiot would sell a bottle of booze to a couple of strangers.

The enforcement of the law against "moonshiners" was quite another matter. Illegally distilling alcohol was a federal offence and was not related to provincial Prohibition. The provincial and the city police were involved only when the homebrew moved into the retail market. If they blundered onto an illicit still a most cumbersome procedure had to be followed. They would notify their superiors, who would notify the Attorney General, who would notify the

Federal Customs and Excise Department, who would authorize the obtaining of a search warrant and the staging of a raid by the R.C.M.P.

In an effort to bring a measure of common sense to bear on liquor enforcement, the Alberta government suggested to Ottawa that its liquor inspectors be enrolled as special constables for the Excise Department. Then, when they discovered illicit stills being operated, action might be taken at once, before all the evidence could be destroyed. At a time when efficiency was the last thing the Canadian Department of Customs and Excise wanted, the offer of co-operation was naturally spurned. [25]

There was a good deal of home distilling of booze on the prairies — before, during, and after Prohibition. The peasants who were settled in their German, Polish, Ukrainian, and Scandinavian blocs were only doing what their forefathers had done for a thousand years when they made their own "ceremonial" refreshments. Turning surplus harvests of potatoes into vodka was as natural for the settlers from Russia as making sauerkraut was for the Germans.

It seems a safe assumption that in the early years of Prohibition most of the illegal stills were operated for home consumption. They had small capacity, consisting of a few salvaged vinegar or flour barrels in which the potatoes, grain, etc., were fermented with a makeshift boiler and condensing coil. One ingenious farmer salvaged a copper-cored radiator from an old Model T Ford and used that for his coil. But from a money-making perspective, the whole operation was so time-consuming, and often downright expensive as sugar and honey were used in the process, that it was not worth the trouble. In later years, when increased excise taxes raised the price of alcohol far above what it had been at the outbreak of Prohibition, illegal distilleries sprang up in the hinterland with capacities running into the hundreds of gallons.

Except in such isolated areas as the Crowsnest Pass on the Alberta-British Columbia border, the volume of liquor involved in the illicit traffic must have been infinitesimal compared with the flow prior to Prohibition. In the Crowsnest Pass, there was alleged to have been a great deal of illicitly distilled homebrew made by the coal miners. Seemingly, wherever there were pockets of "foreigners" during wartime there was widespread suspicion that laws of all kinds were being violated. The production from the illegal stills was run into southern Alberta and down to Montana over several well-used back-country trails. A respectable body of legend has grown up around this area and stories of gun battles between police and rum-runners, and rum-runners and hijackers abound. It was in the Crows-nest Pass that Emilio Picariello gunned down an R.C.M.P. constable in 1922 after a hectic chase through the Pass with a convoy of liquor. [26]

It is possible that during the driest years there was more interest in booze in Alberta than in either Manitoba or Saskatchewan. Alberta had managed the smallest majority for Prohibition in the Laurier plebiscite and was by no means as keen for it in 1916. It was adjacent to Montana, one of the last states to vote for Prohibition, and after 1917 there was some trade in American whisky being run into the province. Little of this traffic ever got above Lethbridge, however. In the Peace River country, a correspondent of the *Edmonton Bulletin* noted that so little whisky was sold outside the drugstores that a bootlegger would go broke.

Yet despite the achievement of a very high level of sobriety over most of the prairie society the Prohibitionists were far from happy or satisfied. Premier Walter Scott of Saskatchewan, after he retired to British Columbia, said he believed the people of Saskatchewan wrong in voting out the government liquor stores. He was sure that the system could have been made to work if it had been given a chance. Certainly it had reduced public drunkenness to nearly zero, and had vastly improved the quality of the liquor which was available for those who could not reform their appetites. [27]

The Temperance zealots, no less than the general public, seemed, however, to share the conviction of the governments that the Prohibition law should result in province-wide total abstinence. In a sense, the Banish-the-Bar crusade was followed by an enforcement crusade. There was an incessant clamour for more rigorous enforcement. Even the newspapers which supported Prohibition gave full play to such violations of the law as came to their attention, adding point to a common phrase of the time, which was used in connection with the brothels as well as booze: "Everybody seems to know what is going on right under our noses except the police." At each session of the legislatures the liquor acts were tightened and tightened. In 1918 the provincial laws were augmented by federal Prohibition as well. The federal Order-in-Council of March 11, 1918, outlawed the manu-

facture of beverage alcohol and the transportation or sale of it anywhere in Canada.

The usual exceptions were there, of course: "for use for medicinal, scientific, mechanical, industrial or sacramental purposes
under terms of this license". Even with these exceptions, it ought to
have been possible to turn the whole country into a drinking man's
Sahara. In fact it just about did, save for the breweries and their
Temperance beer, and the now greatly reduced and better controlled
leakage through the drugstores.

As time passed, the country seemed to be becoming accustomed,
if not totally reconciled, to the arid way of life. How permanent the
cure would have been if the treatment had been allowed to continue
is a fascinating speculation. Unfortunately, for the sake of such
philosophizing, the federal government abandoned the treatment
long before the disease had run its course.

The 1918 Order-in-Council was to run until the end of the war and
one year beyond. With the end of the war the Dry provinces of the
west bombarded Ottawa with appeals to have the provisions of the
Order-in-Council embedded in the statutes of the country. But in
1919 Ottawa had a great deal besides booze on its mind. Besides
attending the peace conference in Paris, struggling with a seemingly
uncontrollable inflationary spiral, dampening down labour unrest
that was getting out of control on a hundred fronts, and trying to
pacify the angry agitation of the prairie wheat growers, the warring
politicians of the Union Government were in the process of destroying it from within.

The federal government was being pushed and pulled from all
directions, and by no means the least of the pressure for removal of
all wartime restrictions came from the distillers. The United States,
which had been drifting steadily toward Prohibition since the turn of
the century, was poised for the final plunge. In December 1917,
both houses of Congress had approved by the required two-thirds
majority the submission of the Eighteenth Amendment of the Constitution to the states for ratification or rejection. By January 16,
1919, the necessary three-quarters of the states had ratified the
Prohibition amendment and, in accordance with its provisions, Prohibition would come into full force on January 16, 1920. It would
thereafter be illegal to import, manufacture, transport, or sell beverage alcohol in the United States. In October 1919, the Congress

passed the Volstead Act, which created the federal enforcement agency.

While all this was going on, Canada's arid condition was being maintained under the 1918 Order-in-Council. But as it was based on the emergency powers of the War Measures Act and would expire in November 1919, pressure mounted both from the Drys and from the provincial governments for a Canadian Prohibition act which would follow American precedent and make the suppression of boozing a federal responsibility.

When the Canada Temperance Act was passed in November 1919, it fell short of that goal. It did, however, make it illegal to ship beverage alcohol into any province that voted to forbid the importation or sale of liquor. As all the provinces save Quebec had already voted for Prohibition, the assumption was that the act would continue the status quo of that November. Oh no, said Ottawa; the act required each province to hold a referendum on the question before it came into full force.

The need for another vote was shattering news to the Drys. Even worse news was the date picked by Ottawa for the prairie referenda — October 25, 1920. The effect of that decision was to open the floodgates for booze to flow from all directions. Mail-order boozoriums which had bloomed briefly in 1916 could quickly be re-established. Beverage alcohol of all kinds could be shipped into Manitoba from Ontario and Saskatchewan, into Saskatchewan from Manitoba and Alberta, into Alberta from Saskatchewan and British Columbia.

And that in fact was what happened. In 1920 the prairie towns immediately broke out in a rash of small-bore mail-order whisky dealers, all eager to capitalize on the demands of the neighbouring provinces. It was Harry Bronfman, a prospering auto-dealer and hotel owner in Yorkton, however, who saw where the real pot of gold was located — across the border in the United States. Between the expiration of the federal ban on interprovincial shipments of booze and the holding of the plebiscite, he would have almost unlimited freedom to stock up with supplies. During that hiatus he could develop connections with American rum-runners to establish markets which might survive long after the interprovincial flow was stopped.

For the Prohibitionists of Manitoba, Saskatchewan, and Alberta, it was "Once more unto the breach, dear friends, once more." The battles of 1915 and 1916 would have to be fought all over again, for if the chaotic conditions which had prevailed in 1916 were to be permitted to return, Prohibition, as the Banish-the-Bar zealots conceived it, could be filed as a noble experiment that went wrong, and forgotten.

Yorkton, where Harry planted the money tree

Of all the 3,500,000 immigrants who came to Canada between 1885 and 1914 a few may have come with less, but none went further, than the family of Yechiel and Minnie Bronfman who in 1889 fled from the pogroms of Bessarabia to a homestead north of Wapella in what would become Saskatchewan. They were among the vanguard of several hundred Jewish families that came to the Manitoba-Saskatchewan borderland, many of whom the Baron de Hirsch rescued from Russia and settled in colonies in the Canadian west, as well as in South America and Australia. The baron helped to save many thousands of Jews from death in the pogroms then sweeping eastern Europe, but his plan to create viable Jewish colonies in the hinterlands of the world was doomed to failure. The rescued Jews were people of diverse qualities and skills, but peasants they were not. Of the half-dozen groups he settled on the Canadian prairies, none stayed for much more than a decade.

For the Bronfman family, there must have been many times during their two years at Wapella when they wondered which turned the cruellest face upon them, the peasants of Bessarabia or the climate of western Canada. Certainly the virgin wilderness of the Wapella area, part bush and part prairie, was an unfriendly environment for immigrants lacking in basic farming skills or instincts for agriculture. The elder Bronfman, who had operated a grist-mill in his native Napovda, was particularly ill-equipped for a sod-busting career. Other settlers came with half-grown sons who could assist in the task of clearing the bush and breaking the soil to the plough. The Bronfmans had only Abe who was six, Harry who was three, and Laura who was a babe in arms.[1]

But Yechiel, whose name was quickly Anglicized to Ekiel and would be further Anglicized to Ezekiel, had something infinitely more valuable than a strong back or a green thumb. His was a family that had survived for more than a thousand years in the vicinity of the Black Sea coast, over which the Turks and Russians and Romanians had fought for centuries. As Jews they had been fair game for the genocidal impulses of whatever power reigned over the land. To survive in such an environment required a rare coupling of native cunning and a high order of intelligence. The Bronfmans had both in abundance. When it became apparent to Ekiel that there had to be a better way of making a living than homesteading at Wapella, he loaded his family and his possessions on his farm wagons and moved to Brandon, a town of 3,500 located 120 miles to the southeast. There two more sons and three more daughters were born before the family moved on to Winnipeg fifteen years later.

With only a rudimentary knowledge of the language, and lacking any salable skills, Ekiel Bronfman would have been ill-equipped to storm the commercial battlements of Brandon even if he had not been a Jew. But if he had not been a Jew, he probably would not have identified and seized upon the one avenue to success open to him. He had his horses and his wagon, which were all he needed to set himself up in business as a peddler, as many a displaced co-religionist would do. As he looked around Brandon for something to peddle, he discovered a great pile of slabs which had been trimmed from the logs by the local sawmill. They were for sale cheap, almost for the taking. Bronfman was in the fuel business, which, given Manitoba's winter climate, was sure to be a thriving one for at least six months of the year. The details of the Bronfman life in Brandon are understandably sketchy, but it is known that soon after his arrival Bronfman bought a vacant lot near the C.P.R. station and turned it into a combination woodyard and horse corral.[2]

In the summer horse traders often came through western Manitoba with herds they had rounded up in Montana and North Dakota to sell to the homesteaders. Some were farm horses that had wandered from home in winter storms; others were "green-broke" mustangs — "green-broke" meaning they could be haltered and led without trampling a farmer to death. Ekiel expanded into the horse business as a natural extension of his fuel business. He would buy half a dozen wild horses and break them to harness by hitching them, one by one, in a team with one of his well-trained animals. The quiet horse would act as a brake on the untrained horse and the latter would soon be worn into tractability by the weight of the heavy loads of coal and wood. After a few days on the fuel wagon the new horse was ready for sale to farmers at a good profit.

What with horse training and dealing, wood slabs, and whatever other work came his way, Ekiel Bronfman prospered in Brandon, and was able to buy a comfortable red brick house for his family and keep the Bronfman table well supplied with food. But it was far from easy, and as soon as Abe and Harry were able to work they went to work. How much exposure either had to formal education is unknown but in the nature of things it had to be minimal. Manitoba in 1891 was just switching from its religious school system to secular public schools and there was no place in the Catholic or Protestant schools for Jews. The switch, moreover, was taking place without a compulsory school attendance act. What book learning Abe and Harry acquired was most likely obtained at home or at the synagogue. In any event, both were at work before they were out of their teens, sometimes on the business end of a pick or shovel on railway construction or maintenance. By the time Sam, the third son, reached school age, the public schools were in operation in Brandon and he attended until the family moved to Winnipeg when he was fifteen. Allan, the sixth child and youngest son, continued through high school and the University of Manitoba to a law degree.

Ten years after the family moved to Brandon family finances had improved to a point where Ekiel could afford to send his two eldest sons off to Winnipeg to learn a trade. Abe's chosen calling was cigar-making and he apprenticed to the Lee Cigar factory on Main Street for six months. Harry studied harness-making. In their off hours Abe hung around the Main Street poolrooms, where he could more than hold his own with the city slickers, and Harry fell under the spell of Annie Gellerman, their landlady's daughter, whom he was ulti-mately to marry.[3]

Winnipeggers who can recall the apprenticeship days of the Bronf-man boys remember how much they resembled each other in both size — they were of medium height and build — and looks despite the three years' difference in their ages. The family resemblance was a striking characteristic of all the Bronfmans. Forty-odd years later the four brothers and four sisters sat for a formal family group photograph and they were still as alike in size and shape as the proverbial peas in the pod. It was recalled, too, that the Yiddish translation for Bronfman is "whiskyman" and the boys of his age frequently teased Harry by shouts of "Hey, whisky man!"[4]

Whether Harry ever pursued the harness-making trade is open to question. For a time after he returned to Brandon on completion of his training, Abe worked at his trade, and then gravitated into the occupation that was to found the family fortune. What more ap-propriate trade could there be for a family named "whiskyman" than the hotel business, which survived in the west on the profits from whisky? As previously noted, the urgent need of the country hotels for all the profit they could get out of booze was one reason given by both Manitoba and Saskatchewan for resisting Temperance pressure for greater restrictions on the bars. In Saskatchewan, the government even flew in the face of Temperance sympathy. In 1909 it set back the closing hour by thirty minutes to improve the eco-nomics of the country hotels. The hotel which gave Abe Bronfman his start was either the Arlington in Brandon or one at Emerson, Manitoba.

Abe Bronfman's apprenticeship was short; by the age of twenty-one he had acquired sufficient expertise to launch the Bronfman family into the hotel business. In 1904 he took over the Balmoral Hotel in Yorkton, Saskatchewan, a substantial brick building of sixty rooms. The choice of the town and the hotel was a felicitous one on every count. As one of the earliest settled villages in eastern Saskatchewan, its population doubled and redoubled during the next decade, and so did the population of the surrounding country-side. The railway construction boom would give Yorkton, which was on both the Canadian Pacific and the Canadian Northern railways, a direct connection with all the important centres of Manitoba and Alberta. The hotel itself was on Livingston Avenue, directly across the street from the C.P.R. express sheds through which Bronfman whisky would flow by the carload after the re-opening of interpro-vincial trade in the 1920 hiatus.

No details of the purchase survive, but the size of the hotel — 60 rooms — does not by any means indicate that the investment was necessarily a substantial one. Most of the hotels, and a great deal of other construction on the Canadian frontier, were built by entrepre-neurs who were long on optimism but shy on capital. As the inevit-able collapses followed the booms, many enterprises were taken over by mortgage companies. In the case of the hotels, the furnishings were frequently seized separately by holders of chattel mortgages. Thus a hotel proprietor might own the building and contents, the building alone, or the contents alone. In the parlance of the times, a hotel proprietor was most often the person who owned "the in-sides".

When foreclosures occurred, the mortgage companies had but one desire — to unload the property and its contents as quickly as pos-sible on somebody who would take care of it, operate it, and, hope-fully, pay off the mortgages. It was thus possible to become a hotel proprietor with little more than enough capital to make a down-pay-ment on the furniture. Given the kind of furniture that was typical of the average hotel room — a bed, a chair, and a washstand — an entire hotel could be equipped for surprisingly little. An outlay of thirty dollars a room would have bought everything up to and in-cluding window blinds, essential crockery, a fire-escape rope to hang under each window, replenishments for the bar and pantry, and a repainted sign for the front door. The terms on which the Bronfmans acquired the Balmoral probably died with Harry, if not with Abe. Two years after he took possession Abe was able to advertise that his hostelry had been completely renovated and refurnished and now contained sixty good rooms, steam heat, electric lights, electric bells, sample rooms, and hot- and cold-water baths.[5]

Two years after Abe took over the Balmoral, Harry moved to Yorkton and joined him in its operation. They shared joint billing as the Bronfman Brothers — proprietors of the hotel. That they profited mightily from the boom that gripped the Yorkton district from 1905 to 1915 can be demonstrated by a single fact. By 1910 they had expanded their nest-egg to a point where Abe could move to Port Arthur, Ontario, to become proprietor of the Mariaggi Hotel, the fanciest hostelry between Toronto and Winnipeg. It was a four-storey structure with verandahs running the entire length of the front and side on two levels. It had "110 Comfortable and Commodious rooms, 30 rooms en suite with bath, large and well lighted sample rooms with telephones and an elevator that runs to every floor".[6]

The departure of first Abe and then Harry for Yorkton marked the end of the Bronfman domicile in Brandon. Ekiel sold out whatever modest interests he had acquired there and moved his family to Winnipeg, to a five-roomed house with a store-front at the corner of Pacific Avenue and Isabel Street across from the site of the Midland railway yards. A year later they moved to less cramped quarters at 514 Alexander Avenue. Both locations were in an old, but well maintained, working class district, as would befit the status of both Ekiel and his son Sam, whose occupations were given as labourers by the city directory.

Some question must arise over the accuracy of the description of Sam as a labourer. In 1907 he was sixteen years old and suffered, as he had from birth, from a weakened left arm. There would be little work as a labourer that he could do in Winnipeg. The best guess is that he swung into the role he would play for the next twenty years as a sort of utility infielder or free safety for his elder brothers. He went where he was needed and did what had to be done. He first went to Yorkton to help Harry after Abe left. Then he moved to Port Arthur and worked for Abe. Then it was back to Yorkton for a spell with Harry. Ekiel, after he moved to Winnipeg, seems to have retired

from active work, but he too spent long periods with Harry at Yorkton and Abe at Port Arthur, until his death in 1919.[7]

The Bell Hotel, which was located in the very heart of Winnipeg's
drinking district, a hundred yards down Main Street from the new
Royal Alexandra Hotel, came onto the market in 1913. It was added
to the Bronfman chain and Sam, who had just turned twenty-one,
was placed in charge, though it is safe to assume that Ekiel, who had
moved his family to a large house on nearby Lily Street, kept an eye
on the operation. Jewish boys may come of age, religiously, at thirteen at Bar Mitzvah but few Jewish fathers of that era would have
conceded that their sons reached maturity in a business sense before
they were at least thirty. According to the well-laundered Sam
Bronfman legend, Sam bought the hotel himself "with $190,000 in
family money and loans". In his autobiographic sketch . . . *from
little acorns* . . . he casually assumes credit for everything else that
ever happened to the clan.[8]

It is more probable that in 1913 the Bronfman family decisions
were being made by the troika of Ekiel, Abe, and Harry. But however the decisions were made, the entire enterprise then, and until
Harry's crippling illness and Sam's takeover twenty-five years later,
was a joint venture in which all members of the family, including the
four daughters, shared. How the shares were divided has never been
revealed. But as late as 1922, when Harry made a $200,000 settle-
ment with the Income Tax department for the profits earned from
1917 until 1921, the arrangement was between the government and
the entire family as a unit.[9] The relative interests of the various
members of the family were ultimately sorted out and divided when
its operational base was moved to Montreal. All that, however,
occurred at a time that is well beyond the scope of this book.

The Bell Hotel, which had seemed such a potential bonanza when
the Bronfmans acquired it, never quite achieved that status, for it
was bought at the top of the market. It was one of the best of the
smaller hotels on Main Street and it could hardly have been better
located to catch both the transient and the resident trade. It was
within two hundred yards of the C.P.R. station and midway between
transfer points of half a dozen streetcar lines. But the pre-war real
estate boom that was gripping all of western Canada was headed for
an imminent collapse. The First World War would soon drain away
thousands of the young single men who spent their off hours in the

Main Street bars. The influx of immigrants ended abruptly. A size-
able depression settled over the land, and out of it emerged the
Prohibition crusade which would bring ultimate bankruptcy to
many a western hotel owner.

If it had not been for Prohibition Harry would probably have been
content to spend the rest of his life in Yorkton. Of all the Bronfman
brothers he was the easiest going, most patient, and slowest to anger.
He was hence the opposite of Sam, whose hair-trigger temper, physically violent reactions, and blistering vocabulary of gutter oaths
made him the terror of family and business alike. One Yorkton
acquaintance remembered Harry as "a nice guy, really. You know,
always pleasant, a real Kiwanian or Rotarian type, but, my God, was
he sharp with a mind like a steel trap!" In the fourteen years he spent
in Yorkton, Harry grew from one of the smallest tadpoles in a puddle
to a well developed frog in a modest pond. Under his management
the Balmoral Hotel became a favoured stopping place for the commercial travellers and grew into something of a social centre to which
the gentry frequently repaired for Sunday evening dinner. "Harry,"
they said, "always set a good table." [10]

Not only did he clear off the mortgages on the Balmoral in short
order, he bought out his main competitor, the Royal Hotel, which he
tore down and planned to replace with a much larger hostelry. He
also acquired the hotels at Sheho and Saltcoats, two nearby towns,
and as his other interests expanded he brought in Frank Brunner
from Regina, to run his hotels. He bought the entire city block on
which the Balmoral stood and put up a half-dozen stores. He bought
out the City Garage and became the largest Grey Dort dealer in
Saskatchewan. He even established the Western Prudential Investments and Trust Company, Ltd., a high-sounding enterprise that
never did come to fruition.

Harry Bronfman was a lifelong supporter of the Liberal party of
Saskatchewan, a fact that would return to haunt both him and the
Liberals long after he left Saskatchewan. On one occasion he even
toyed with getting into politics himself. That was toward the end of
the First World War when he was bitten by the mayoralty bug. As
one of Yorkton's most successful businessmen and largest taxpayers,
he could have been persuaded that he owed it to the town to become
its mayor. He first tried the idea out on Sam Wynn, the editor of the

Yorkton Enterprise. Wynn did not discourage him but suggested that the best procedure would be to talk it over first with Levi Beck, the town's richest man, a successful farmer and nearest approach to merchant prince. As Bronfman was a good customer of Beck's he expected a favourable reaction. Instead, Beck was appalled at the idea.

"Harry," he roared when he recovered his breath, "I'd give everything I own to keep you or any other Jew from ever becoming mayor of Yorkton."

The confrontation gave rise to a couple of Bronfman legends. The first is that Harry Bronfman was so outraged at Beck's reaction that he vowed to destroy him; and did. It is a fact that Beck lost his huge farm-spread to the mortgage companies and his business interest to the banks. He spent his last days living on a compassionate pension of fifty dollars a month granted by the bank in consideration of past business. The likelihood is, of course, that it was over-extension in the post-war economic collapse that did Levi Beck in, rather than Harry Bronfman.[11]

The second legend is that Harry Bronfman took such a scunner against the town after the Beck reaction that he vowed never to return when he left for Regina in 1921. The basis for that legend is that the Bronfman brothers scattered their largess widely around Montreal and Winnipeg and never returned a dollar to Yorkton which gave them their start. There is a minor factual flaw here. Harry did leave five thousand dollars in his will to the Yorkton Synagogue, and the sadly decimated Jewish community of Yorkton was hoping for a similar bequest from Sam in order to replace the synagogue's heating system. They were disappointed, perhaps because Sam, unlike Harry, had never looked on Yorkton as home.

It must be noted in passing, of course, that Harry Bronfman may not have enjoyed the same pleasant image in the eyes of the Yorkton townsfolk that he had in his own. He was the hotel owner, which automatically classed him with the forces of evil for half the people of the community. In the pre-Prohibition era, his hotel, like hotels everywhere, lived with the vexing problem of the interdicts, the confirmed drunkards who could not be legally served in any saloon. In the smaller communities, most hotels were able to identify the interdicts from the names on the lists which the government sent around every month. In towns such as Yorkton, which was a bustling and expanding centre with a substantial floating population, identification was much more difficult, particularly for new bartenders.

When an interdict staggered home full of booze there was a good chance that the neighbours would complain to the provincial liquor police if the man's family did not. In that case few remorseful and hungover drunks could resist the urge to squeal on the architect of their misery, the local saloonkeeper. There was, on the other hand, a natural antipathy toward the whole interdiction system on the part of the liquor trade. The boozers were always full of excuses for the behaviour that led to the charge of habitual drunkenness and blacklisting. As they could be placed on the list without trial by a liquor inspector, there was always the chance that spitefulness was involved. With the treating custom so widely in vogue, an interdict could accompany a friend into the bar and be well on his way toward saturation before a busy bartender was aware what was going on. There was an even better chance that most bartenders turned blind eyes to the regulations and treated interdicts like everyone else. Harry Bronfman, ergo, could well have been a law-abiding plaster saint and still have run afoul of the law. The prosecutions of the Balmoral and Bronfman's appearances in court before and during Prohibition did nothing to endear him to the Temperance zealots of Yorkton, of whom Levi Beck was numbered among the leaders. As a cynical resident explained, "Harry Bronfman couldn't have been elected dog catcher of Yorkton, even if he hadn't been a Jew." [12]

Though the depression, the war, and Prohibition combined to impede the Bronfman climb to the heights of affluence, the family was not one to accept defeat without a struggle. Certainly not with the loopholes which had been built into the Prohibition laws. When Prohibition shut down the Mariaggi bar in Port Arthur, Abe moved to Kenora and set up a mail-order house to supply the Winnipeg market. Once it was well established he moved on to Montreal to set up another company to supply eastern Ontario. The government put the mail-order houses out of business at the end of 1917. Harry then got a licence to establish a wholesale drug company in Yorkton, and in 1919 the Canada Pure Drug Company became the vehicle on which Harry rocketed the Bronfman clan to fortune.

At first glance the move made little sense. If the main business of the drug wholesale was to supply booze to the retail druggists, it was being set up to serve a steadily declining market. If the handling of a full line of drugs was intended, Yorkton was hardly the best location. Yet the choice of the vehicle was a measure of the Bronfman acumen and vision, for a complicated set of reasons.

Regardless of what measures Ottawa took in 1919, nothing would be done to prevent an export trade being developed in whisky. Unhappily, the measures taken in 1917 in an effort to conserve food supplies had created a serious shortage of alcohol in bond. With the United States on the eve of closing down its distilleries, vast post-war markets seemed to be beckoning. To assist the Canadian distillers, the government cut the required aging time of the booze from twenty-four months to twelve months. There was, however, a vast surplus of whisky in Scotland. A wholesale drug firm in Saskatchewan, if it held a provincial licence, could obtain a bonded-warehouse licence from Ottawa. With both licences it could import alcohol from abroad without limit as to quantity, if it was importing it for re-export. Some of Harry Bronfman's Liberal friends in Saskatchewan had become powers in the Unionist Government in 1917 and were highly placed in Ottawa. He was quickly granted bonded-warehouse status for the Canada Pure Drug Company warehouse which had been constructed next to the Balmoral Hotel.

On Christmas day, 1919, on the eve of interprovincial exports' becoming legal, Percy Dallin, the customs agent at Yorkton, was called by the C.P.R., who said that five carloads of Scotch whisky was on track for Canada Pure Drug and would he come down and release it so it could be transferred in bond to the company warehouse? Dallin had previously protested that the Bronfmans' poorly built structure was unsuitable for a bonded warehouse but his warning was ignored. He notified his superiors in Regina that the floor of the building, and perhaps the walls as well, would collapse if they tried to unload five carloads of alcohol into it. Dallin was told, in effect, to stop being difficult and release the whisky. They filled one warehouse until the floors creaked, then another and another. Then, with all facilities overflowing, another twenty-seven cars of whisky arrived on the siding.[13] Harry Bronfman and his brother Sam, who had moved to Yorkton, worked twenty-hour shifts.

The customs department bent its rules to allow Bronfman to ex-warehouse the bonded booze to customers from the railway cars. That meant that it could be reshipped to the export houses that were springing up all over western Canada, including those which the Bronfmans were themselves establishing in Alberta, British Columbia, and Ontario. There were approximately 1,600 cases of whisky to a car, and twelve bottles to the case. Within a matter of weeks the Canada Pure Drug Company had moved over 30,000 cases of whisky through Yorkton. As Harry Bronfman said, "Our big business was with imported whisky. We shipped it by the carload to the Hudson's Bay Company, etc."

Not all of the trade was in bottled stock, however. The public had not yet cultivated a taste for branded lines. At least a quarter of the business, and perhaps more, was in straight alcohol shipped in two-gallon and five-gallon cans. The purchasers could then water, flavour, and mix their drinks to their own tastes, and cut the cost of their booze by about a third to a half, depending upon the mixture they drank.

With the pent-up demand there was for whisky in the west in the booze holiday before the 1920 plebiscite, sixty mail-order houses went into operation in a matter of weeks in Saskatchewan. A somewhat smaller number of Alberta houses were supplying the demand of the people of Saskatchewan and British Columbia. Manitoba, throughout this entire period, did not permit any new mail-order houses to be established and hence was mainly an importing province, though perhaps a dozen Winnipeg houses found a way into the business. The volume of the interprovincial trade that was done out of Yorkton frequently delayed the Great West Express, the C.P.R.'s Winnipeg-to-Edmonton train, by as much as thirty minutes to complete the loading of Bronfman shipments to the thirsty customers in the neighbouring provinces.[14]

Percy Dallin became genuinely alarmed at the way things were developing in the previously quiet customs port of Yorkton, and he consulted his Regina supervisor for advice.

"Percy," his superior responded, "I am sorry I ever got you to come here. With this thing starting you won't last six months! If you do what the liquor interests want the department will get you; if you don't do what they want, they will get you!"

It was a Hobson's choice that was to confront more than one government official as time passed, and when the crunch really came those who put the government's interest second survived best.

Despite the frantic pace of their whisky-selling, the Bronfman brothers were far from satisfied. There was little save financial satisfaction in merchandising other people's goods, and even this was diluted by the realization that their efforts were yielding large profits to others. By manufacturing their own booze they could undersell their competitors and increase their own profits into the bargain. They went on a shopping tour for mixing vats, bottling equipment, labels, and a reliable supply of alcohol needed to launch them into the business of mixing, bottling, and labelling Scotch, rye, and bourbon whisky in their Yorkton "distillery". The project almost became an instant disaster and might well have become known to history as "the blue-black rye caper" or "the mystery of the discoloured vats". Out of it all there emerged a side of the Bronfman character which was probably basic to the family's success. That was a monumental stubbornness beyond all understanding, coupled with a visionary, venturing spirit that in another time and another context would have done a Cortez proud.

Harry at thirty-three and Sam at twenty-eight together probably knew as much about chemistry as they knew about chiropractic or choreography. They had stumbled into a business in Yorkton that was earning them at least fifty thousand dollars a month, distributing the products of other men's genius, competence, or just simple know-how. And yet, not satisfied with this, they risked the entire enterprise by launching themselves into a business about which they knew so little.

Their equipment search seems to have begun, and ended, at the office of the Brewers and Bottlers Supply Company in Winnipeg. There they bought ten one-thousand-gallon redwood vats which they would use for mixing their booze. They bought a bottling machine that would fill a thousand bottles an hour. They negotiated for a labelling machine that would fix two labels to the side of each bottle and one over the cork. They negotiated deals with Kentucky and Ontario distillers for carloads of ethyl alcohol from which whisky is made.

Ordering alcohol in carload lots may leave an impression that huge sums of money are involved. Such was not quite the case. In 1920, 65 overproof ethyl alcohol wholesaled at less than $2 a gallon, so that a carload would be worth about $8,000. However, the liquor was subject to excise duty, depending on its end use. If it went into beverage alcohol, it would be taxed at $2.40 a gallon. If it was used in the manufacture of vinegar the excise tax would only be twenty-seven cents a gallon. Because the end use was not known to the distiller shipping the alcohol it was shipped in bond, and the purchaser only became liable to duty when the substance was taken from the bonded warehouse in which it was stored. A customs or excise officer was always on hand to measure the quantity taken and collect the excise tax from the processor at the applicable rate. Thus the Canada Pure Drug Company could store all the alcohol or whisky bought by the Bronfmans until it was shipped out without their having to tie up large sums in excise taxes.

The whisky business of 1920 was done not with cash on delivery but mainly by cash before delivery. The only capital that the Bronfmans required was, in the main, for the booze that was tied up in inventory. This was minimal for the imported whisky because it was frequently shipped directly from the incoming cars at Yorkton to the mail-order customers who had sent cash with their orders. Once the brothers got into the blending business they did require a large capital investment for inventories, but they kept that to a minimum because they only aged their liquor in the vats long enough to allow it to become thoroughly mixed.

To round out their supplies, the Bronfmans needed labels, and they discovered that a large Winnipeg printing company, Bulman Brothers, was already in the business of printing what were called "stock labels" for anybody who wanted to buy them and paste them on liquor bottles.[15] Long before Prohibition they were doing a profitable business with a number of small-time blenders who were importing booze in barrels and ladling it into bottles out of ordinary washtubs. Among the labels which the Bulmans offered were:

GOLD LABEL
Special Blend
Scotch Whisky

Munroe and Company
Inverness, Scotland

SPECIAL VAT
Old Scotch

SOLE PROPRIETORS
D. Macgregor and Company
Glasgow.

There were, of course, no such whiskies and no such distillers. Bulman's had simply discovered and adapted an old trick of the Scotch whisky distillers, who did not care what their whisky was labelled as long as their customers kept coming back for more. A good way of assuring themselves of repeat business was to provide their agents with exclusive trade names for each agent's Scotch. The prairie wholesalers who bottled their own booze were not interested in having their own branded lines. They were satisfied with whatever names Bulman's had chosen for their labels. The label was not yet a designation of contents of a special quality. It was simply a facility for helping to convert a barrel of whisky into easily salable quarts and pints.

To go with their bottling plant, the Bronfmans laid in a supply of Bulman labels. But why should they, who were prepared to go first class, be content to market the same brands as every other minor-league blender in the west? They would not; and while they were prepared to use Bulman's standard stock labels to get into business they wanted some brands of their own. They called in a designer and with a bow to royalty they selected "Prince of Wales" as the name for their best Scotch and "Glen Levitt" for the lower grade. They chose "Superior" for their best rye and "Black Knight" for the cheaper kind. Eventually they got around to names for their brandy, bourbon, and gin lines as well.

By the spring of 1920, everything was in readiness to launch the Bronfmans on their career as whisky blenders. Into one of the one-thousand-gallon vats Harry supervised the pouring of 100 gallons of aged rye whisky, 318 gallons of 65 overproof alcohol, and 382 gallons of water, which would produce 800 gallons of whisky at a total cost of around $5.25 a gallon, tax included. It would sell, depending on whether wholesale, in bulk, or bottled to exporters or druggists at $11.40 a gallon and $18 to $20 a gallon. When the liquor had been sufficiently aged for bottling, a couple of days later, Harry dipped into the vat to inspect his brew and almost collapsed in shock. Instead of the nice amber colour of whisky, his beaker held a bluish-black substance. Something had gone desperately wrong, but what? As a neophyte whisky blender, Harry failed to recognize that discoloration was a not unknown, and usually a harmless, aberration in the distillery process.

The Bronfmans blamed the discoloration on the tanks and refused to pay the $3,200 which the Winnipeg firm had charged for the vats and the labelling machine which the brothers said would not do the job it was bought to do. The suppliers sued and the Bronfmans, incomprehensibly, allowed the suit to go to trial, where the detail of their operation was set out in the public record. That record was unearthed a year later by the *Winnipeg Tribune* which, on October 27, 1922, ran the following lead to a six-column summation of the transcript.

REGINA. Oct. 26 — A surprising index of the profits in the Saskatchewan Liquor business is found in the record of evidence given by Harry Bronfman in an action which took place in the King's Bench court at Yorkton, in November last year.

He testified that his company, the Yorkton Distributing Co., mixed 100 gallons of rye whisky, 318 gallons of raw alcohol and 382 gallons of water, to make 800 gallons of "whisky". The cost of this mixture was $5.25 a gallon.

The company's sales amounted to 16,000 to 20,000 gallons per month, he said.

Computing upon this basis, any reader who knows anything of border conditions will readily agree that $50 a case is around the average selling price to rum-runners. There are 2 gallons to a case; 20,000 gallons would be 10,000 cases a month — a gross revenue of $500,000 a month, the cost being $109,000 — a profit of $391,000 a month.

"DIRTY BLUE" STUFF USED

When one reflects that the basis of this computation was brought out in an action to recover $3,200 from Bronfman, which he refused to pay for a bottling and "blending" plant, the comparison is the more astonishing. It is more than merely astonishing, however, in the light of the fact that the first mixture . . . turned a dirty bluish color and, far from being thrown away, was afterwards worked off in lots of 10 gallons to every 100 of other

mixture, as what was euphemistically termed "the alcoholic content."

QUESTION OF CHEMICALS

The tanks, against paying for which Mr. Bronfman
fought, were of California redwood, and an expert
chemist testified that a "dirty bluish color" could not
react from that wood by contact with alcohol, water or
whisky. He had made experiments to prove it. Blue, being
a primary color, could come about by chemical reaction
from "something such as sulphuric acid."

Incidently, it may be mentioned that there exists such a
thing as "beading oil" — an oil used for putting an artifi-
cial "bead" on cheap liquors, or for artificially ageing
liquors. It contains a considerable proportion of a distil-
late of sulphuric acid, according to a high authority on
chemistry in Winnipeg.

Whatever it was that turned the first batch of whisky blue, the
suppliers were able to prove to the court's satisfaction that it was not
the fault of the redwood vats. Judgment was entered in favour of the
suppliers. The problem never arose again, giving weight to the suspicion that somebody had added something else to the mix in addition
to the whisky, alcohol, and water. It was common practice among
blenders to bring whatever they were bottling as close in taste to
what the unsophisticated tastes of the customers might expect. As
Harry Bronfman said, caramel was frequently added to the mix to
bring the colour of their rye whisky up to the accepted norm. When
the mix was Scotch, a base of dark-coloured Scotch was used instead
of rye to give the whisky at least a trace of its peat smoke taste.
Straight alcohol and water could be transformed into imitation rum
by adding rum caramel and blackstrap molasses. [16]

The widely circulated story of the blue-black whisky gave credibility to stories that would keep arising to torment Harry Bronfman
for as long as he was in business — that all bootleg booze was rotten
booze. In court and out, he insisted always that Bronfman whisky
was good whisky and he boasted that when the Manitoba govern-

ment ran out of pharmaceutical whisky they bought from him. Jack
Diamond, whose family ran a large export business in Calgary during
the hiatus period, said he seldom had any complaint with Bronfman's brands. "In fact," he said, "we did a lot of business with Sam
Bronfman, who was the one we dealt with. We could get their brands
for fifty cents or a dollar a case less than the Hudson's Bay or the
Montreal wholesalers would charge. We thought it was every bit as
good but then, as you know, Jews have never cultivated a taste for
whisky so we had to rely on what our customers told us."[17]

It may well have been that the first experience with the blue-black
whisky made the Bronfman brothers more aware of the need for
quality control than some of their competitors. From then on, very
close watch was kept on the Yorkton mixing plant while Harry was
concentrating upon the creation of his monopoly in Saskatchewan.

Only people who carried stubbornness to the ultimate degree
would have gone to court over such an unimportant sum and sub-
jected their business activities to public scrutiny. There was, for
example, the cross-examination of Sam Bronfman about their competence as liquor blenders, which produced the following exchange:

> Cross-examination by Mr. Locke:
> Q. Have you been employed in some place where there is a
>   large blending business done? I suppose there is a place
>   of that nature?
> A. A distillery is not blending; they do not do blending.
> Q. I do not suggest they do. I understand there are places
>   in Canada and in the United States where there are large
>   blending businesses?
> A. I do not know anything about such a business.
> Q. You were not employed in one?
> A. No.
> Q. Your experience has been?
> A. In my own business.
> Q. Your brother is an expert liquor blender? Is he?
> A. In so far as our own business is concerned.
> Q. What do you mean by that qualification?
> A. Probably, if I understood your question right — so far
>   as blending he has blended whiskey all his life and met
>   with general success.[18]

Harry a whisky blender all his life? Harry, whom everyone in the courtroom knew as a hotelman, car dealer, and real estate developer, a whisky blender all his life?

Here it is,
you come
and get it

Whether Harry Bronfman dodged newspaper publicity, or whether the newspapers simply ignored Harry Bronfman, is almost impossible to determine. Certainly each got along without the other very well. One of the rare exceptions, if not indeed the only exception, to their mutual neglect was a two-hour interview which Bronfman gave to the *Winnipeg Tribune* on Sunday morning, October 15, 1922. The newspaper had been running a series of exposés on the "liquor situation" in Saskatchewan, with special attention to bank hold-ups, rum-running, illegal distilling, and crimes of violence, including one murder. The interview is important in that it provides an insight into Harry Bronfman's own assessment of his domination of the booze business in the Wheat Province.

"Any slap at the liquor business in Saskatchewan I regard as a slap at me," he said at the outset. "With the exception of two small concerns in Saskatoon which have practically run out of stock, the liquor business in Saskatchewan is controlled by me."

The secret of his success, he maintained, was commercial integrity. He had established a reputation of standing behind his goods and insisted that his customers everywhere knew and relied on the fact that, if they dealt with Bronfman, they would get what they paid for. As a result, he said, American rum-runners would take Bronfman liquor in preference to others and reject others in favour of Bronfman's. He insisted, moreover, that this was the way he had always done business, whether it was selling automobiles in Yorkton or whisky in Regina. And he predicted that when the liquor business was over, Harry Bronfman would be as successful in any other mercantile line he chose to pursue. Of that, he said, he had not the slightest doubt.

There can be no reason to cavil at Harry Bronfman's self-assessment. Time and again, in the hotel business, the automobile business, and as a small-town real estate operator, he had demonstrated an uncanny ability to select the right key to unlock the door to success while his competitors fumbled and failed. From the beginning, at the Balmoral, he had made a special effort to attract the commercial-traveller trade to keep his rooms full during the long winter when farm trade dwindled. He turned a marginal garage into the largest Grey Dort agency in Saskatchewan by financing his farmer purchasers, when auto financing was almost unknown. It was the liquor business, however, in which his commercial genius reached its fullest flower. Of the legions who stampeded into it in 1920, Harry Bronfman was almost alone in his concentration on the source of the biggest profits — wholesale distribution. Moreover, he was sharpening that focus long before anybody else. The carloads of booze that began clattering into Yorkton in December of 1919 did not materialize out of nowhere as a result of spur-of-the-moment decisions. Their arrival was the product of Bronfman prescience, coupled with a willingness to risk his family's fortune on the soundness of his judgment. It may not have have been much of a fortune, but it was stretched to the limit to launch the liquor business and it was committed many months before the government's post-war liquor policy had been firmly established.

In the interview, perhaps his strongest emphasis came when he insisted that throughout his entire participation in the liquor business he had operated completely within the law. He denied all knowledge of such things as illicit distilling in his Regina warehouse, the use of forged labels, and misbranding of whiskies. He had only done what the law permitted him to do. As the law changed he changed his operations to conform to the law. When the law made the liquor business illegal, he would get out of it and, from the way he was feeling that Sunday morning, the sooner the better.

In 1922 Harry Bronfman could look back on perhaps the most remarkable three years in his life. From operating a small-time wholesale drug warehouse and makeshift liquor-blending plant in Yorkton, he had grown to dominate completely the whisky trade on the prairies. Of the more than sixty competitors who had rushed to get into the mail-order booze business during the 1919-20 hiatus, only he and a half-dozen others remained. A several-times-over millionaire he was now established in the biggest house in Regina at 2326 Sixteenth (College) Avenue.

Nothing comparable to the rash of export houses that broke out in Saskatchewan during the winter of 1919-20 occurred in Manitoba, for the simple reason that the Attorney General of Manitoba refused to sanction any additional bonded warehouses. Alberta followed the Saskatchewan pattern, but with much less proliferation of enterprisers in the business. Nor were the "boozoriums", as they came to be called in the south country, confined to the larger towns. Any village with a vacant store, house, or shed could become the site for a liquor export house. North of Regina, the warehouses existed mainly on the trade they did by mail and express with customers in Manitoba or Alberta.

From Regina southward the stores supplied the rum-runners from the United States, and in the southeast became the base from which thirsty Winnipeggers drew most of their supplies. The extent to which the liquor export houses dotted the Saskatchewan landscape can be gauged from the following list of companies which were in operation in the fall of 1920.

Town

Bienfait	Bienfait Export Co., Bienfait Export Liquor Co., Globe Wine & Spirit Co.
Broadview	Andrew Murray Ltd., John Shaw & Co., Winnipeg Wine Co.
Canora	Canora Export Co. (changed to North Star Liquor Co.)
Carievale	Carievale Export Co.
Ceylon	J. D. McMunn, Ltd.
Consul	J. D. McMunn, Ltd.
Estevan	Beaver Wine & Spirit Co., Estevan Exporters Wine Co., Southern Export Co.
Gainsborough	Liquor Exporters, Ltd.
Glen Ewen	Macdonald Liquor Co.
Govenlock	Govenlock Export Co., Ltd., Maple Creek Export Co.
Hatton	Diamond Liquor Co., Hatton Export Co.
Kamsack	Kamsack Export Co.
Kerrobert	Hughes Export Co., Ltd.
Lloydminster	Yale Liquor Co.
Macklin	Lee Wine Co.
Maple Creek	Capital Wine & Spirit Co., Great West Liquor Co., Maple Creek Export Co.
Maryfield	Crown Liquor Co., Maryfield Liquor Co., Ltd.
Melville	Melville Export Co., Ltd.
Moose Jaw	Consumers Export Co., Montreal Wine Co., Ltd.
Moosomin	Algoma Liquor Agency
Oxbow	Yorkton Distributing Co., Ltd.
Regina	Bolvin, Wilson & Co., Dominion Liquor Co., Great West Wine Co., Ltd., G. W. Griffiths & Co., D. Hunter & Co., Ltd., T. P. Kelly Co., North Star Liquor Co., Prairie Drug Co., Regina Wine & Spirit Co., Ltd., James Buchanan Wallace
Saskatoon	Lee Wine Co., Metropolitan Liquor Co., Saskatoon Liquors, Ltd.
Senate	Beaver Wine & Spirit Co., Ltd.
Swift Current	Nat Bell Liquor, Ltd.

Tribune	J. D. McMunn, Ltd.
Vidora	Capital Wine & Spirit Co.
Weyburn	Capital Export Co.
Yorkton	Yorkton Distributing Co.

Many of these localities were little more than whistle-stops, which was in fact all they had to be. As long as the trains stopped, one place was as good as another; it only had to have a building substantial enough to be turned into a liquor store. Ken John, who was a resident of Bienfait at the time, recalled that the liquor stores were more secure than the banks. "They all had iron bars on their windows and enough locks on their doors to protect the mint," was the way he described them.[1] In 1920 Bienfait was a two-and-a-half-street town, which distinguished it from such places as Ceylon, Macklin, and Senate, which were only one-street hamlets. The stores themselves fell into several categories. Those in Maple Creek were established by Calgary men for the purpose of supplying their Alberta customers. The Diamond brothers, who had a large liquor warehouse in Calgary, established a branch at Maple Creek to which they sent all the orders received from Alberta residents.

Under federal law it was perfectly legal to ship booze from Alberta to Saskatchewan and then ship it back to Alberta. But it was illegal to ship it from one point in a province to another point within the same province. This created an amusing situation in Lloydminster, Sask., and Lloydminster, Alta., which is in reality one town bisected by the provincial boundary. There was a liquor store on the Saskatchewan side but none on the Alberta side. There was, however, only one post office and one railway station and both were on the Saskatchewan side. The export house delivered the booze for Alberta residents to the railway express agent or post office and they could pick it up and take it home. But there was no handy system for the Saskatchewan residents, so they adopted the address of the bank on the Alberta side where they kept their savings accounts.

Some of the export houses were locally owned, but many were established by people from outside the province, and some, perhaps most, were run as joint ventures between a local resident and one of the larger companies such as the Bronfmans, the Diamonds in Calgary, or Nat Bell, who had warehouses in Saskatoon, Edmonton, and in the British Columbia Interior. In Saskatchewan in particular the form in which the ownership was established was vitally important. There was a good deal of leakage from the export stores into the throats of the thirsty natives. These leaks, curiously enough, were as sternly frowned on by the Bronfmans as by the government. The export business was of such magnitude, and so profitable, that it was folly to bring it into jeopardy for the sake of the small profit to be made from the local trade. Of course what the rum-running purchasers did with the booze once they hit the road was none of the suppliers' concern.

In the event that the provincial liquor enforcers of Saskatchewan could convict an export dealer of selling liquor in Saskatchewan, the entire stock of his warehouse became forfeit. The Bronfmans quickly devised a system to prevent the loss of their boozorium inventories if a local manager was caught bootlegging. They adopted the consignment system for stocking the stores — the liquor remained the property of the supplying company until it was sold to the rum-runners. The managers of the boozoriums, therefore, were merely commission agents for the suppliers. In the nature of things, a great deal of booze that was consigned to the States never reached there. Indeed, there were many complaints from the Temperance people that cars loaded with booze were frequently spotted headed away from instead of toward the border.[2] There can hardly be any question that the boozoriums welcomed this business as much as they did the American buyers, as long as the local bootlegger took all the risks.

There were several occasions on which stocks valued in excess of ten thousand dollars were seized as a result of arrests of local dealers for bootlegging. In all instances the whisky was returned when the cases were appealed and the seizures quashed, but it was a nuisance to the exporters and bad public relations generally. It was, indeed, the blundering ineptitude of his agents in Moose Jaw that gave Harry Bronfman his closest brush with the penitentiary during his years in Saskatchewan. His brother-in-law David Gellerman, who was a partner in the Moose Jaw export business, was charged with selling whisky by the bottle to a local enforcement agent. Extricating Gellerman from his offence ultimately led to Harry Bronfman's being charged with jury tampering.[3]

A conversation between Bronfman and Sam Tadman, who was the other partner in the Moose Jaw operation, is clearly indicative of

Bronfman's general attitude toward the sale to local people. Tadman approached Bronfman with an accounting for the expenses he had incurred during a prosecution for bootlegging. Tadman said he had spent over six hundred dollars and thought Bronfman should reimburse him. "Six hundred dollars?" shouted Bronfman. "Why I spent six thousand dollars and do you know what is going to happen to that six thousand dollars? It is going right onto your account." It was no idle threat. That amount was charged to the Moose Jaw operation and Tadman and Gellerman had to pay it out of the profits of the store.[4]

Not all the enterprisers who rushed into the liquor business at the dawn of the hiatus year had Harry Bronfman's magic touch. Archie McCorvie and Joe Bonfadini, who had been in the hotel business in Lethbridge, took Sid Doe, a onetime bartender lately back from the war, to Maple Creek, Saskatchewan, to help run their new export store.[5] The volume of business they were able to develop with Alberta customers turned out to be less than a bonanza. Their next step was to try to get into the business of supplying American rum-runners. Maple Creek, unhappily, was sixty miles north of the border and the Bronfmans already had a store at Govenlock, fifty miles southeast of Maple Creek. However, the McCorvie-Bonfadini partnership found a vacant store in Govenlock and opened an export store. It was even less successful than the Maple Creek enterprise.

Many other small-time operators fell by the wayside and on June 1, 1922, the Saskatchewan government finished them all off. It passed an order-in-council which restricted liquor export houses to cities of ten thousand and over. Complaints from Prohibitionists over the leakage from the small-town export stores, not only to the surrounding communities but back into the major centres, convinced the government they were more trouble than they were worth. The effect of the order was to limit export stores for the last half of 1922 to the cities of Regina, Saskatoon, and Moose Jaw.

While some of the competing boozoriums which concentrated on the Canadian market had a thin time of it, the Bronfmans were getting rich at a rate that must have astounded even them. Sam had opened branches in Calgary and Edmonton and had moved into joint deals in British Columbia. The Kenora Wine Company was re-activated in the northwest Ontario town which had a convenient all-water outlet to northern Minnesota. Dedicated as they were to achieving what latter-day economists would call "an economy of scale by maximizing sales volume", the Bronfman brothers restructured their operation. Abe became the operating head of everything east of Ottawa. Sam became the boss of Ontario, Manitoba, and British Columbia, while Harry stayed at the centre of the action in Saskatchewan.[6]

None of Abe's operations in Quebec were ever opened to public scrutiny but there is no reason to suppose that he did other than contribute a full measure of success to the family operation. Certainly he moved into the management of the huge Maritimes export business with the quiet skill of an accomplished operator when the time came for the family to move their base to Nova Scotia.

From his Winnipeg headquarters Sam flitted continually to Port Arthur to Kenora to Calgary to Edmonton to Vancouver to Chicago to Louisville and back to Winnipeg. In his spare time he filled in for Harry at Yorkton and Regina and made doubly sure that the Winnipeg carriage trade knew that their shortest line between thirst and gratification was the one that ran from Yorkton to Winnipeg. In January 1921 a reputation as a super-salesman was easy to acquire in the booze business in Winnipeg, for private importation of liquor into the province would end on February 1. There was an understandable rush by Winnipeg's leading citizens to get their cellars well stocked before the long drought settled over the province.

Chief of Police C. H. Newton bought his Scotch by the case. Pat Shea, the millionaire brewer, ordered his in twenty- and forty-case lots. A. J. Andrews, K.C., the Bronfman family counsel in Winnipeg, once placed an order for seven cases of wine, six cases of brandy, five cases of Scotch, ten cases of gin, two cases of liqueurs, and a case of rum. A fellow ornament of the Conservative party of Manitoba, C. P. Fullerton, K.C., was more frugal. He bought his Scotch in one-gallon cans at a cost of eleven dollars a gallon compared with the forty-six dollars Andrews was paying for a case of two gallons. The tastes of Travers Sweatman, K.C., another Tory stalwart, ran more to liqueurs. He ordered twenty-seven cases of the stuff at one time. W. P. Fillmore, K.C., his partner, was more modest in his purchase and pedestrian in his taste. He included a request for seven cases of Scotch with his partner's order.[7]

Such purchases serve to underline the class aspect of the Prohibition legislation. The working class was effectively cut off from access to booze in the manner to which it was long accustomed – knocking it back while standing at a hotel bar. The upper crust, which seldom frequented the watering holes of the workers, could still obtain stocks for their cellars as readily as they ever had. Before the Prohibition era, they had sent their orders around to any one of a dozen wholesale liquor dealers who were in business in all the main centres and it was delivered to their doors. After Prohibition they put the order in the mail and it was still delivered to their doors.

While many individual purchases were impressively large, the truth was that this business was at most peripheral to the Bronfman operation. It was the wholesale business that bulked largest at Yorkton and elsewhere. Thus, in the same month of January 1921, the Kenora Wine Company ordered almost 1,400 cases of liquors of all types, and the Hudson's Bay Company's Calgary store in one order took 550 gallons of rum, 300 cases of Bronfman Scotch, and 20 cases of brandy. F. T. Anderson of Kaleida, Manitoba, a point most convenient to the U.S. border, ordered 35 gallons of Scotch, 35 gallons of Irish, 15 gallons of gin, and, curiously, 3 bottles of rye.[8]

Important as it was, however, the Canadian business did not provide the family with either the profits or the notoriety that was to flow from their domination of the export business with the United States. It was the borderland export stores which between 1920 and 1922 created the mythology of Saskatchewan as the "wild" in the Canadian wild west. It is a mythology that is rooted, if not in the soil, at least in the geography, of Saskatchewan.

The area south of the Canadian Pacific Railway main line is the heart of the Palliser triangle, which encompasses the area bounded by a line from Waterton Lakes to Olds, Alberta, to Saskatoon, and then to Boissevain, Manitoba. This semi-arid, treeless plain was as sparsely settled in North Dakota and Montana as it was in Canada. A sizable pocket of the uninhabited Montana badlands extends close to the southern border of Saskatchewan. Because of the sparsity of settlement and scanty railway construction, towns were few on both sides of the 49th parallel.

There was little north-south communication except where there were railways, and where the towns in Montana and North Dakota were closer to the farmers than the Canadian towns. Throughout this area, roads of a sort existed, but only in dry weather. In the main, roads in Saskatchewan connected one town with another parallel to the railway lines and tended to fade into little-used trails at the dividing point for traffic for each town. The surveyors of the 1870s had laid out the entire country on a grid system of road allowances, separating the farms with sixty-six-foot interspaces every two miles north and south and every mile east and west. Few of the allowances were graded into proper roads and in the 1920s, if used at all, were little more than trails between neighbours.

Strung along the Canada—United States boundary at fifteen-, twenty-five- , fifty- , and one-hundred-mile intervals were the customs houses where the officials vegetated between the random visits by neighbourhood farmers and the enforcement patrols which they were required to take. The farmers who lived between the ports were supposed to call in and pay duty on anything they purchased in the United States. As this meant a journey of ten or fifteen miles the matter of duty-paying was one that slipped the minds of many farmers along the border.

With the impact of the motor car on rural as well as urban society at the end of the First World War, it became increasingly easy for the borderland farmers to slip down to the States on shopping excursions, particularly to buy automobiles, trucks, tires, batteries, parts, and farm equipment. The farmer-smugglers ran almost no risk of getting caught. The Royal Canadian Mounted Police were not yet a part of the Customs Department Enforcement Branch and became involved only when help was requested by the department's preventive service. As that service consisted mainly of one man and a secretary in Winnipeg it was not expected to prevent individual smuggling along the border. Its main concern was with ferreting out the tricks employed by Winnipeg merchants to get their carloads of imported goods through customs without paying proper duty. A common dodge was to have American exporters supply false invoices which substantially undervalued the goods so as to reduce the duty payable by seventy-five or eighty per cent.

The main hazard to the farmer-smugglers was an unfriendly neighbour who might report the smuggler to the customs department and be rewarded by half the penalty imposed upon conviction. However, it was a comparatively simple task to change the registration numbers on smuggled cars, trucks, and tractors, and vehicles were easily hidden under straw stacks until the job was done. The customs department was aware of all this, of course, and one of the contemporary agitations was for the hiring of trained mechanics for the preventive service. Only they knew how to locate the secret numbers American makers stamped on their machinery and parts to catch imitators who were pirating their patents and supplying customers with imitation parts. The fact that most farmers made their smuggled purchases in the fall when they were cashing in on their wheat crops is probably the basis for a Saskatchewan legend: In the south country after the First World War, every second straw stack dotting the landscape sheltered a car waiting to have its numbers doctored.[9]

"Mostly," an early settler recalled, "the farmers only burned their straw stacks after a rain had wetted down the stubble so that the fire would not spread. If you saw a stack going up in smoke at any other time you wondered whether a back-firing car, being run out from under its straw-stack hiding place, had set the straw ablaze."

In the reverse direction there was little smuggling of anything but booze, for North Dakota had a state prohibitory law long before Prohibition came to western Canada. Before the First World War, illicit exports from Canada seldom amounted to much as the state seemed to rely mainly on Montana and Minnesota for its bootleg liquor supply. State Prohibition, however, did give rise to a clandestine network to supply the needs of the drinkers prior to the war.

There is little doubt that this network became a rung for Harry Bronfman's sharp climb to financial eminence. There is some question, however, as to the particular route he would choose to follow. At first he seemed inclined to favour a fleet of Bronfman trucks and cars which would carry the booze from Yorkton and his border warehouses into the United States, as well as into Alberta and Manitoba. In 1920 he obtained a federal charter for the Trans-Canada Transportation Company Limited, and then approached the United Grain Growers with an offer to join with it to move grain by truck in competition with the railways.

In the context of the times, this was as visionary a scheme as ever came down the pike. Saskatchewan highways, in any real sense, were rarely more than coloured lines on maps in the office of the minister of highways. The Department of Highways existed primarily to ensure that loyal supporters of the Liberal party got a share of the province's roads maintenance budget. All-weather highways were few and far between, consisting mainly of graded roads given a thin veneer of gravel from time to time. A list of a dozen such roads between the larger centres would have sufficed to describe the Saskatchewan highway system of 1920. The trucks of the same era were becoming quite common in the cities, but they were still unwieldy, mainly chain-driven affairs that moved at a lumbering gait, and tended to freeze up in November and stay frozen until March. It was hardly surprising that Harry Bronfman's grandiose proposal for a trans-Canada truck line was filed and forgotten by the U.G.G. But it did not take him long to have the value of his idea demonstrated in court.

An automobile full of booze being shipped from Yorkton was seized by the Saskatchewan Liquor Commission. The car was leased to the Trans-Canada Transportation Company and had all the forms needed for an export shipment had it gone by rail. The prosecution held that inter-provincial trade meant rail shipments by express or parcel post. Bronfman's lawyers argued that shipment by car was just as legal. The judgment in favour of the Bronfmans set the stage for the adoption of the automobile as a favoured means of moving booze around the Canadian prairies.[10]

By the time the case was processed through the courts Bronfman had substantially revised his plans for delivering booze to American bootleggers. Instead of transporting the stuff to them in his own or hired vehicles, he adopted a "here-it-is, come-and-get-it" system. He established a string of export stores in the towns most convenient to the border. His customers were invited to bring in their own vehicles and load them at his store, thus avoiding splitting their profits with truckers. It also reduced the risk of having a double-crossing driver steal either the bootleggers' money or the Bronfmans' booze.

The North Dakotans at first were reluctant to venture north of the border into the wilds of Canada where North West Mounted Policemen were reputed to be lurking behind every bush. In plain truth the Mounties were so thinly scattered across the prairies that few natives, let alone American rum-runners, ever caught sight of them. To allay their fear, Harry Bronfman set up an all-coverage insurance scheme. If the liquor were seized while the Americans were in Canada, he would replace it. If their cars were seized, he would put up the double-duty bond required by the customs department for the release of their vehicles. In later years Bronfman disclaimed credit for devising this "free ingress and egress" insurance plan.[11]

The testimony of those who operated under it, however, leaves little doubt as to the scheme's inventor.

The Bronfman plan was by no means the only method used to encourage the Americans to come and get their own whisky. The Sair brothers at Oxbow went even farther. They provided guides who knew all the border-crossing trails within a hundred miles and would pilot the rum-runners to safety in the United States. The Sairs, Isaac and Jacob, had other imaginative innovations to their credit. It was they who stumbled onto the idea of converting dollar-a-gallon undertakers' rubbing alcohol into potable twenty-five-dollars-a-gallon booze.

Like Harry Bronfman the Sairs had come to Canada with their parents from Russia as refugees from pogroms and were settled on a farm near Oxbow. Unlike the elder Bronfman, the elder Sair had elected to stay farming, and survived under the most appalling conditions. To help the family, Isaac and Jacob as mere children drove ox-teams hauling coal from the Roche Perce mine to Oxbow, a distance of forty miles, for a dollar a ton. Instead of fleeing to the city at the earliest opportunity, the boys took up homesteads themselves as soon as it was legally possible. They prospered both as farmers and as enterprisers in the boom before the First World War. Isaac built a huge horse barn in Estevan and became heavily involved in Estevan real estate. Jacob took a quick course in horse-trading from Isaac and picked up enough veterinary medicine en route to establish himself in the horse business in Moose Jaw. There he reached heights of affluence by taking sick horses in trade on healthy ones.[12]

The outbreak of the First World War ruined the Sairs' horse business and knocked the bottom out of real estate values. In fairly short order the Sair brothers were back where they started. Their properties in Moose Jaw and Estevan were gone and only the timely intervention of an elder brother saved their farms from tax sale. They went back to their farms for the duration of the war and like all other farmers reaped the financial harvest from bountiful crops and high farm prices. Their farms on the Souris River hills less than a dozen miles from the border could hardly have been more advantageously located when rum-running began in 1920. The Grand Trunk Railway line from Regina to Northgate, where it connected with the Northern Pacific, ran within sight of the Sair farms.

The Sairs opened liquor export houses at Gainsborough, Oxbow, and Glen Ewen, all villages reasonably handy both to their farms and to the United States border. Jacob took charge of the stores while his brother Isaac went down to the States to drum up trade. Customers were easy enough to get and so were supplies as long as the Sairs relied on the Bronfmans. By patronizing them, however, the Sairs were supporting their main competitor. They decided to go into the distilling business for themselves on one of the farms. Instead of running a standard homebrew operation which began with grain mash and ended with alcohol, the Sairs short circuited all but the last phase. They arranged with an undertaker in Minneapolis to supply them with rubbing alcohol by the ton in five-gallon cans. Undertaker's alcohol differed from drinking alcohol only in that a bruicine sulphate denaturant had been added. Undertaker's alcohol could be bought for around a dollar a gallon because it was free of U.S. excise tax. They had it shipped to a nearby border point and smuggled it into Canada. On the farm they ran it through their still, removed the denaturant, and had potable alcohol which they could turn into whisky, as the Bronfmans were doing at Yorkton with ethyl alcohol. [13]

Despite such imaginative antics, booze was not really the Sairs' forte, for they seemed to have a built-in affinity for disaster. Hijackers stole their cars. Their customers paid for their booze with forged cheques and counterfeit money. Jacob was arrested in Minot and it took most of the family profits to extricate him from the Americans. When the government put an end to export they were left with an unsalable stock of booze and became embroiled in a costly lawsuit with their partners. The Sairs, like so many who had floated to affluence on the flood tide of whisky, left the rum-running era as they had entered it, with little to show but experience. They went back to the horse business. [14]

The actual running of the booze across the border, while not completely an American monopoly, was nearly so. Occasionally adventurous Canadians drove carloads of whisky as far south as Omaha and Denver. Despite the blood-and-thunder tales of hijacking and murder of the later years, such risks were not great. The main problem for Canadians was to find buyers for their smuggled booze, once they got to population centres, without running afoul of local law enforcers in a strange and unfriendly environment. After the business had shaken down into established avenues of trade, Canadians did begin to participate more, but much more often as hired drivers and guides rather than as principals in the traffic.

The Americans gradually overcame their fear of Canadian officialdom, but they were never really comfortable until they were back in their own country. They usually came into the country in the late afternoon and in summer hid out in their cars until it was time to load their cargoes. That was invariably done at night after the natives were long since in bed, and it was done in pitch dark both by choice and by necessity; few of the towns had street lights. The financial arrangements would be completed and the liquor collected in the boozoriums behind well-draped windows. Then it was lights out while the stuff was carried outside into the cars. On bright moonlit nights they often drove without lights and otherwise took great pains to attract as little attention as possible. They kept always to the back roads and trails and when they saw cars following them they had lengths of heavy chains bolted to the rear axles which they could drop down to drag along the dirt roads, creating such clouds of dust that pursuers were forced to slow almost to a halt.

"You know if you weren't paying attention, you could live and die in any of these country towns and not know what was going on. And I guess many people did," Ken John said. "It stood to reason! None of these guys wanted to advertise what they were up to. All they wanted to do was to get their cars loaded with the stuff and get out of town and out of the country before anybody saw them. There was none of this roaring in and roaring out of town and firing off guns and that sort of stuff, though they did carry guns. I once went up to one of the rooms in the hotel to see Jimmie LaCoste and there was this rum-runner lying on the bed in his shirt sleeves and his guns were hanging on the bed post. Aside from that, the only time you'd see these guys was if, as happened sometimes, one of them came up and stayed at the hotel for several days, probably hiding out from some trouble in the States. One time there was a gangster named Dutch Schultz, who later got to be quite famous, who spent a week at the Bienfait hotel." [15]

The reports of rum-running shoot-em-ups being staged all over the Saskatchewan countryside may have made good reading in eastern and western papers, but the nature of the trade dictated that the facts would be otherwise. There is no doubt, however, that the

Americans rum-runners in the early months did come into Canada well-armed. They did so probably from force of habit because to many of them their revolver and holster were as much a part of their clothing as their shirts. [16]

They ran thousands of loads of whisky across the border in the thirty months the export stores were open. The wonder is not that there was a rare act of violence; it is that acts of violence were so few. The main trouble the Americans got into sprang from their efforts to stay completely out of contact with Canadians. There was a fairly good road from Minot, North Dakota, the reputed gangster centre of the west, to Estevan, and thence to Regina. It was a simple matter for the Americans to get a border-crossing permit for themselves and their cars at North Portal, the border-crossing point below Estevan and Bienfait. They could then go in peace to the liquor store of their choice, load their Hudson super sixes or Studebaker whisky specials full of booze, pocket a sheaf of official forms, and head back home. Because they were violating no Canadian law, they had nothing to fear from the police, or from anybody else.

The regulars in the trade who patronized the stores at Bienfait or Estevan followed that procedure. But for those lured northeastward by better prices at Oxbow, Gainsborough, Glen Ewen, or Carievale, going through customs was a nuisance that took them miles out of their way, so they gambled on getting into Canada and out without being caught. Most of the time they succeeded but once in a while they would be caught up in police action of some kind. If they blundered into Manitoba en route from Gainsborough back to North Dakota, they ran the risk of being pounced on by Manitoba law enforcers and in that case would lose both their cargo and their car. When that happened none of the Saskatchewan "free ingress and egress" guarantees applied.

It was not long before a number of extra-legal aspects of the North Dakota booze trade began to spill over into Canada. The American rum-runners were reluctant to carry around the large quantities of cash needed in their Canadian purchases. A fully stripped-down Studebaker whisky six could carry up to thirty or forty cases of whisky when fully loaded. Three or four such cars in a convoy would be carrying five thousand to six thousand dollars' worth of whisky at fifty dollars a case. In the first transactions cash was demanded and produced. Then the practice developed of paying with cashier's cheques drawn on United States banks. These were similar to Canadian marked cheques and the forerunners of traveller's cheques. It took the small-town banks, and the liquor stores, time to become accustomed to United States cashier's cheques. As they were doing so they were cheated out of tens of thousands of dollars. Several pads of blank cheques were stolen in a hold-up in the United States and then passed to the rum-runners, who used them to pay for Canadian whisky.[17]

As time passed and the Americans lost some of their fear of Canada they moved farther north for their supplies. In the process they discovered the small-town banks. They noted that the banks carried substantial quantities of currency and seemed able to cash bank drafts for any amount. Yet they went completely unguarded, except for a revolver lying in a corner of the teller's cage, which was empty most of the time as tellers doubled as ledger-keepers, accountants, and janitors. Sooner, rather than later, the vulnerability of the Canadian small-town banks became bruited about the North Dakota and Minnesota underworld, with the inevitable result.

Until 1921, the small towns of the Canadian west had little need for local police protection. In the rare event of a crime being committed somebody telegraphed the nearest Mounted Police post and a Mountie caught the next train. Robbing banks was therefore the merest child's play for American bandits. They cut the telephone and telegraph wires, brandished their guns at the bank managers, scooped up the available cash, and left. By the time anybody in the town could make his way to the nearest working telephone or telegraph office, the bandits had a long head-start back home. Sporadic bank robberies in the small towns of both Manitoba and Saskatchewan had occurred in 1920 and 1921. In 1922, two Manitoba towns were raided in August, another, along with three Saskatchewan towns, was held up in September, and there were more robberies in Saskatchewan in October and November.

An example of the vulnerability of the prairie towns occurred in the hamlet of Ceylon, Saskatchewan, in September 1922. The robbers arrived, and cut the communications, and while two men entered the bank the third stood on guard outside with gun drawn. Several residents of the town watched the robbery from across the street and were able to furnish the Mounted Police with a full description of the holdup men. Why then, if they were that close to the

scene of the action from beginning to end, had nobody done anything to stop it? To that question the Ceylon people had a most
convincing reply:

"What on earth could we do against three armed men? Nobody in
Ceylon owns even so much as a shotgun!" [18]

In the town of Estevan in the fall of 1922, there were enough
people with guns to organize a posse which began patrolling roads
and questioning strangers. They pushed their search with utmost
vigour but succeeded only in making life miserable for the native
duck hunters whose pleasure they disrupted. The newspapers reported that the authorities were going to ship a load of machine guns into
the district and move a detachment of Mounties down to guard the
border. Another story told of how the station agents were to be
supplied with surplus Very pistols and flares from the late war. At
the first sign of a break in their telegraph line they were to rush onto
the station platform to fire the gun into the air in the hope that
somebody would see the flare and notify the Mounties.

No evidence of the identity of the bank-robbers was ever brought
to light because none was ever caught. Yet the newspapers were able,
often on the basis of anonymous informers, to identify the bank
robberies with the liquor traffic. The single event that enabled everybody to zero in on the whisky-runners was the murder during the
night of October 4, 1922, of Harry Matoff at Bienfait. Matoff was
married to Harry Bronfman's eldest sister. He had been in charge of
the Bronfman stores at Gainsborough, Carnduff, and Bienfait, which
were out of business by 1922. [19]

Life was following its normal even-tempered way in Bienfait that
night. There was the usual quota of uncommunicative strangers
registered at White's Hotel, waiting in their rooms, or whiling away
the time trying vainly to beat Fat Earl at his own game. Fat Earl had
the restaurant concession in White's Hotel and offered his customers
a double-or-nothing gamble for the price of their meal. Fat Earl's
game was throwing fifty-cent pieces at a crack in the floor and he was
so accurate at it that he seldom lost one throw in five. The natives
were well-acquainted with Fat Earl's prowess and they usually refused his challenge, but the rum-runners who frequented the area sometimes could be lured into tossing coins, and losing.

In the Bienfait poolroom the high-stakes snooker game had given
way to a modest poker game which was generating little excitement

until Jimmie LaCoste wandered in with the word that something would be cooking at the railway station that night. Jimmie LaCoste was a dapper local sport, pool player, and whisky-runner who occasionally sold some booze on the side. LaCoste reported spotting a couple of big cars near the grain elevator, which meant that some booze would be loaded up as soon as Harry Matoff turned up to arrange for its release. There was always more than an academic interest in whisky shipments in the Bienfait poolroom. Sometimes the cars were loaded so heavily with whisky, or the cargo tied so inadequately, that a case would be jolted loose in the dark as the cars hit bumps on their way out of town. There were some who said that the potholes were deliberately dug on strategically located curves to accomplish the unloosening of the cargo.

The closing of the liquor stores along the border had reduced only slightly the flow of booze to the States. When the weather was dry the rum-runners loaded their supplies at the Dominion Distributors warehouse in Regina and headed southeast along a graded road to Weyburn and Estevan. In bad weather the whisky was shipped by rail and consigned to the purchaser in Minot, "via C.P. express to Bienfait". Upon reaching Bienfait it was unloaded and stored in the express office until Harry Matoff arranged for its release to his customers. The operation had long since shaken down into a normal routine. The rum-runners waited at the hotel until well after midnight when Matoff would send word that he was at the station. He would take their money, and the expressman would assist the buyer to load up and provide all the documents required to prove to Canadian authorities that he was a common carrier moving a legitimate cargo to the United States.

LaCoste visited with the poker players for a while and when somebody at the front of the poolroom noted that the lights were on at the station he went over to see who was in town. It turned out to be Lee Dillage, an important North Dakota liquor dealer and sponsor of an outlaw baseball team that toured the Saskatchewan border towns in the summer. Among Dillage's stars were Happy Felsch and Swede Risburg, two of the disgraced members of the Chicago Black Sox team of 1919. LaCoste stayed briefly. Matoff was busy in the office checking the cash he had received from Dillage, and Dillage and the expressman were busy loading their cars. LaCoste headed back for the poker game and was nearing the door when a gun was poked through the station window and Harry Matoff was murdered by a single charge from a 12-gauge shotgun at a distance of about ten feet.[20]

The shotgun blast broke up the poker game at the poolhall and the players exploded onto the street to see what was happening. They met Jimmie LaCoste coming back from the station. Through the darkness, against the station light, they could see a solitary figure pacing the platform with a shotgun under his arm. They retreated into the safety of the poolhall, the blackness of the night swallowed the murderer, and somebody phoned Estevan to notify the Mounted Police. Jimmie LaCoste, who said he had seen the murderer taking off in a car, volunteered to lead the police in the direction he had gone, then veered in another direction. This diversion provided Dillage with enough time to get across the border with his loads of whisky. LaCoste and Dillage were ultimately charged with Matoff's murder and were acquitted.

The Matoff murder, coming as it did in the midst of the bank robberies and a couple of warehouse lootings blew the lid off the export business. The Government of Saskatchewan applied to the federal government for leave to outlaw all exports of liquor from the province except from breweries and distilleries. Permission was quickly granted and orders went out to the Bronfmans to dispose of their stocks by December 15, 1922, and get out of the business.

There remained, however, the mystery of the murder of Harry Matoff, and the more and longer it was discussed the wilder became the theories. To Harry Bronfman, there was no mystery about it. Somebody had shot his brother-in-law to rob him of the six thousand dollars in cash, and his diamond ring. What more motive did anybody need? It was surely not unheard of for people to be killed and robbed for so large a sum of money. It had, in Bronfman's view, nothing whatever to do with the liquor business. Bronfman must have been a minority of one holding that opinion. Much more widespread was the conviction that Matoff was the victim of a reprisal murder, that the money was taken only to divert the investigation from the real murderers. Reprisal for what?

One theory was that it was in reprisal for Matoff's part in having a couple of American hijackers returned to Canada and a term in the penitentiary. The men had stolen one of Bronfman's cars full of whisky and were picked up in Omaha. Matoff had appeared in court

at their extradition hearing and identified them, and they were returned to face the Canadian courts. Organized gangsterism had not
at that time developed to a point where it controlled bootlegging in
the United States. The rum-runners who were transporting liquor
into North Dakota, Minnesota, and Nebraska from Saskatchewan
were for the most part individual enterprisers who were supplying
jobbers and retail bootleggers in the American cities. Even if the
convicted hijackers had powerful gangster friends in the United
States, a dubious assumption in itself, it was unlikely they would
have waited a year to "get" Matoff if that had been their determination.

Another theory was that Harry Matoff was killed by mistake by
slayers hired to do in Harry Bronfman — allegedly by a customer
who had been sold inferior booze. This theory is obviously far-
fetched, spawned no doubt by the general belief that all bootleg
booze was rot-gut and worse. Certainly the newspapers of 1922
worked hard denigrating the quality of bootleg whisky. Most victims of alcoholic poisoning could die with confidence that they
would get their names in the paper. Many, perhaps most, of the
poisonous concoctions, however, were produced by the drinkers
themselves, sometimes by adding generous shots of wood alcohol
to alcoholic tonics that were advertised so widely for sale in the
drugstores.

It can also be conceded that some very low-grade bourbon was
shipped to the United States with a taste that was guaranteed to
outrage any old-time bourbon drinker. The fact must remain, withal,
that most of the liquor being compounded in the Bronfmans'
Dominion Distributors warehouse in the old Craftsman Building in
Regina was good liquor, and it was good liquor for a very simple
reason. Given the raw materials they used and the equipment they
had, it was much easier for the men running the plant to turn out
reasonably good booze than bad booze. They had begun at Yorkton,
and continued at Regina, with straight-grain, overproof, medicinal-
quality alcohol as their basic ingredient. The Royal Commission on
Customs and Excise estimated that the Bronfmans had imported
300,000 gallons of alcohol from the United States in 1920 alone.
True, the products of their inexpert blending were sold without
proper aging. The taste may well have resembled that of carbolic acid
as it trickled from the tongue to the throat. Many Bronfman cus-

tomers who thought they were buying Bronfman bourbon might have wound up with Bronfman rye, or rum or Scotch. Accuracy in labelling the bottles as they came from the machines was never a long suit at the Regina plant. [21]

There is, finally, little reason to doubt the statement of Harry Bronfman to the *Tribune*, that he threw away cases of essences and thousands of labels when he took over the stocks of his competitors after the governments closed the small-town export houses. Many of these dealers were buying alcohol by the drum and doing their own blending. Some of them may have laced their stuff with wood alcohol to improve its bite and others may have used a variety of essences to doctor up the taste and improve the colour. It seemed an immutable law of whisky that when an opportunity arose to dilute and adulterate it, it was diluted and adulterated. That law had applied to the bar managers before Prohibition as it applied to their bartenders when the bar manager was not looking. On the weight of the evidence of the business they did alone, it is difficult to believe that the Bronfmans would have knowingly permitted really bad whisky to go out to their customers. It is probably at least half true, as Harry Bronfman pleaded before the Royal Commission, that he paid little attention to what went on in the warehouse side of the Dominion Distributors operation in Regina. But that anything could go on in any aspect of their operation of which Harry Bronfman was totally unaware would have been completely out of character. [22]

In the fall of 1922, however, the murder of Harry Matoff was giving the Bronfmans second thoughts about the Saskatchewan environment, and it was also a part of the catalyst which would draw all the opponents of Prohibition into a cohesive force which would ultimately destroy it. And they would do it by standing all the facts on end. They would begin by blaming the violence along the Saskatchewan border, which culminated in Matoff's murder, on Prohibition; not on the loopholes which the authorities had built into the Prohibition law.

Sue
the bastards!

Of all the partnerships that emerged in the Prohibition era, none was more improbable than that of Harry Rabinovitch, Zisu Natanson, and Meyer Chechik. Three more unlikely operators of a wholesale drug company would have been difficult to imagine. Harry Rabinovitch was on the lam from a manslaughter charge in Minneapolis.[1] He had jumped $15,000 bail in connection with the death of a trucker in a liquor hijacking case. Natanson was the owner of a Regina junkyard who had become mildly affluent on the wartime boom in metal prices. Chechik was a wholesale chicken merchant in Winnipeg whose cold storage warehouse had enabled him to prosper in the liquor business. He was, on his own testimony, the financial man in the operation because he had an open line of credit of $150,000 with Boivin, Wilson, and Company of Montreal, Canada's largest liquor importers and wholesalers. The vehicles for the partnership were the Prairie Drug Company Limited and the Regina Wine and Spirits Company which obtained licences from the federal government to operate bonded warehouses in Regina in which alcohol could be stored.[2]

This partnership would set a behaviour pattern for Prohibition-era liquor operations in western Canada which was the antithesis of the American system. As the American system matured, and disputes arose between partners, the disputants went for their guns and settled the argument with bullets. As the struggle for control of the illicit liquor trade intensified, it was reflected by a steady escalation in gang warfare until the peak was reached with the St. Valentine's Day massacre of 1929, when one gang in Chicago machine-gunned to death seven members of a rival organization.

It is impossible to imagine Al Capone being sued by Dutch Schultz over sixty cases of booze that went bad; or Schultz dropping the suit at the examination for discovery when Capone apologized for the mistake and refunded the purchase price. Yet that is precisely what happened in Regina in one dispute that arose between Natanson and Harry Bronfman. If a dispute comparable to that between Bronfman and the Brewers and Bottlers Supply Company had developed a few years later in any American city, the contract would have been enforced by a man with a machine gun.

In western Canada, nobody even punched anybody else in the nose. Violence did flare occasionally along the 49th parallel, of course, but it was imported American violence and almost never involved Canadians. There was an occasion, for example, when two groups of American liquor dealers got into a hassle over the ownership of a large stock of whisky in one of the border warehouses. One of the disputants came to Canada, stormed the warehouse, and made off with the booze.[3]

The closest Canadians ever got to settling arguments violently was probably the time Harry Bronfman offered to fight a customs officer for the three-thousand-dollar deposit he was demanding on some smuggled cars. In Canada the disputants ran to the nearest lawyer's office and tried to settle their arguments in the courts. Mostly they failed because the courts would not settle any argument which involved illegal activity.[4]

The penchant for involving the courts in the liquor traffic disputes was climaxed, in 1925, by the most complicated, extensive, and expensive libel suit in prairie history. The *Regina Morning Leader* in a series of articles accused the chairman of the liquor commission of accepting bribes, dereliction of duty, and generally turning a blind eye to the wide-open sale of booze in Regina. The chairman sued the newspaper for $50,000 damages on an eight-point bill of particulars. The suit lasted for two weeks and recorded 400,000 words of testimony, mostly from king-pins in the liquor business. The jury acquitted the *Leader* on every count, the presiding judge awarded costs to the newspaper, and the government fired the liquor board chairman in a matter of hours.[5]

When the Jewish liquor dealers resorted to legal action to settle their disputes they were breaking one of the oldest of Jewish traditions: When a dispute arises between Jews, they must settle it among themselves. The first step was to select a mutually satisfactory arbitrator. If that failed the rabbi of the congregation to which the disputants belonged became the binding arbitrator. He decided what should be done and that was the end of it. Yet despite this almost sacred tradition, the Bronfmans, Chechiks, Sairs, Rabinovitchs, and Natansons all went to court, quite possibly because no rabbi could be found who would arbitrate any dispute of dubious legality.[6]

Whether Meyer Chechik would ever have gone to court, or would even have had much to complain about, if he had not become involved with the Bronfmans, is a moot point. Certainly the Prairie Drug Company and Regina Wine and Spirits Company were able to more than hold their own in the export—mail-order business which developed between December 1919 and February 1921. Following the October 1920 plebiscites, the prairie provinces stepped into the vacuum the Dominion had left and outlawed liquor importation, either by private drinkers or by the export stores. At least in theory, this not only restricted the liquor dealers to the United States export market, but it cut off the supplies with which to fill the demand of that market. Clearly the bloom was off the heather for the merchandisers of Scotch and rye, though there would still be business to be done as long as their stocks of medicinal alcohol and branded booze lasted.

Some time between the October 1920 plebiscite and the February 1921 cut-off for interprovincial imports, the Chechik partners got together with Harry Bronfman and worked out a joint venture of sorts. While each group was loading their own premises to capacity and supplying their own stores and customers, they decided to pool the supply end of their operation. The first step was to lease the old Craftsman warehouse at the corner of McIntyre Street and Sixth Avenue in Regina. It was a huge building on C.P.R. trackage and convenient to the main road out of town. Each group supplied liquor on a quantity and quality parity with the other. Harry Bronfman became the operating head of the enterprise, specially concerned with sales, while Rabinovitch ran the back shop, warehouse, and bottling plant.[7]

About this time the federal government decided it was time to increase the excise tax on alcohol, from $2.40 to $9.40 a gallon. The bonded drug companies did not actually have to pay the duty until they removed the alcohol from bond, but so large an increase in duty would severely reduce profit margins. Whether it was a factor in pushing the Bronfman-Chechik partnership to completion is unknown but it must have been a consideration. At the very least, it resulted in an immediate and drastic cut in the amount of alcohol that went into Saskatchewan Scotch whisky, coupled, of course, with a sharp increase in the volume of distilled water.

Putting the partnership together required some fancy legal footwork to stay within the law. For the partners to have sold their stocks of liquor to a new company was a violation of the Saskatchewan Temperance Act. The courts had processed enough cases to establish that it was illegal for anybody in Saskatchewan to sell liquor to anybody else in Saskatchewan. So the partners set up the unincorporated Dominion Distributors Company to export each partner's liquor and, presumably, to turn the proceeds over to the partner companies.

An immense business was done from the old Craftsman warehouse, although it is impossible to put a dollar value on it. How much actual profit was made, as distinct from estimates worked up by accountants for the government's tax department, was never revealed. The partners kept several sets of books, some in Winnipeg and

some in Regina, so that the operation was most effectively camou-
flaged from any prying governmental eyes which might have become
inquisitive.[8] There is evidence, however, that the informal partnership did not work smoothly. Bronfman brought in his chief account-
ant from Yorkton, W. H. Read, to become *de facto* manager. Two of
Chechik's employees from Winnipeg were given subsidiary positions.
Sam Bronfman floated in, out, and around the operation.

The dissension in this alcoholic Eden became apparent when
Chechik became impatient with the paucity of financial information
he was getting. In October 1921, he blew into Regina on an inspection tour and was barely through the front door of the Craftsman
Building before he was faced by his Winnipeg employees in a near
panic. Chechik's partners, they said, had been burglarizing the bonded warehouse, had removed thousands of gallons of alcohol from
bond without paying duty, and had filled the thus emptied barrels
with water. Here is Chechik's own description of the meeting as he
recalled in 1927 for the Royal Commission on Customs and Excise:

> Mr. Rodriguez and Mr. Gorman came up to me. They look
> to me as I am the financial man. I had very big credit in the
> east in the banks where I financed myself all this money.
> They said to me:
> "Mr. Chechik we have to go to jail."
> They are only employees. They have only one or two
> shares. I said, "I am not running a business for anybody to
> go to jail. What is wrong?" They make a statement to me
> what shows Rabinovitch and Natanson to syphon out by
> pumps or by pipes from the drums, alcohol, where they
> substitute water. As soon as the government finds out I
> am the president and this is the treasurer and this is the
> secretary and most of the directors will have to go to jail.
> . . . They told me how it was done. They took out the pins
> [from the door hinges]. The government lock is there.
> They do not move or interfere with the government lock
> or seal but they removed the pins [which enabled them]
> to [open] the door.
> The [next] thing I called a meeting of these three men,
> and I wrote a letter to the collector of customs in Regina
> not to allow any more clearing of these goods or any

goods from bond. [I have] money in the Imperial bank to cover the government interests and then I start to bring action against Rabinovitch, Natanson and Bronfman.[9]

The conspirators had emptied some twenty drums of alcohol and filled them with water and hence owed the government $37,000 in excise taxes. To make sure that the deficit was not increased further Chechik hired a team of bailiffs and put them on round-the-clock shifts while his lawyers were preparing papers for his suit. At this point Sam Bronfman entered the picture and made a sales pitch to Meyer Chechik that must rank with the outstanding sales talks of all time. At the very least it ought to nail down a claim for Sam Bronfman's being one of the great salesmen that Canada has produced. Unhappily the text of his speech is lost to history because it lost everything in translation into Meyer Chechik's impossibly laconic summary of the conversation in his testimony to the Royal Commission. His report of his conversation, completely expurgated, took only three or four lines.

Sam Bronfman was never slow to anger, and if ever anybody had a cause for anger Sam Bronfman had it that day as Meyer Chechik, in a rush of self-righteousness to the head, was threatening to ruin everybody, himself included, by involving the authorities. It was not an occasion when the volatile Sam Bronfman could ever have confined himself to saying, as Meyer Chechik told the Royal Commission:

"It would be better, Meyer, that you should go and pay the duty rather than cause so much trouble."[10]

Only those who had once felt the cut of the Bronfman anger and vocabulary would have been able to reconstruct the torrent of abuse that must have poured down on the hapless Chechik. In their mind's eye they would see Sam Bronfman circling Chechik with arms waving and head shaking.

"Meyer Chechik," they could imagine Sam screaming, the pitch rising with his anger, "You Goddamn stupid son-of-a-bitch, you must be out of your — mind! In the whole — world, do you know the worst — — thing you could have done? The worst — — thing you could have done, you have done – bringing the — government into it! How much — liquor do we have in stock? A half a million? a whole — — million? And how much do we owe Montreal? Half a — — million?"

"So what happens when you bring the —— government into it? They will seize all the —— liquor in the warehouses. They discover the shortages and then we all get arrested. Then you stupid —— —— you tell me how we pay all the —— creditors when the —— government confiscates our stock!''

There would be more, and somewhere along the way the tirade would become physical. Things would be thrown on the floor, there would be much jumping up and down and arm-waving. It was all highly effective.

Meyer Chechik, overwhelmed by this logical summary of the situation, took a personal cheque from his pocket, filled it in for $37,000, signed it, and handed it to the bookkeepers to give to the government's excise tax collector.

Nor was that all. Chechik not only paid the duty, he abandoned his threatened lawsuits and returned to Winnipeg, while his partner, Harry Rabinovitch, proceeded to negotiate a new deal with the Bronfmans. Instead of each partnership company supplying liquor on a quantity-for-quantity and quality-for-quality basis, it was agreed that it should be supplied to Dominion Distributors on the basis of an agreed price list. This, the court concluded, so varied the arrangement that it took the operation outside the law, for it became a purchase and sale of whisky between two Saskatchewan companies.

Once the duty was paid it was no longer useful or wise to keep the drums of water in the government bonded warehouse. They had it officially released and the employees ripped a hole in the warehouse floor and dumped it through the hole. This, seemingly, was easily accomplished without the Customs and Excise Department becoming privy to what had happened. It was *that* kind of a department, from top to bottom, in the 1920s.

Despite the super-sales job that Sam Bronfman had done on Chechik, the brothers were by no means free from trouble with their Winnipeg partner. Or perhaps it should be the other way around, Meyer Chechik was by no means free of trouble with his Regina partners. In fact Chechik's problems were only beginning and would not end until two years later when the Saskatchewan Court of Appeals threw his suit against the Bronfmans out of court.[11]

Once the October tempest blew over, the Chechik-Bronfman partnership seemed to rocket along, with the former reduced to the role of silent partner. In the spring of 1922 he was back and forth to Regina from Winnipeg for prolonged discussions about further amendments to their agreement. With the decision taken by the government to close all the outlying export houses in June, the indications were that the operation would further contract. According to Chechik they worked out a verbal agreement in which he agreed the Bronfmans should have sixty per cent of the shares in the now incorporated Dominion Distributors Company Limited and he and his partners would take forty per cent. However, when everything was sorted out, he later discovered that Rabinovitch, in violation of his instructions, had given the Bronfmans eighty per cent and reduced the Chechik group's interest to twenty per cent.

In 1923 Chechik filed a multi-pronged suit to have the sixty-forty relationship restored. He demanded an accounting of profits and the appointment of a receiver for the whole operation. He also sued Harry Rabinovitch for special damages. What triggered the suit was apparently his suspicion that the Bronfmans were supplying local whisky bottled at Yorkton to Dominion Distributors and charging imported whisky prices. The local booze should have been invoiced at twenty dollars a case. As imported stuff it yielded the Bronfmans forty dollars a case.

Unhappily for Chechik he could never get the case to trial in the ordinary sense. The Bronfmans, with a stable of lawyers that included A. J. Andrews, K.C., and F. L. Bastedo, K.C., of Winnipeg, and D. A. McNiven, K.C., of Regina, moved quickly to drive Chechik out of court. They applied to the Master in Chambers for a hearing on whether the alleged causes for action set forth in the Statement of Claim were illegal and hence contrary to public policy.[12]

For Chechik, whose understanding of the English language stopped this side of perfection, something had surely gone awry. He had gone into the deal with the Bronfmans vaguely understanding that the legal niceties were well taken care of and that it would be perfectly lawful to do what they had been doing. He had hired a lawyer to draw up his Statement of Claim. How was he to know there was a difference between "proceeds from" and "profits from", and between a "joint sales venture" and "partnership"? How was he to know that his lawyer did not understand too clearly what he was talking about and did not get it into the kind of English that would protect his interests? Was it Meyer Chechik's fault that the words never came out right? The unanimous opinion of the Saskatchewan Court of Appeal was that it was. It refused to allow him to amend his Statement of Claim so he could get his case into court:

> . . . . the allegations contained in the original statement of claim set forth transactions contrary to the provisions of the Saskatchewan Temperance Act. They show a sale, barter or exchange within the meaning of that act. The transactions upon which the claims of the plaintiff are founded are therefore illegal, and no action can be brought for the purpose of enforcing an illegal contract either directly or indirectly, or of receiving a share of the proceeds of an illegal transaction. Where the object of a contract is illegal, the whole transaction is tainted with illegality and no right of action exists in respect of anything arising out of the transaction.

Nothing but disaster ever happened to Chechik. He lost his law suit and then was driven to the edge of bankruptcy when the government of New Brunswick seized over a million dollars' worth of his liquor for non-payment of provincial taxes.[13]

In 1927 he pleaded inability to pay a $1,400 claim the federal government made for income taxes.[14] In addition he was being dunned by Ottawa for $87,000 for excise taxes on another eight thousand-odd gallons of alcohol that had been removed illegally from the bonded warehouse of Prairie Drugs. He went to elaborate pains to prove to the Royal Commission that he had nothing to do with the management of anything in Regina. Somehow he had been deluded into thinking that the Royal Commission had power to free him from the clutches of the federal tax collectors.

He got no assistance and less sympathy. Would the commission please ask the government to give him back the $37,000 Sam Bronfman had talked him into paying in excise taxes? The commissioners were almost contemptuous in dismissing that appeal. Would they, then, authorize the government to furnish him with copies of letters it had received from the Bronfmans in connection with Prairie Drugs to assist him in a suit he was going to launch against the Bronfmans? Again he got an abrupt and unsympathetic "no".[15]

The Supreme Court of Canada was more friendly. After the exodus from Regina, Harry Rabinovitch went to Halifax and became involved in exporting booze to the United States. With new lawyers and a new statement of claim, Chechik sued in Nova Scotia to have his partnership with Rabinovitch terminated, asked for an accounting, and was awarded $309,000 in damages. The award was upset on one appeal, reinstated on another, and confirmed by the Supreme Court of Canada.[16]

All this, however, would come much later. The partnership in Regina ended not with a roar, not with a whimper, but in such a flood of booze from the partnership warehouses that it almost swept the city away. In the early autumn of 1922 when it became clear that the Saskatchewan government was serious about wiping out the domestic export trade, the warehouses of the drug companies were loaded with alcohol. In order to clear the several premises before the December 15 deadline the government had set, Harry Bronfman launched the greatest fire sale of booze in the annals of the west.

While the Liquor Commission chairman benignly turned his attention elsewhere, just about anybody who could carry a case of whisky trooped in to purchase unlimited quantities from the partnership. Until then, sales to rum-runners had been restricted to the Dominion Distributors warehouse on McIntyre Street. To handle the increased business it was decided to open a sales office a couple of blocks away in the Regina Wine and Spirits Company warehouse. From ten to twelve men were steadily employed at Dominion Distributors blending and bottling the whisky from the alcohol transferred from the drug storage vaults. Then it was carted back to the newly established cash-and-carry sales office at Regina Wine and Spirits.

Between the start in 1920 and the finish in 1922, the mix that went into the booze was, as previously noted, substantially diluted to maintain profit margins despite the whopping increase in excise duty. At Yorkton, Harry's original mix had been 100 gallons of rye whisky, 318 gallons of alcohol, and 382 gallons of distilled water. In Regina during the last ninety days of legal export, the mixture was reduced to 40 gallons of water, 10 of alcohol, and 2 of malt whisky, with a shot of caramel for colouring. On the basis of simple arithmetic alone, it is easily demonstrated that the partnership, in that period, was one of the greatest forces for Temperance in Saskatchewan. It had certainly reduced alcoholic consumption on the part of its customers by a good thirty per cent. In doing so they established a precedent which governments were to follow twenty-five years later to satisfactorily increase their profit margins.

Out of each vat containing that emaciated mixture there poured forth four separate brands of Scotch — Dewar's, Johnny Walker, Black and White, and "no fame". The brand of whisky in each bottle depended not upon the mix but upon the supply of labels which the workers on the assembly line had stacked beside them at the moment. The liquor was identical in all the bottles. The prices were not. Customers who thought they were buying Johnny Walker paid three dollars a case more for it than those whose preference ran to Dewar's or Black and White. Customers who were not too much concerned with brand names could get "no fame" whisky — a catch-all term for all the other labels, real and counterfeit, the company carried in stock. "No fame" whisky sold for thirty-five dollars a case compared with the forty-five dollars charged for Johnny Walker. [17]

Soon after the warehouse sale at Regina Wine began the company was doing an average of six thousand dollars' worth of business a day. It had previously been the practice to provide each purchaser with all necessary customs entry forms. That procedure was scrapped, for so great was the rush toward the latter days of the sale that there was barely time to count the money, which for the period exceeded $300,000.

The climax for the entire operation came on December 14, the day before the deadline. The bonded drug warehouses had been cleared but there were still thousands of cases of whisky unsold at the Dominion warehouse, together with several hundred barrels of alcohol. The public sale was phased out and the partners decided to liquidate the company by dividing up its liquid assets. The entire stock was divided into eight portions. Chechik, Rabinovitch, and Natanson got an eighth each, as did Harry and Sam Bronfman. Where the balance went was never disclosed but on the basis of the Chechik lawsuit it can be assumed it went to the Bronfmans.

It "went" to the Bronfmans and the other partners literally. They rounded up a fleet of truckers and draymen and for the next two days the hauling business of Regina was concentrated on transporting booze along the route between the Dominion Distributors warehouse at McIntyre and Dewdney and the homes of the partners on St. John Street and Fifteenth and Sixteenth avenues. Harry Rabinovitch lived at 2322 St. John Street, Natanson at 1326 Fifteenth Avenue, and Harry Bronfman at 2326 Sixteenth Avenue. All were substantial houses. They had to be, to accommodate all the booze that was carried into them during that forty-eight-hour period.

Ed Waite, who could carry sixty cases on his dray, made eighteen trips to Harry Bronfman's on December 15. Others carried similar loads to various addresses around the city. There was nothing clandestine about the operation. It was carried on in broad daylight in full view of the working population. To get from the warehouse to the homes of the partners the route led directly through the downtown business district. [18]

There were other things to be divided up besides the booze. There was the bottling plant at the warehouse. Natanson took that, dismantled it, and set it up in his basement. He also bought $100,000 worth of Harry Bronfman's share of whisky, but whether he took delivery of it that day or later is not clear. The purchase would have amounted to at least four thousand cases — enough to fill two railway box cars and far beyond the storage capacity of the Natanson basement. It may well have been that the extra purchase was for alcohol in barrels, for Natanson continued the bottling business in his basement until 1924.

The result of the 1922 fire-sale was that everybody in southern Saskatchewan who could afford forty dollars for a case of booze, and wanted a case of booze, got a case of booze. The extent of the saturation of the Saskatchewan market may be gauged by an answer Natanson made to a question over a year later. He was asked whether he had got rid of all the liquor that had been removed from the Craftsman Building. No, he said, he still had quite a bit left, at least sixty cases in his basement. [19] Things were very slow in the booze business and it was taking much longer than expected to get rid of the stuff.

The editors of the *Regina Morning Leader,* whose reporters had noticed the steady flow of booze through the streets, decided that there was something rotten at the Saskatchewan Liquor Commission. Indeed the December 15 events had only reinforced that opinion, for rumours had been rampant for months about an illicit liaison between the law enforcers and the Dominion Distributors.

The practices of the commission would have generated rumours even if nothing untoward had been happening. All the prairie provinces permitted the hotels to sell "Temperance" beer, which could contain only two per cent alcohol in Manitoba and Saskatchewan but up to four per cent in British Columbia. One of the primary tasks of the Liquor Commission was to enforce the law against "strong beer". Because beer was transported and mainly merchandised in kegs, the seizure of strong beer often occurred in very large quantities — up to a carload in many cases.

Little beer was sold by the bottle for home consumption. It went by kegs and barrels into the hotels and was sold by the glass "on draft" for twenty-five cents, compared with fifty cents for bottled beer. It was no trick at all for an amateur plumber to devise a system by which the hotels could run one connection to their faucets from Temperance beer and another connection to the same faucets from well hidden strong beer. When any suspicious characters arrived at the hotel looking for a drink, the flick of a tap could switch supply sources and if he was a government spotter he would get the legal draft.

While the country hotels were raided periodically, they were seldom caught with illegal beer or liquor on hand. They had little need for fancy plumbing. When a liquor inspector boarded a branch-line train at Regina, Moose Jaw, or Saskatoon, every station agent on the line got the word from the telegraph operator in time to warn the bootleggers.

In the cities successful beer raids were seldom managed in secret. The weight and sheer bulk of the contraband was bound to attract public attention, whether the booty was a few barrels or a carload. There was, of course, a natural urge on the part of the law breakers to discredit the law enforcers. When a bootlegger got a barrel of beer with a government seal and the initials of the chief inspector still on it — sure proof that it came from seized stock — rumours of official corruption spread rapidly through the drinking community.

The reappearance of the seized beer on the bootleg market was a natural result of the system adopted in Saskatchewan for disposal of confiscated beer. The commission had two choices. It could dump the stuff down a convenient drain, as the Mounties once did with contraband, or they could sell it for export to a province which permitted the sale of strong beer. The latter policy was usually the one followed.

And who was its prime purchaser? None other than Harry Bronfman, who bought it for four dollars a barrel from the commission and had no trouble unloading it on his partners at Dominion Distributors for seventeen. They frequently sold it back to the Saskatchewan hotels for twenty-five dollars a barrel.[20]

In Manitoba, a different system was in vogue. There the liquor enforcers favoured dumping the beer they seized, but they disposed of the booze by shipping it to charitable institutions.[21] Thus F. T. G. White, who was chief of enforcement in Manitoba, once made a large haul at a local bootlegger's and noted in his official report that he had disposed of it as follows:

> 8 bottles of gin to Old Folks Home at Gimli
> 3 cases of Scotch to the Children's Hospital in Winnipeg
> 1 keg of Scotch to St. Adolph's Orphanage
> 1 barrel of Scotch to St. Joseph's Orphanage
> 1 barrel of Scotch to Old Folks Home, St. Boniface.

One can easily imagine the old folks having a use for the gin and Scotch so generously donated. But what would the orphanages do with Scotch by the barrelful? Bathe the kids in it? The question never arose in Saskatchewan. The question that did arise there, with increasing insistence in the columns of the *Morning Leader*, was: Where were all the liquor commissioners and their minions when the transfer of booze from the Dominion warehouse was taking place?

It seems clear, *a posteriori,* that much of the booze that was sold from Dominion Distributors after the border export stores were closed was diverted to domestic consumption, if not in Saskatchewan then in Manitoba and Alberta. From December 1922 onward there is no doubt of it. The editors of the *Morning Leader* would have been kept aware of the situation in Regina from the sobriety or otherwise of their reporters. The trade of journalism in that era was overrun with drinkers, if not with drunks, who had an unerring nose for booze as well as news — frequently one led to the other, and from either direction. It was not long before the *Morning Leader* had reached the conclusion that Chief Commissioner R. E. A. Leech was the villain of the piece. Instead of zeroing in on him, however, it took a decidedly circuitous approach. It attacked the commission in most vigorous terms for dereliction of responsibility in connection with non-enforcement in Regina. Then it ran stories specifying that nothing of its criticism was directed to commissioners W. J. Bell or A. G. Hawkes. That left Leech sitting amidst the brickbats and dead cats all by himself.

The *Leader* for twenty years had been an ardent advocate of Prohibition. It was also equally ardent in its support of the Liberal party. Almost from the outset, however, it had been critical of the enforcement of the Prohibition law in Saskatchewan and particularly from the onset of the hiatus to the end of the export boom to the United States. Here in part is the *Leader* in the days before the libel action was launched:

> Anyone not blinded by a determination not to see knows that with respect to the sale and consumption of liquor conditions in this city are absolutely rotten — and have been rotten ever since the present Sale of Liquor Act went into effect.
>
> The responsibility for this state of affairs rests squarely upon the Saskatchewan Liquor Commission — and upon no one else.
>
> When the present Sale of Liquor Act was put into effect its administration was entrusted to the Saskatchewan Liquor Commission. This commission drew its authority from the most drastic law ever placed upon the statute-books of the province. At every subsequent session of the legislature this law has been tightened up until the power vested by it in the Commission challenges all previously accepted theories of personal liberty and inviolability of domicile. The Commission has armed itself with inspectors and spotters and operatives and agents sufficient to clean up every blindpig in this city in twenty-four hours if it were so minded. Still it is possible for a brother of the chairman of the Saskatchewan Liquor Commission to stand before a district court and state that he is "appalled" at the extent of the liquor traffic which the Commission of which his brother is chairman has permitted to continue all these months unchecked.
>
> The bulk of the liquor with which this city has been running wet for the last sixteen months can be traced directly back to the stocks contained in the local liquor warehouses when those establishments were put out of business by federal order-in-council on December 15, 1922.
>
> The Morning Leader submits that the traffic in liquor that has been going on in this city for the last sixteen months all but wide-openly has been conducted with the connivance of the Saskatchewan Liquor Commission; and

it further submits that the operations of the Saskatchewan Liquor Commission during those sixteen months should be investigated by a royal commission without further delay.

As every newspaper editor knows, once any sort of crusade is launched it automatically brings a lot of information pouring in from a miscellany of informers — from outraged idealists to vindictive former employees and spiteful competitors. Within a matter of months the *Leader*'s file on Leech took on impressive bulk and it was emboldened to become specific.

Among its specifics were statements from the teamsters that they were told when loading up with whisky at the Dominion Warehouse that they had nothing to fear because Bronfman had fixed it with Leech; that Leech had sold beer seized by the Commission to Dominion Distributors for give-away prices; that the Bronfman confederacy had subscribed $1,250 apiece to a $10,000 fund with which it had purchased a weed-grown farm from Leech at five times its value. [22]

Eventually the *Leader* succeeded in provoking Leech into his libel suit. The testimony at that trial filled in the details of the close friendship that existed between Leech and Harry Bronfman, of direct payments to Leech in connection with beer sold to dummy purchasers in British Columbia, of Leech's substantial deposits of large-denomination banknotes in his bank account in Regina.

By this time the partnership between Chechik, Rabinovitch, and Natanson was long since dissolved. Chechik and Rabinovitch were gone to greener pastures and Natanson was in jail. The police had raided his home and discovered his basement bottling plant in full operation. Upon conviction he was fined five hundred dollars and sent to jail for two months. He appealed the conviction and the jail sentence was increased to six months at hard labour.

But for Harry Bronfman there was to be a dramatic footnote to these free-swinging years of the early 1920s.

In the Customs Department, who told the truth?

As Harry Bronfman relaxed in his study in Montreal's gathering gloom of November 28, 1929, the farthest thought from his mind would have concerned a chance meeting in the village of Gainsborough in the now dim and distant past. The Saskatchewan chapter of his life was long since done and finished. He had made the long climb from a room in the Balmoral Hotel to a castle on Mount Royal and such odious expressions as "boozorium", "bootlegger", and "rum-runner" seldom fell upon his ears any more. He was now a well-established millionaire who, like Shakespeare's Caesar, bestrode the Canadian distillery industry like a Colossus.

A maid entered the room and announced quietly that two men, who said they were policemen and wished to speak with Mr. Bronfman, were at the door. He went to see the men whose announcement cut Harry Bronfman down to size.

"Mr. Bronfman? We are Royal Canadian Mounted Police officers and we have two warrants for your arrest signed by the Attorney General of Saskatchewan. We are instructed to have you proceed with us in custody to Regina."

His requests for a delay to attend to urgent business matters, for permission to call his lawyers or his brothers, were refused. The "kidnapping" of Harry Bronfman had begun. He was whisked to the Windsor Station and aboard a train for Regina. There, three days later, he was arraigned on two criminal charges. The first was attempting eight years before to bribe Cyril Knowles, a customs enforcement officer. The second was attempting to obstruct justice by tampering with the witnesses who were to testify against his brother-in-law on bootlegging charges seven years before. He was released on $50,000 bail and returned to Montreal.

To many western Canadians, particularly partisan newspaper publishers and their political allies, the arrest of Harry Bronfman was the penultimate act of a drama that had been receiving newspaper reportage for the previous two years. Bringing Harry Bronfman to trial was a cause to which the Conservative party of Saskatchewan had been dedicated during the lately completed election campaign that brought it to office for the first, and the last, time in Saskatchewan history. His arrest followed with all reasonable, even unseemly, haste, as soon as the new government was settled in power. Like everything else about the affair, the way in which the arrest was made was what might have been expected from the background to the Bronfman saga. Nevertheless the kidnapping aroused angry protests even from the newspapers which had been leading the pack in pursuit of the Bronfman hide.

The *Winnipeg Tribune*, in a leading editorial, denounced the manner of the arrest as unbecoming to Canada. It asserted in part:

UNBECOMING TO CANADA

The Tribune has no particular sympathy with Harry

Bronfman or his ilk. In various articles several years ago it exposed and directed public attention to the practices of the export liquor business in Saskatchewan, which was carried on to a large extent under his auspices.

The Tribune takes it for granted . . . that Bronfman escaped prosecution on serious charges made against him by the Customs Commission chiefly because the late government in Saskatchewan feared the political consequences of such a course. . . . Law enforcement in Saskatchewan was almost habitually prostituted to political advantage. The new government and the new Attorney-General, Major M. A. MacPherson, are to be congratulated on efforts to remove the stain that rested on the province by reason of the fact that Bronfman was not prosecuted.

At the same time the newspaper reports of the manner of Bronfman's arrest are disquieting. If it is true that he was arrested in Montreal, rushed by auto across the border into Ontario*, and then taken aboard a train for Regina, the fact is far from creditable to those responsible. The proceeding savors far too much of kidnapping to suit the dignity of law and justice in Canada. There are ordinary processes of law established for the protection of both individuals and the authorities. They cannot be violated without repercussions that will tend to destroy the high respect in which Canadian law is held.

If Bronfman could not be arrested in the manner prescribed by law and brought before the courts to answer to the charges against him, he should not have been arrested at all. If he could be so arrested he should have been. The excuse suggested by Regina newspaper correspondence, that a long battle might have taken place in the courts of Quebec on habeas corpus proceedings, is no excuse at all.[1]

*This turned out not to be true.

The charges which brought Harry Bronfman to the criminal dock arose almost incidentally from public hearings that occurred long after he had shaken the last of Saskatchewan's dust from his shoes. The shutting down of the liquor export business in December 1922 ended the big-money phase of the booze business on the prairies. Harry stayed on in Regina only long enough to liquidate the huge stock of liquor he had stowed away at his home. That took him well into 1923 and he then left for Winnipeg, where he lived until 1924. His next move was to Montreal to build the first Bronfman distillery at Ville La Salle.

Harry Bronfman embarked on distillery-building the same way he had gone into whisky-blending in Yorkton — from pure ignorance. Instead of turning the job over to specializing architects, engineers, and contractors, he became his own Mr. Everything, letting his own contracts as the work progressed. He was joined on the site by his brothers Sam and Allan, who divided their time between helping to get the distillery built and assisting their brother Abe with the Atlas Shipping Company and Atlantic Import Company in Halifax. The family which had once thought carload shipments were something special was now exporting booze by the boatload from the Nova Scotia port.[2]

By the time the Ville La Salle distillery began shipping its own production to market, the storm clouds in the form of a major scandal were gathering over Montreal and Ottawa. The already notoriously inept and corrupt Department of Customs and Excise was being reduced to total nullity by the blundering, bumbling administration of the Honourable Jacques Bureau. Smuggling along the 49th parallel had reached such proportions that the Canadian Manufacturers Association and the Toronto and Montreal Boards of Trade organized the Commerical Protective Association. Its agents became free-lance customs detectives and provided information for a general attack on the customs department. Smuggling, the Toronto *Saturday Night* had written, had reached such proportions as to be a national menace. At least fifty million dollars' worth of goods were being smuggled into the country annually, putting Canadian factories out of business and Canadians out of employment.

In the early days of the agitation the spotlight had been focused on the chief enforcement officer of the customs department in Montreal, J. E. A. Bisaillon, whom Ralph Allen described as "one of the most incredible sitting-ducks in the history of public malfeasance". Among other things Bisaillon ran a customs brokerage business on the side and was a prominent landowner in Rock Island, the smuggler's-cove village astride the U.S.-Canadian border. Bisaillon owned one house on each side of the line, both of which, gossip had it, were used extensively for two-way smuggling. He had been the centre of several notorious cases involving smuggled whisky and narcotics, but held onto his job nevertheless.[3] Bisaillon's activities triggered a parliamentary committee investigation into the department. That investigation directed public attention to another and even more serious flaw in the enforcement structure, one which had cost the Government of Canada fifty-two million dollars in lost revenue during the three years ending in 1925. In the 1920s it was no trick at all to blow fifty-two million dollars into a major scandal, which, save for the adroit footwork of Prime Minister Mackenzie King, would have destroyed the Liberal government.

The outflow of booze from Canada to the United States was then at its peak. Rum ships left the Maritimes, Ontario, and west coast ports daily, returning for repeat cargoes within a matter of hours. The liquor which supplied this vast trade was shipped from bonded warehouses and as it was going into export it was exempt from the nine-dollars-per-gallon excise tax which had to be paid on alcohol going into domestic beverages. In order to qualify as excise-tax-exempt, the exporters were required to file with the Canadian customs officials a sworn declaration, from the port to which it was consigned, that the cargoes had reached the foreign ports of entry. This rule also applied to the exports which were made by railway express and automobile from Saskatchewan. It was a regulation to which nobody paid the slightest attention, least of all the customs officials.

If the rum-runners had been willing to trust the United States customs officials they could easily have had their papers rubber-stamped officially. The American customs agents were as scandalously corrupt as the Canadian. Examples of the willingness of the U.S. agents to be bought are legion. After one protest from Washington about rum-running from Canada there was an abortive attempt by Canadians to co-operate. After clearing shipments of rum from Canada the customs officials would phone their American counterparts and warn them that a load of booze was on its way. The ringing telephone became a nuisance to the Americans who put an end to the attempted assistance.

"Why don't you quit worrying about the telephone and just mail us a report at the end of the week?"

On the western run from the interior of British Columbia, the roads into the States were hemmed in by the mountain ranges. There could therefore be no casual meandering across endless prairie going from one country to the other, as there was in Saskatchewan. There was but a single narrow road which was easy to blockade if anybody was interested in combating smuggling. In practice, the Canadian transporters pulled up to the border in full sight of the customs houses and transferred their loads to American cars and trucks which moved freely past customs into the State of Washington. A duty of sorts was levied. The rum-runners paid fifty cents a case to a Vancouver Export Company which "took care" of the American customs.[4]

Assuaging the great American thirst was generally accepted in Canada at the time as a legitimate Canadian enterprise, but one that fell somewhat short of qualification as an international aid program. For the exporters to co-operate with American booze importers in supplying the United States demand was one thing; but doing the Canadian government out of its legitimate tax revenue so that Americans could buy Canadian whisky from the rum-runners for less than Canadians had to pay for it in government stores outraged the Canadian sense of the fitness of things. Out of the public clamour for scalps in wholesale quantities came an inevitable royal commission. This was the Royal Commission on Customs and Excise of 1926-7.

Before that commission at its Winnipeg sittings in February 1927 came Cyril Knowles, until then an obscure civil servant, who launched a one-man crusade against Harry Bronfman.

Knowles had been a small-time Conservative party worker in Saskatoon in the 1911 federal election and soon afterwards received an appointment to the Department of Customs and Excise. He proved a reasonably efficient worker and rose steadily in the service. By 1919 he was an assistant preventive officer in the Port of Winnipeg. His duty was not only to prevent smuggling of goods into the country, he also had to ensure that goods being imported through regular channels paid the full duty the law demanded.

Knowles's job was no sinecure. The Winnipeg merchants were a suspicious lot. Every time a competitor put on a big sale, they suspected that there was some smuggling afoot because his retail prices were often below the wholesale cost of their own goods. The odds being at least even that they were right, they kept a steady stream of complaints flowing across Knowles's desk. In hard-to-identify things such as boots, shoes, tires, tubes, watches, and electrical goods, the merchants were each convinced that nobody was paying duty but themselves.

The faking of invoices had been developed into a fine art. It was common practice for American exporters to supply their Canadian customers with two sets of bills, one for payment and one, listing much lower prices, for dealings with the customs department. One enterprising Winnipeg church-goods importer did a big business with the St. Boniface religious orders in under-valued rosaries. The most expensive prayer beads, which were dutiable at jewellery rates, were billed through as the cheapest variety. The dealer was thus able to supply his customers with highest-quality products at a lower price, and profit handsomely into the bargain.[5]

It was, of course, an era in which the concept of honest weight or honest dealing was all but unknown. Only the most gullible of travellers on the branch lines of the railways paid full fare for their tickets. A friendly conductor would "slip them the wink" on the platform and they would board the train without buying a ticket at the station agent's wicket. The conductor would hand them a stub of a ticket and let them ride for half-fare, which he pocketed for himself. The oldest C.P.R. joke on the prairies was that the conductors used to throw the fare they collected in the air and what landed on the bell-cord belonged to the company, what fell to the floor was theirs. An Estevan harvesting contractor recalled that he once moved two harvest gangs totalling forty men from Estevan to Rosetown, along with two carloads of machinery. He paid full freight on the machinery, but the men were carried for half-fare over two different lines by co-operative conductors. The return journey in late fall was made under the same arrangement.[6]

The notoriously elastic standards of the railroaders have spawned a hundred prairie legends. In the days when pipe-smokers bought their tobacco in plugs, and cut and palm-rolled it to a desired fineness, a pocket knife was an essential tool. The knives usually were fitted with tampers and corkscrews, and railway expressmen carried a special knife on which a gimlet replaced the tamping blade. Much of the booze that was shipped around the country went by railway express. It was no trick at all for an express messenger to use his gimlet to bore into a keg of whisky and drain off a quart of the liquid between stations. It was a trick which draymen, warehousemen, and hotel janitors all across the country adapted to their own use.

Nor was minor pilfering the railroaders' only peccadillo. One of the most widely accepted legends of southeastern Saskatchewan concerns the neatly contrived hotboxes which regularly developed on the Grand Trunk Railway line between Regina and Northgate on the North Dakota border. A great deal of booze was shipped over this line to Vancouver via the Northern Pacific which joined it at the border. While on record the liquor was consigned to Vancouver for export, it was actually intended for North Dakota consumption.

As the train pulled out of Regina a railway employee would toss just enough sand into the journal of the boxcar to turn the oil-soaked waste that lubricated the axle into an abrasive substance which would create a hotbox by the time the car reached the border. The last station on the line before Northgate was the hamlet of Openshaw where all trains were stopped and inspected before starting on the long, steep downward grade to cross the Souris River. When the hotbox was discovered, the car would be cut from the train and spotted on the siding where the faulty journal could be serviced.

The American bootleggers could quickly slip into the car through an improperly sealed door, make off with the booze, and re-seal the door. The car would be repaired, picked up by another train, and carried empty westward to its fictitious consignee at the coast.

On one occasion the operation ended in tragedy. A howling two-day blizzard descended on the country while the empty car was still sitting on the Openshaw siding with its faulty journal unrepaired. A snow plough that was stalled by drifts hooked onto the car to give it additional momentum as it worked down the river hill. The car again developed the hotbox and jumped the track. An oncoming freight train, its engineer blinded by the blizzard, crashed into the plough and killed the crew working to free the derailed car. According to legend, that put an end to the hotbox caper.

Elevator operators habitually short-weighted their farm customers who were delivering their grain. City merchants did likewise on the provisions they sold, while their customers, if they worked in the retail stores, dipped into their employers' tills with nary a twinge of conscience. In an effort to raise the percentage of the sales that stayed in the tills, the till-makers equipped the machines with bells which clinked when the drawer was opened. It was a device which was added to the cash registers after they became popular. Schoolboys being launched on banking careers took over the "stamp concession" and the stamps they were able to purloin and sell helped make up for the starvation wages they were paid.

There was, in truth, nothing unusual about the rather casual morality of the commercial world in an era when "with two fires and a failure, a man's fortune is made". It was the hallmark of politics as well. An honest politician, in the cynicism of the times, was one who stayed bought. It was taken for granted that politicians took advantage of whatever opportunities arose for profitable investment. Sir Clifford Sifton, who was a struggling lawyer from Brandon when he entered the Laurier cabinet in 1896, left it with a substantial fortune in 1905. In his life of Sifton, J. W. Dafoe is authority for the following:

> Nothing could be more characteristic of him than the account of how, when he changed residence, he moved his securities from Ottawa to Toronto. The problem was to transfer securities for a very substantial amount from the vaults of a trust company in Ottawa to the vaults of a similar company in Toronto. If Sir Clifford had followed the customary course he would have turned the job over to the trust company, at the same time heavily insuring the securities; and the trust company would have transferred them in a heavily guarded express car. But Sifton did the business differently. On a certain day he, in company of one of his sons, appeared at the trust company in Ottawa with two suit cases and a trunk into which the securities were shoveled. He then departed for the station. The trunk was checked to Toronto and the suit cases carried into the parlour car. Upon arrival in Toronto the suit cases and the trunk were delivered to the vaults of the trust company which had stayed open to receive them.[7]

In Manitoba, a decade later, the Parliament Buildings scandal, in which construction graft was rampant, was an important factor in driving the Roblin government from office and banishing the Conservative party to the political wilderness for forty years.

In an era when political coloration was the essential consideration in civil service appointments, maintaining an acceptable standard of honesty and efficiency in the public service was exceedingly difficult. The customs department, long before the days of Jacques Bureau, had adopted the moiety system of the N.W.M.P. It held out the payment of rewards for effort by the employees and information from the public to assist in law enforcement. Half the proceeds from the sale of goods seized by the customs officer making a seizure went to the officer. Half the fines collected from Customs and Excise violators were paid to informers.[8]

Under the moieties system, a conscientious and energetic official could make more money from bonuses than he could from his salary. Cyril Knowles was such an officer. He could have made a great deal more than he did if the department had not been split between customs and excise. His duty began and ended with the customs work. If, in the course of tracking down smugglers, he came across an illicit still, for example, he had to get special authority and the assistance of the Mounted Police to seize the still. And the Customs Department being what it was, it sometimes took a long time to get necessary authorizations. However, from the information that came to him, Knowles had built up an efficient network of informers along the Canadian border, particularly in the three-corners area where Manitoba, Saskatchewan, and North Dakota came together.

It was while pursuing smugglers of shoes and cigarettes in this area in December 1920 that Knowles came upon a convoy of three American rum-runners who had lost their way between Gainsborough, Saskatchewan, and the U.S. border and had blundered into Manitoba by mistake. The Americans had not checked through the Canadian customs to obtain their visitors' permits on the way in, so their cars were subject to seizure. When Knowles and Constable C. B. Piper of the Mounted Police apprised the rum-runners of that fact they protested loudly that the liquor agent at Gainsborough had guaranteed them free ingress and egress. They demanded to be taken to Harry Bronfman.[9] Knowles and Piper accompanied the rum-runners back to Gainsborough, where they located Bronfman at the liquor store.

The practice which the Canadian officials followed when they encountered Americans in the country illegally was to demand a deposit of double the regular customs duty on their car. The car was then released and when the Americans furnished proof they had returned it to the United States the Customs Department refunded the deposit. The rum-runners, having used up all their cash buying booze, asked Bronfman to put up the forfeit so that they could be on their way. Knowles computed the deposit at $3,025 and Bronfman agreed to provide it.

Up to that point the stories of Harry Bronfman and Cyril Knowles are in perfect agreement. Bronfman went to the safe and got out the cash, and Knowles got busy filling in the receipts for the money. According to Knowles, it was while he was making out the receipt that Bronfman made his celebrated bribe offer. He suggested to Knowles that he make the receipt out for "$1,000 or $1,200 or whatever amount he thought he could get away with with the government". Bronfman would then pay him $3,000 in cash and he could keep the difference. What was more, if he would get out of the district and stay out, an envelope containing a similar pay-off would be slipped under the door of his apartment every month.[10]

Piper confirmed Knowles's story in all the important details. It was denied in every detail by Bronfman and his partners in the liquor store who were there when the episode occurred. Bronfman said that what had happened was that he had challenged Knowles to a fight for the money because he was so angry over the seizure.

"Oh no," said Knowles, "that was not how it happened." The challenge to fight was not made until after the financial transaction was completed and the drivers were preparing to take off for the States with their loads. Knowles refused to let them go. Their liquor, he told them, was seized in Manitoba and consequently it would have to be held in custody until the Manitoba government was notified and gave its permission for it to be released. The thrust of that announcement must have put Bronfman's emotions into orbit.

The flow of booze across the borders to North Dakota raised few objections from that sovereign state. But Manitoba took the dimmest view of the way in which Saskatchewan whisky was finding its way into the illicit markets in Winnipeg. The Manitoba Provincial Police paid special attention to the roads of the western reaches of the province and occasionally set up ambushes at the bridges over which the rum-runners travelled. Whenever a good haul was made it gained favourable attention for the police. Unhappily such coups were infrequent, for early in the game the rum-runners laid out roundabout routes which kept them well away from the bridges.

The export papers, which kept the Provincial Police in Saskatchewan from interfering with the whisky trade, were a liability in Manitoba, since they were positive proof that the vehicle was not going to the customs point named in the printed form. That point was already behind it. Policing the liquor trade, to repeat, was none of Knowles's business. Nor was it something with which even the R.C.M.P. was concerned unless specifically instructed to do so. Liquor was the responsibility of the provincial liquor police, and the liquor police alone.

That Knowles would have concerned himself in the least with Manitoba's enforcement problem would have been difficult enough for Bronfman to understand; that the Mountie and the customs officer would have actually seized his whisky and held it for the Manitoba government must have been totally flabbergasting. When Bronfman recovered from the shock of Knowles's announcement he would have been less than human if he had not flown into the sort of violent tantrum that would have done his brother Sam proud. His denunciation of Knowles concluded with a challenge to go outside and fight for the deposit and the liquor. Knowles refused the challenge and that was the end of the matter until February 25, 1927, when Knowles retold the story for the benefit of the Royal Commission.

Knowles claimed he reported the bribe offer to his superior, who, if he paid any attention at all, gave it only a cursory glance before throwing the report away. A similar fate overtook another communication — that his home had been burglarized and his notebooks and files stolen. Bribe offers, of course, were by no means unusual. The Mounted Police testified that it was a common practice for the rum-runners, when stopped and questioned, to offer the officers a bribe, almost automatically.

For Knowles the immediate result of his confrontation at Gainsborough was a small increase in pay. It was the costliest raise he ever got because it lifted his income above the point at which civil servants ceased to be eligible to receive moiety payments. With that raise the department was able to wipe out over three thousand dollars in moieties which Knowles had earned but had not yet been paid.

It becomes difficult here to resist the temptation to engage in some soap-opera-type speculation. Did Bronfman use his influence

in Ottawa to rob Knowles of his moieties? Did Knowles concoct the
story of the bribe offer after he had lost his moieties and blamed
Bronfman for it? Did he bear a grudge against the Bronfmans and
embark on a deliberate campaign to destroy them? Was Harry Bronfman the sort who would offer a customs official a bribe in front of a
police constable in a roomful of people?

That Knowles was far from the usual trouble-avoiding civil servant
who stayed within his official parameters and "kept his nose clean"
can be conceded at once. He could have kept himself fully occupied
behind a desk in Winnipeg. Instead, some weeks later, he got information that the Bronfmans were "compounding" booze in the
Dominion Distributors warehouse in Regina. Both the Regina Wine
and Spirits Company and the Prairie Drug Company had bonded
warehouses. Under the terms of the incorporation of the latter it was
empowered to engage in the mixing and blending of alcoholic spirits.
Compounding alcoholic beverages, which on the face of it seemed to
be the same as blending, required a special licence, which neither
had. The difference seemed to be: Blending was mixing one whisky
with another to produce a slightly different whisky; compounding
was mixing alcohol with water, flavouring, essences, and other ingredients to produce distinctively different products, such as rum,
gin, and Scotch and rye whiskies.

That the Dominion Distributors were compounding booze with
enthusiasm was an open secret in Regina in the winter of 1922. On
an earlier occasion W. F. Taylor, head of the preventative service at
Ottawa, had journeyed all the way to the Saskatchewan capital to
raid the place. The journey was so well advertised that when he and
the collector of customs from Winnipeg arrived on the scene they
found no evidence upon which to lay charges.

On the raid that he staged on Dominion Distributors in 1922
Knowles managed to strike without warning, but he had the bad luck
to arrive after the compounding operation was temporarily shut
down. Nevertheless, he was able to seize twenty-six cases of wrongly
labelled bottles of liquor, some counterfeit labels, and other equipment. Then he raided the premises of the Regina Junk Company
which was owned by Zisu Natanson, a partner in the Dominion
Distributors. There he was able to seize a truck full of compounding
equipment along with cartons of counterfeit United States government excise tax stickers, counterfeit liquor labels, and jugs of es-

sences used to colour and change the taste of the booze being produced. He even located the dies from which the counterfeit labels
and stickers were made.

Knowles packaged a sample of the seized liquor in a wooden
carton, tied the carton with iron strapping, locked the strapping, and
placed an official seal on it. It was then ready for shipment to
Knowles's superiors in Ottawa. But instead of taking it to the express
office himself, Knowles accepted the offer of Harry Bronfman to
take care of it for him that night and deliver it to the railway the next
day. Knowles wired Ottawa for instructions about the next step in
connection with the counterfeit seizures. He was told to proceed at
once to Ottawa for consultation.

The first action taken in Ottawa was to open the case of liquor,
and when this was done Knowles said that two bottles were missing,
although nobody could explain how that could have happened.
When he returned later for an appointment at the office of the Hon.
Jacques Bureau, he was forced to wait in the corridor while Sam and
Allan Bronfman were ushered in ahead of him. His interview with
the minister consisted mainly in being cross-questioned about his
having some kind of a spite against the Bronfmans.

Upon his return to Winnipeg he received the following letter from
R. R. Farrow, the Deputy Minister of Customs and Excise:

> As explained to you when in Ottawa recently on offic-
> ial business the Department is unable under present
> conditions, namely those caused by your lack of dis-
> cretion and judgment in connection with the recent
> Inland Revenue cases at Regina, to continue your assign-
> ment to duty in excise work.
>
> You are therefore instructed that until otherwise order-
> ed, your duties are to be confined to Customs work, at the
> Port of Winnipeg only and performed under the direction
> and control of Mr. W. F. Wilson, Chief, Customs Preven-
> tive Service.
>
> For the present the Department cannot authorize you
> to make investigations regarding Customs matters outside
> the Port of Winnipeg except as specially authorized by Mr.
> Wilson.
>
> You are directed to communicate to Mr. A. Code,

> Inspector of Customs and Excise any information which
> may be in your possession or may be communicated to
> you regarding infractions of the Inland Revenue laws and
> regulations so that investigations may be made in respect
> of these by Mr. Code when he deems it advisable to do so.

Clearly, what Harry Bronfman had been unable to do with his
alleged bribe offer at Gainsborough, to get Knowles to stay out of
Saskatchewan, somebody had done with pressure exerted in the
right place in Ottawa. If Knowles was to be believed, that pressure
developed after the visit of Sam and Allan to Jacques Bureau.

But was Cyril Knowles to be believed? Despite the denials of
everybody concerned except the R.C.M.P. Constable C. B. Piper, the
Royal Commission believed him. One of the factors which, if it did
not add to Knowles's credibility, certainly destroyed that of the
Customs Department hierarchy was their testimony before the
commission concerning another raid staged by Knowles a year later.

Information came to Knowles that not even Abraham Code, his
superior in Winnipeg, could ignore. It was that the Sair brothers were
running a smuggling barter ring from their farms south of Oxbow,
Saskatchewan. It was alleged that whisky from Canada was being
exchanged for silks, watches, automobiles, and cigarettes being
smuggled into Canada. Knowles asked for and got permission to
make the raid along with William Stubbs, his opposite number in the
excise branch, and two special constables.

In August 1923 they raided several farms in the Carnduff area. On
the farm of L. Barnblatt, Isaac Sair's brother-in-law, they seized a
smuggled Cadillac car and two stills. Then they raided the home of
Isaac Sair and discovered two secret rooms carefully hidden in the
upper part of the house. There they picked up notebooks containing
details of transactions in American watches and other merchandise
and a large stock of whisky.[11] Further investigation revealed that
the merchandise was shipped to a fictitious company at Sherwood,
North Dakota, where delivery was taken by one of the Sairs. Sherwood was a small community just south of the Canadian border.
Knowles also seized a trunk filled with invoices, correspondence,
and even I.O.U.s from neighbours for watches sold by the Sairs.

Clearly this was one of the great coups of the Customs and Excise
Department on the prairies. W. F. Wilson fired off a letter of congrat-

ulations to Knowles. It was followed, three days later, by a telegram ordering him to drop the investigation.[12] This action followed a complaint by the Sairs to Senator J. G. Turriff of Saskatchewan about the manner in which the raid was conducted. Despite the mass of evidence that Knowles had uncovered, nothing was ever done to bring the case to court.

For all practical purposes, Knowles was thereafter confined to his desk in Winnipeg until his death in 1932 ended his service with the government. Nor was the shackling of Knowles all that happened. The Customs Department restricted him to Manitoba but did nothing to provide anyone to take the responsibility for policing the North Dakota border in Saskatchewan. About all that was unequivocal about the testimony of the Ottawa officials to the Royal Commission was that Wilson had ordered Knowles off the case on instructions from Farrow on instructions from Bureau. The *Winnipeg Tribune* suggested editorially that Knowles's service to his country was such that some tangible reward should be offered to him in appreciation. The government spurned the suggestion.

On its journey across the west the Royal Commission had heard enough to cause it to issue an interim report, and in it it urged that Harry Bronfman be prosecuted for his attempt to bribe Knowles. The recommendation seemed to interest only the opposition Conservatives in Ottawa and in Saskatchewan. The Hon. Ernest Lapointe, the Minister of Justice, managed to duck for cover in the House of Commons with excuses that the Crown's witness was in ill health, that it was a matter for the Attorney General of Saskatchewan, and that law officers of the Crown did not consider there was enough evidence to justify prosecution. In Saskatchewan the Attorney General shunted responsibility back to Ottawa by claiming the entire affair was a federal matter.

All this changed abruptly with the onset of the Saskatchewan provincial election of 1929. That election would have been bitter enough without the Bronfman issue being added, but added it was.

The province had been torn by religious and nationalist controversy for two full years. It had come to a head when the French-Catholic minority in the province petitioned for the government to provide some sort of course for training French teachers for the schools system. The existence of a minuscule minority of Roman Catholic Separate School Districts — 23 compared with 4,776 public schools districts — was always anathema to the Loyal Orange Lodges of Saskatchewan and it had rankled the other militant Protestant groups for twenty years. The United Grain Growers and the Conservative party both worked diligently to keep the language-religious issue bubbling and burbling. For years, scarcely a question arose in Saskatchewan which did not get dragged eventually through the mud of racial and religious prejudice.

This was the environment which the Ku Klux Klan encountered in its invasion of the west in 1926. Its war cry of "One Flag, One School, One Race, One Language" was a perfect reflection of the faith the militant Protestants had lived by for two generations. How many members the Klan actually enrolled in Saskatchewan is anybody's guess. It could hardly have been less than thirty thousand and might have exceeded fifty thousand. Certainly it attracted the enthusiastic endorsement of a number of country weekly newspapers and a surprising number of United Church ministers. How it would have fared if its promoters had not decamped with its funds cannot be estimated, but while it lasted the Klan found the soil of Saskatchewan fertile ground on which to scatter the seeds of bigotry. [13]

In June 1927 the *Moose Jaw Times* reported that the Klan Konclave there had attracted a crowd of thousands, that four hundred had come by special train from Regina, and that there were groups present from active Klans in Melville, Biggar, Creelman, and Regina. At this gathering J. H. Hawkins, a Regina clergyman of unidentified persuasion, keynoted the meeting with an attack on Catholics and foreign immigrants, a twin theme that was to become dominant in the election of 1929. By this time the organizers had made off with most of the Klan's funds, but the residual camp followers still toured the province stirring up hatred against everything that was not Anglo-Saxon, Protestant, gentile, racially pure, and purely patriotic. The strength of the sympathy which existed with Klan ideas, if not with the Klan itself, may be gauged from this fact: when the United Church attempted to get a resolution condemning the Klan through its convention, it was unable to do so.

There were Liberal as well as Conservative Klan sympathizers in Saskatchewan in 1929, but Premier J. G. Gardiner spearheaded a determined Liberal attack on organized bigotry. The Conservatives, on the other hand, with only four seats in the legislature, went out to harvest votes wherever they could and their spokesmen heated up the religious-racial controversy wherever a favourable possibility developed.

In the endless public disputation over Prohibition, overt anti-Semitism was quite common, and because the Jews were so prominent in the liquor export business "the Bootleggers" and "the Jews" became interchangeable synonyms. Fifty years after the end of Prohibition in Saskatchewan, this writer in his researches frequently encountered aging witnesses who still recalled the exporters as "the Jews". During the 1920 plebiscite campaign the Anglican Bishop the Right Rev. G. E. Lloyd had singled out the Jews for special chastisement in the following terms:

> Of the 46 liquor export houses in Saskatchewan, 16 are owned and run by Jews. When the Jews form one half of one percent of the population, and own 16 out of 46 export houses, it is time they were given to understand that since they have been received in this country, and have been given rights enjoyed by other white men, they must not defile the country by engaging in disreputable pursuits." [14]

In 1921, as another example, the Rev. E. H. Oliver, of the Presbyterian Theological College at Saskatoon, and the Rev. H. B. Johnston, the Presbyterian minister at Assiniboine, wrote a joint letter to the *Saskatoon Star* [15] which began:

> There are certain Jews in this province engaged in the liquor trade who could contribute a great deal to Saskatchewan by leaving it at once.

In a lifetime of failure to persuade their own co-religionists to enact laws which would eradicate the liquor traffic once and for all, it was understandable that the zealous Drys would look for a scapegoat on whom to work off their frustrations. The Jews, who dominated the export business, and the "foreigners", who persisted in operating home-made distilleries, were the handiest around.

And then, hard on the heels of the Ku Klux invasion, came the Royal Commission on Customs and Excise with a rushed-out recommendation that Harry Bronfman be prosecuted for attempting to bribe Cyril Knowles. It was, to say the least, a curiously ambivalent recommendation when it had nothing to say about the *opéra bouffe* performance of the Ottawa mandarins whose treatment of Knowles was as scandalous as the offering of a simple bribe.

Though the waffling of the Liberal federal government on the Commission recommendation became a bone in the craw of the Parliamentary Conservatives, the issue eventually lost its savour and was expiring from inattention until the closing days of the 1929 provincial election in Saskatchewan.

On May 8, the *Regina Star* the Conservative organ in Saskatchewan, published the first of a string of blistering editorials attacking the Liberals for refusing to prosecute Harry Bronfman. In its first editorial, headed "Above the Law", it wrote:

> It is now six months and 23 days since Attorney-General T. C. Davis pledged his word in the town hall in Craik to the Arm River electors that the prosecution of Harry Bronfman, wealthy Regina bootlegger, as recommended by the Royal Commission on the Customs Scandals, would be "carried through to the end".
>
> On that pledge the electors gave a majority to the Liberal candidate.
>
> What is the explanation of this betrayal? Is it true that the Gardiner Government dare not prosecute this case for fear of consequences to itself? Has the machine a stranglehold on justice in Saskatchewan?

From that day onward until the election on June 6, the *Star* rang the changes daily on that editorial, usually beginning with a first paragraph that added a day to the elapsed time since the Arm River by-election. Other Conservative papers naturally joined in the campaigns. The influence which the *Star*'s attack had on the outcome of the election would be difficult to assess. It was a fact, nevertheless, that the Conservatives swept every city seat and the Liberal candidates in Regina and Saskatoon were very badly beaten. The Liberal strength, over all, was cut from fifty-two to twenty-eight, the Conservatives rose from four to twenty-four while the Progressives carried five ridings, and there were six anti-government independents. When the legislature met in September the opposition carried a non-confidence motion, the Conservatives came to power, and Harry Bronfman landed in the dock in criminal court in Regina, not just on the one charge arising out of the Knowles accusation but also on a second one in which he was accused of spiriting government witnesses out of the country to save his brother-in-law from jail.

In the context of the bigoted times, Harry Bronfman was ideal fodder for the wolves. He was the perfect symbol of everything that was wrong with society in the eyes of the extreme Orange-Prohibitionist-Ku Klux Klan coalition that had helped bring the Conservatives to power. It might well have been that the lunatic fringe of bigotry in Saskatchewan was an unwelcome ally of the Tories. But the bringing of Bronfman to justice would still have been good politics in Saskatchewan without any such coalition in existence. He was rich, he was a Liberal, but most of all he was a "bootlegger" and a Jew.

As befitted a millionaire distiller, Harry Bronfman gathered as imposing a tableful of lawyers as the courts of the west had seen: A. J. Andrews, K.C., of Winnipeg, A. A. McGillivray, K.C., of Calgary, and P. M. Anderson, K.C., of Regina. Opposing counsel were C. E. Gregory, K.C., H. E. Sampson, K.C., and F. R. Bagshaw, K.C.

With such a team as Andrews, Anderson, and McGillivray for the defence it was only to be expected that a search would be made for a handy loophole that would get their client off without the nuisance of a trial. They thought they had found one in the way in which the Knowles charge was laid. He was being charged under the Criminal Code, which carried upon conviction a maximum penalty of eleven years in prison. If laid under the Customs and Excise Act, it would not only carry a shorter penalty, but the act itself required that a charge of attempted bribery of a customs officer had to be laid within three years of the commission of the offence.

The defence contended that the common law required, where a crime was covered by a specific law, that the charge of committing that crime had to be laid under the specific law and not under a general law, such as the attempted bribery section of the Criminal Code. In the Bronfman case, if the change could be made it would be tantamount to acquittal, since the statute of limitations would apply because the three-year limit for laying charges had long since passed.

The defence lawyers decided that the best move into this gambit was by way of habeas corpus proceedings. That required that Bronfman be placed in jail. So after Bronfman was committed for trial at the preliminary hearing on the Knowles charges on January 18, 1930, the defence refused to put up bail. Bronfman was taken to jail and habeas corpus proceedings were launched before Mr. Justice Lyman Duff in the Supreme Court of Canada. This required that the Mounted Police transport Harry Bronfman all the way to Ottawa for the hearing. The indignity of being confined to the Regina jail, carried to Ottawa, figuratively if not actually in chains, and then incarcerated again, was hardly the sort of thing that would appeal to any millionaire. But it was characteristic of Bronfman that when he hired high-priced help to advise him he did what they advised. As it turned out, all he got out of the experience was the experience. The Supreme Court Justice took two weeks to ponder the matter and then denied the habeas corpus motion. The defence put up the twenty thousand dollars' bail, got their client out of jail, and wrote finis to that effort.

The trial on the bribery charge was held at Estevan in the first week of March and was quickly over. The defence brought in both W. F. Taylor, who by now was Commissioner of Excise, and C. E. Blair, the assistant commissioner, to swear that no bribe offer had been reported and no such Ottawa meeting with the Bronfmans as Knowles had described had ever occurred. The jury took only four hours to believe the Ottawa mandarins rather than Knowles, and Bronfman was acquitted.

But Bronfman was far from out of the woods, for he had already lost an important skirmish on the witness-tampering charge. The case went to trial prior to the Knowles case and after forty-eight hours of wrangling the hung jury was discharged and another trial ordered. This must have come as a great shock to the defence. If there was ever a prosecution that beggared credibility, this was it.

Included in the string of liquor export houses that Harry Bronfman had been legally operating in Saskatchewan in 1920-2 was one in Moose Jaw which his brother-in-law David Gellerman managed along with a former Moose Jaw junk dealer named Sam Tadman. Despite their legality, there was a suspicion abroad that too much of this "export" booze was leaking from this warehouse into the gullets of thirsty residents of Moose Jaw. As a result, there must have been pressure exerted on the Saskatchewan Liquor Commission from the

Moose Jaw Drys to "get Bronfman". To that end the chief inspector hired a couple of skid-row characters as special agents to go to Moose Jaw with him and attempt to inveigle the manager of the boozorium into selling them half a dozen bottles of whisky.

Instead of accompanying his hirelings and watching for their emergence from the warehouse, so that he could corroborate their evidence in court, the inspector pointed them in the direction of the warehouse and went off to a hotel for a nap. He was awakened a couple of hours later by the arrival of his agents with their evidence, which they were drinking up at a great rate. On the basis of this performance, the inspector arrested David Gellerman and seized the entire stock of the warehouse — thirty thousand dollars' worth of liquor.

How the agents would have fared in court will never be known. They disappeared before the trial, and the prosecution had to be abandoned and the liquor returned. That was the end of the episode until either during or following the 1929 election William St. John Denton got the ear of the Conservatives with a story of inter-provincial derring-do. Denton, on his own testimony, was as complete a scalawag as Prohibition had produced, in Saskatchewan or anywhere else. [16]

Denton was everything that Knowles was not, a man without a trace of character. He described himself best in a wisecrack from the witness stand: "There may be honour among thieves but there's none among bootleggers." He was, among other things, a former bootlegger. He identified himself as an engineer and in the immediate post-war years had operated a trades school in Regina. His next job was as an undercover agent for the Saskatchewan Liquor Commission. He discovered there was more money on the other side of the law and joined Zisu Natanson in the rum-running business. Then he and Natanson had a falling out and he informed on Natanson to the Liquor Commission; a raid and seizure of a large stock of Natanson liquor resulted.

If David Gellerman had in fact sold the booze to the skid-row agents, it was truly an act of monumental stupidity that was out of character for any of the Bronfman clan. An ordinary employee who did some sideline bootlegging from an export house had very little to fear from the law. If caught, he might be fined two hundred to five hundred dollars, depending on the number of times he had been caught. But as previously noted, for an owner of a warehouse to be caught bootlegging placed the entire stock in jeopardy. David Gellerman was a partner in Southern Exports, Ltd., which owned the business. Gellerman, if he sold liquor locally, made the stock subject to seizure.

To save his liquor stock, Denton testified, Harry Bronfman decided that the witnesses must be spirited away until after the trial, and had hired him to do the job. He, the past-master of the double-cross, had been entrusted by a gullible Harry Bronfman to take the special agents on an expense-paid tour of several Bronfman hotels. Their first stop, he said, was the St. Regis Hotel in Winnipeg where they stayed cost free and well supplied with booze. Next they moved to the Bell Hotel, likewise in Winnipeg. Then he took them to the Mariaggi Hotel in Port Arthur for another extended stay, and finally escorted them to the United States and abandoned them. By this time the danger to Gellerman and the threat to the Moose Jaw liquor stocks had evaporated with the abandonment of the charges.

Was the story true? Or had it been concocted by Denton in an attempt to shake down Harry Bronfman? Or was it true and he was trying to blackmail Bronfman? The jury at the first trial could not make up its mind. Then the defence got to work in earnest. With the help of Jacob Sair, a meeting was arranged between Denton and Bronfman in the Leland Hotel in Winnipeg. At this meeting Denton offered to "tell the truth" at the new trial and get Bronfman off in return for a payment of thirty thousand dollars. They haggled for a long time, during which Denton had come down from thirty thousand to nine thousand dollars. Unknown to Denton, the defence had hidden a shorthand stenographer with an ear to the keyhole in an adjoining room. The entire conversation was taken down and used to confront Denton at the new trial. Denton did not shake easily. He claimed that he had gone to the room to discuss the offer which Bronfman had made, and it was Bronfman who was trying to buy him off, and not the other way around.

This time the defence prevailed, Bronfman was acquitted and returned to Montreal and the obscurity of the distillery business which was gearing up for the day when the United States would repeal the Eighteenth Amendment to its Constitution. So well did he succeed in avoiding the limelight thereafter that in Saskatchewan many of the legends that arose from the bootleg era became identified with his brother Sam, or simply with "the Bronfmans".

As visionary and off-beat a character as ever grew out of the soil of Saskatchewan, Harry Bronfman was an authentic child of his generation. His energy was boundless, and a combination of native cunning and incisive intelligence enabled him to spot, on the far horizons, opportunities for profitable enterprise. He was an Alger hero of the Prohibition era — the poor immigrant boy who, by his own initiative and daring, rose from rags to riches on the wings of opportunity that the contemporary Establishment created for him. Not the least of these opportunities were the gaping loopholes which the legislatures, by accident or design, built into the liquor laws of the land.

The first crack
in the dike

No prairie legend is more deeply entrenched or more widely spread than the notion that Prohibition was an outgrowth of the suffragette movement and was ended by the returned soldiers as soon as they could get their hands on a ballot when they came home from the war. As previously noted the reform was achieved in Manitoba before women obtained the franchise. Far from being any short-term phenomenon, Prohibition lasted for a full eight years. And it was ended not by any outpouring of public indignation but by a heavily financed drive by the breweries to sell repeal as the panacea that would solve the economic ills of the post-war depression.[1] The crowning irony of the brewery conspiracy was that, when the public did make up its mind, it turned thumbs down on the proposal to put their beer back into the hotels of Manitoba and Saskatchewan.

The flow of booze across provincial borders certainly assumed flood-like proportions when the federal wartime Prohibition measure expired in 1919. The resumption of the interprovincial booze trade enabled all the upper-crust drinkers to restock their basement shelves. It enabled the well-heeled middle class to conveniently obtain ingredients for an occasional tipple by mail order. It provided the retail bootleg trade with supplies for customers who, recalling the convenience of the bars, liked a drink or two with their lunch, or after work. And, of course, it led to the development of the huge rum-running trade with the states bordering the Canadian prairie to the south.

In several aspects, however, conditions during the hiatus changed little from what they had been during the two years of bone-dry Prohibition. Drunkenness had disappeared from the streets with the closing of the bars in 1915 and 1916, and it did not return. The treating habit had been broken for all time. Payment of wages in cash by the week had replaced monthly payments by cheque in many segments of the economy. Where pay cheques were still used, the employees no longer stormed into the bars to get them cashed on payday. Public drinking, as it had been known prior to 1916, never came back. Home drinking replaced public drinking, and with home drinking and the absence of treating, excessive consumption and drunkenness became both less noticeable and less common.

The volume of booze consumption during the hiatus probably never approached a quarter of what it had been during the glory days of the wide-open bars.[2] The public thirst was not only substantially reduced, it was kept well within the bounds of accepted decorum. It all added up, as the time approached for ballot-marking on the referendum of October 1920, to a very dull campaign in which neither Wets nor Drys were notably active. Indeed, far from the barricades against the demon rum being stormed by the returned war veterans, the argument in favour of continued importation went almost by default. Here and there a war veterans' convention would pass a resolution condemning Prohibition as an anti-British infringement of the very liberty for which the war had been fought. That was about all. The Drys were only slightly more active, from force of habit if for no other reason. Nellie McClung had moved from Winnipeg to Edmonton and, with Louise McKinney, of Claresholm, tirelessly stumped Alberta. Except for them the orators of the 1915 and 1916 crusades had gone either to their rewards or to greener pastures.

In Manitoba, Saskatchewan, and Alberta, the voters were given a simple choice. Did they wish to prohibit the importation of beverage alcohol into their province or not. A "Yes" vote meant the provinces would revert to the bone-dry Prohibition of 1918-9 when only the druggists were legal dispensers of the forbidden juice. A "No" vote would retain the system intact which permitted the citizens to send to an adjoining province for their supplies.

The campaign to bring out the Dry vote followed the same pattern in each of the prairie provinces. One or two prominent churchmen stumped the back concessions and the Dry leaders in the various strongholds of Temperance pushed the campaign from within. Thus the United Farmers and the United Farm Women in all the provinces supported a "Yes" vote for a total ban on interprovincial booze trade. So did the One Big Union in Alberta, along with the Mormon Church. There was still a cleavage within the Anglican Church. Archdeacon T. G. Lloyd of Saskatoon was a bone-dry Prohibitionist. Archdeacon Burgett of Regina described a vote for Prohibition as a vote of censure on Christ.

In almost all the Protestant churches "Yes"-vote sermons were preached on the Sunday before the voting. In the couple of days immediately preceding the balloting some substantial Dry rallies were staged in Calgary, Edmonton, Regina, and Winnipeg. But there were no confrontations like those of 1915, no debates, no imported exhorters, no broken-up meetings. For all the attention the newspapers paid to it, the issue was resolved with scarcely a ripple of public attention.

Those newspapers which did support a ban on the export houses and cross-border shipments no longer belaboured the arguments of 1915. They were as concerned with provincial rights as with the social cost of saloon drinking. A "Yes" vote, the *Winnipeg Free Press* argued, was imperative to give the province the right to manage its internal affairs as it saw fit. Once Manitoba had closed the door to imported booze it could then reorganize its own Prohibition laws to make enforcement more effective. That, clearly, was not the type of a tocsin call that would send the citizens howling into the streets en route to the ballot boxes.

The truth was that the public mind, that October, was elsewhere. In the countryside the argument of wheat board marketing versus Grain Exchange marketing was boiling over. Anger with the protectionist posture of both the Liberal and the Conservative parties was giving rise to a legion of new-party "Progressives" who were soon to drive the old-line politicians from legislatures and Parliament. The high cost of sugar focussed urban attention on the high cost of living, and the high cost of machinery focussed farm attention on the evils of tariff protection. The grip of post-war inflation was tightening on the working class. For those who could still spare the attention from such tribulations, the Black Sox scandal was beginning to surface that October and shake the faith of every western Canadian baseball fan in the integrity of the game and its veteran heroes.[3]

Far more important to the future of boozing on the prairies than the events of the 1920 campaign itself was the result of the British Columbia plebiscite which was held five days before those on the prairies. British Columbia handled things differently by providing the electors with an alternative to the question of banning, or not banning, booze imports. The B.C. voters could also mark their ballots in favour of establishing a government monopoly of the liquor business, and the sale, in publicly owned groggeries of liquor and beer in sealed packages. They chose that alternative, by a whopping 25,000 majority.

The conditions which prevailed in British Columbia and which led to the big majority for government stores had no counterpart on the prairies. That province's long coastline and its ocean ports made it particularly vulnerable to smuggling. It had gone through a series of scandals in connection with the administration of its Prohibition law, including the jailing of Prohibition Commissioner Walter Findlay for contempt of court after his arrest on a charge of stealing seventy-four cases of whisky. British Columbia was ripe for just such a thing as the Moderation League which came into existence with such political luminaries as Sir Charles Hibbert Tupper and ex-Mayor Fred Buscombe at its head. The league became an irresistible force when the assistance of the war veterans was recruited and the breweries undertook to bankroll the operation. The British Columbia Moderation League campaign was imaginatively structured to gain the sympathy of what might have been called the less-than-totally-committed Prohibitionists. This group accepted the Dry doctrine that boozing was a social and even a religious evil, but they were not given to shouting their convictions from the housetops. To them the Moderationist said:

> We agree with you. The bars were an unmitigated evil and should have been wiped out. We are absolutely opposed to any measure that will restore the bars in any shape or form! All we say is — better a law you can enforce than one you can't.

Whether the law could have been enforced in Vancouver is irrelevant. In fact it was not. Bootlegging and rum-running were rampant and the bars in the downtown clubs operated almost as openly as the pre-Prohibition bars had done.

In the entire west it would have been difficult to find a single prominent advocate of a return to the open bars. The Moderationists were as aggressively anti-saloon as the driest of Prohibitionists. In Vancouver they were able to equate the bootleggers and social clubs with the bars of old and blame their existence on the Prohibition laws.

Of equal potency was the economic argument of the Moderationists. The bootleggers and rum-runners were getting rich at the expense of the treasury of British Columbia, which was in its usual state of disarray. Why should the immense profits being reaped by the bootleggers not be diverted to the government to help provide social services for which the people were starving?[4] Why not, indeed? Then, as a clincher, the Moderationists mounted a scare campaign. Illegal traffic in booze was inextricably bound up with traffic in dope, white slavery, and the smuggling of Chinese and Hindus into the country. It added up to spreading lawlessness that was destroying the fabric of life in Canada's evergreen paradise.

Most of these arguments, curiously enough, had surfaced previously at the conventions of the war veterans who, along with the odd Catholic priest and Anglican clergyman, provided the first, and the loudest, dissenting opinions as to the worth of the Prohibitionist concept.[5] With the help of the war veterans, the British Columbia Wets were able to force the Drys onto the defensive for the first time.

The immediate result of the vote in British Columbia, when the prairie Drys recovered from the shock, was an intensified effort on their part to mobilize the Prohibitionist vote. One solid conclusion seemed to flow from the outcome of the prairie vote: while there was slowly increasing opposition to Prohibition the faith of the voters in its desirability had not been vitiated by five years of half-measures, loopholes, and lackadaisical enforcement of the law. Only in Saskatchewan was there a decline in the Dry vote, and of the prairie cities only Winnipeg, St. Boniface, and Lethbridge voted Wet. In any event here are the comparative figures for the two plebiscites:[6]

	Alberta		Saskatchewan		Manitoba	
	1915	1920	1916	1920	1916	1920
Wet	37,000	44,000	24,000	55,000	28,000	46,000
Dry	58,000	63,000	95,000	87,000	52,000	59,000
Dry Maj.	21,000	19,000	71,000	32,000	24,000	13,000

While the turnout at the polls had been disappointing, and the majority for Prohibition was far from overwhelming, the Drys hoped that the 1920 plebiscite would be the end of the controversy over booze. Instead, it was really only the beginning. The British Columbia result had demonstrated that it did not have to be an either-or proposition. There was a middle way under which the community could Banish-the-Bar and still allow social drinkers to enjoy their booze in the quietness of their homes. Almost on the morrow of the plebiscite, full-blown organizations sprang up to press for the adoption of the British Columbia system on the prairies.

Whether the prairie Moderation Leagues were born of alcoholic inspiration in the clubrooms of the veterans' organizations or were hatched by the breweries and sold to the veterans is a question which must remain unanswered for lack of reliable evidence. By 1921-2 the passage of time was eroding the fine spirit of comradeship that had imbued the returning soldiers in 1919. In that glow they had organized their fraternities: the Great War Veterans Association, the Army and Navy Veterans Association, the Canadian Legion of the

British Empire Service League. They envisioned their clubrooms becoming Canadian counterparts of the English pubs they had become so fond of in their service days.[7] Thanks to Prohibition, however, their pubs were doomed to the indignity of purveying near-beer or risking arrest for bootlegging.

Many of them sold strong beer illegally, of course, and some of them quite openly. While they were seldom raided, the threat nevertheless hung over them, and this was blamed by the enthusiasts for the downward drift in attendance and dwindling memberships. The repeal of Prohibition became a straw at which they clutched when the Moderation Leagues were formed.

In Manitoba, selling League memberships for one dollar apiece became a sideline for veterans with time to spare. It was followed by a chance to earn beer money by soliciting signatures to a plebiscite petition for one dollar a name. There is no question that booze was something about which many an old sweat could work up a fine head of patriotic steam; the addition of a chance to turn an honest profit generated just the sort of drive a Moderation League needed.

The drive was by no means an instant success, although there was an instant reaction of sorts in the form of a rush of comparatively unknown local characters into newspaper offices with announcements that they were launching local branches of the Moderation League. The movement got nowhere, however, until some prestigious names were flushed out to head up the Leagues. The sergeant-majors were pushed aside by the majors, colonels, and an occasional brigadier. In Saskatchewan Brigadier G. S. Tuxford, a well-decorated war hero, was elected president of the Temperance Reform League; Major C. E. Gregory became its chief spokesman; and Major W. T. Hunter, an executive of the Great War Veterans Association, was hired as full-time organizer. In Manitoba the leader was Lt.-Col. William Grassie, his chief aide was Major A. D. Burns, and among the executive members were Col. R. M. Simpson and Col. A. C. Gray.[8]

Providing the financial sinews for the repeal campaign was largely the voluntarily assumed responsibility of the breweries, who poured untold thousands of dollars into the coffers of the Wets. What those contributions totalled is impossible to estimate for the bookkeeping of the beer barons was something to behold. The Royal Commission on Customs and Excise did some probing into the accounts of the

breweries and discovered such things as a racing stable charged up to
the malt account of the Shea's Brewery in Winnipeg.

No very convincing explanation was ever elicited from the brewers as to why they kept their books the way they did. It was not to
avoid income tax. Pat Shea, the Winnipeg multi-millionaire brewer,
paid full income taxes on the hundreds of thousands of dollars he
lavished on his sportsman son, and charged the money to the malt
account. The witnesses for the brewery admitted that it paid the
fines of its agents and customers who were convicted of liquor act
violations. They conceded making payments of $3,000, $5,000 and
$10,000 to the Moderation Leagues, charging the amounts to sales
commissions and malt accounts. Royal Commission accountants
managed to identify four donations totalling $23,000 which the
Saskatoon Brewery made in 1924. The *Edmonton Journal* estimated
the Alberta beer industry's contributions to the Moderation League
advertising campaign at $50,000.[9] The Lethbridge Brewery alone
spent $23,000, so the chances are that the *Journal* substantially
underestimated the slush funds which went into the Moderation
League's campaign for repeal.

Allied with the war veterans and beer barons in the anti-Prohibition crusade were some of the highest-powered stalwarts of the
Conservative parties. That alliance was understandable. Manitoba,
Saskatchewan, Alberta, and British Columbia had brought in Prohibition and kept it on the statute books. All four provinces were
Liberal party monopolies. It was good politics for the Tories to keep
public awareness focussed on the shortcomings of Prohibition so
that public disenchantment could be converted into political capital
for the Tories.

The waters were further muddied by the activities of the political
journalists of the day. The Conservative *Winnipeg Tribune* sent its
muckraking reporters to Saskatchewan to write exposés of the scandalous conditions prevailing along that province's rum-row in 1922.
The Liberal *Regina Leader* later retaliated by sending its reporters to
Manitoba to expose the scandalous lack of enforcement of Prohibition in Winnipeg after the Liberals were defeated.

In the nature of prairie society as well as of prairie politics, all this
stood to reason. If the Liberals were overwhelmingly Dry, then the
Conservatives had to be overwhelmingly Wet. Unhappily for the

Tories, however, the disenchantment that was generated with the Liberals produced no dividends for the Conservatives. In 1921 when the voters turned against the Liberals in Alberta and Manitoba the Conservatives were passed over in favour of the United Farmers or the Progressives.

The governments of the day on the prairies in 1921, though somewhat taken aback by the result in British Columbia, were by no means prepared to surrender with the first shots from the Moderationists. Being ankle deep in trouble trying to manage the booze supplies for the doctor-druggist outlets, none of the governments had any desire to become more deeply involved in the traffic. The first result of the plebiscite in Manitoba was a flurry of increased cracking down on the Winnipeg hotels that were bootlegging beer. The raids were made more frequently and the fines imposed were raised from $200 to $300. When one hotelman was caught with a large supply of two-ounce bottles of whisky on hand he was nicked for $500. But because the breweries were paying the fines of the convicted bootleggers,[10] the aim of the drive — to make the business so unprofitable the bartenders would get out of it — was never achieved. When the Liberal administration was defeated in 1922 enforcement lapsed.

J. R. Boyle, the Attorney General of Alberta, was a mildly dedicated Dry, but he viewed the result of the 1920 plebiscite with deepest trepidation. Without overwhelming public support, he saw little hope of achieving much improvement in law enforcement. The courts, through a series of judgments, had made it almost impossible to get convictions of the principals of the rum-running empires, or to confiscate their supplies. He noted sorrowfully that two chiefs of police who had been convicted of bootlegging were still being maintained on the job by town councils, along with a mayor who had also been convicted. He, like his counterparts in Manitoba and Saskatchewan, brought in amendments to the Temperance act which made evasion more difficult, even though they made enforcement no easier.[11]

In one of his post-plebiscite speeches Boyle noted that the Prohibitionists, while gaining a majority of the votes cast, had the support of only a fraction of the adult population. In Alberta it was 63,000 out of 350,000. This general comparison was also made from time to time by the other attorneys general and it became a major talking-point of the Moderationists and the Repealers. It was seldom noted, even by the Drys, that the same facts could have produced an opposite conclusion. Prohibition had been the law of the land for five years, and if it had been as unpopular as its critics contended, a major uprising of the union of the thirsty and the disillusioned could have been expected. It could well have been argued that the relatively small change in the Wet vote between 1915-16 and 1920 meant that those who did not trouble to vote were satisfied, at least to the extent that they did not care one way or another. From such a standpoint they would be neither an assistance nor an impediment to the enforcement of the law.

Which was the correct conclusion was anybody's guess. The problem in ratiocination arose from the extreme position taken by the Drys, who could never isolate their thinking from the total-eradication-of-booze concept. They could quote the Mayo Brothers, as they did, that alcohol not only had no medicinal properties but was in fact a poison. [12] They could advance all the arguments, which would become clichés fifty years hence, of the addictive qualities of booze. They could stand enforcement officers on every street corner. The fact remained that there were still people around with a developed taste for liquor and an appetite they were determined to satisfy.

These appetites might have been satisfied rather easily, if quite crudely, if everybody had just stopped yelling and let the experiment proceed of its own volition. The upper crust had their cellars full, and for the middle class the prescription service was available, though costly. For the farmers, particularly the immigrants from Central Europe to whom distillation was a household art, barnyard stills would have supplied all the booze needed from the surplus vegetables and waste grains on the farms. For the urban working class, homemade beer and wine could well have been the answer. For the lumpenproletariat at the bottom there were vanilla extract, patent medicines, and rubbing alcohol. When they sought a drunken rendezvous with death, as many did, there was Sterno or canned heat. [13]

Without the relentless pressure from the Drys for total suppression, which may have been generated in large part by the excesses of the hiatus period, liquor control might have evolved into some kind of a compromise that would have satisfied both sides. The times were so far out of joint, the public mind was in such confusion in the stress of massive post-war crisis piled on crisis, that there was no time for letting the experiment work itself out.

There can be no doubt that the authorities, many of whom were convinced Drys, were as determined as ever to make the best fist they could of enforcing the law after the 1920 plebiscite. In 1921 the Stewart government of Alberta, soon to be swept from office by the United Farmers of Alberta, rejected a demand, backed by a petition containing sixty-seven thousand signatures, from the Moderation League for a plebiscite on government liquor stores. Instead it put a ceiling of one thousand prescriptions a month on the medical profession, and dropped the dosage limit to twelve ounces. It provided for cancellation of the licence of any druggist caught bootlegging, and raised the maximum fine to one thousand dollars, with jail and no option of a fine for repeaters. [14]

The Moderation League in Saskatchewan had even less luck, if that were possible. Premier Charles Dunning rejected its request for a plebiscite out of hand. The people had expressed their desires and he would have to have evidence of a substantial change of mind before he would go to the expense of another referendum. The Saskatchewan government beefed up its Liquor Commission, appointed special liquor prosecutors, and brought poolrooms and restaurants within the jurisdiction of the Liquor Commission. It, too, drastically cut the size of the prescription potions and increased the pressure on Ottawa for a complete shutdown of the export stores in the province. As time passed, it had some reason for confidence that the tightening of the enforcement screws were beginning to work. In the six weeks prior to the end of importation Saskatchewan doctors had issued 39,373 prescriptions. Under new regulations the number dropped to 8,998. In July 1922 it was down to 7,126.

After the defeat of the Liberal government in 1922, Winnipeg was dripping Wet. It cannot be emphasized too strongly, however, that it was wetness with a difference. Primarily it was wetness without drunkenness. An eastern clergyman who took up residence in Winnipeg in 1921 was able to report some eighteen months later that he had yet to see his first drunk on a Winnipeg street, and his statement went unchallenged. [15] The volume of booze being sold was down by at least three-quarters and the retail sales facilities were minimal, even with the Main Street hotels serving as sub rosa outlets and the personal, bottle-at-a-time bootlegger becoming a factor; the comparison would be between a chain-store, supermarket-type booze economy which prevailed before the First World War, and a booze economy reduced to pushcart status after the war.

Booze flowed in from Saskatchewan, sometimes in convoys of automobiles from the Estevan area, sometimes well hidden under shipments of coal from the mines in that area. The easiest and safest mode of transportation was the latter. The liquor dealers in the lignite area could stow a hundred cases of whisky under planking in each end of a boxcar and then fill the car to the doors with coal. Shipped to a Winnipeg or St. Boniface fuel dealer it had every appearance of being what it was reputed to be, a carload of coal. In order to get at the contraband, the liquor police would have to shovel out all the coal, and shovelling dust-laden lignite from a boxcar was not the kind of work relished by any special liquor policeman.[16] Whatever attenuated natural instinct for ferreting out booze the law enforcers started with would soon have been wiped out by false tips supplied by prankful bootleggers. Tipping off tyro enforcers that booze was hidden in carloads of flour, sugar, lumber, coal, and best of all, green cowhides, was a Prohibition era refinement of the sending of apprentice plumbers for left-handed monkey wrenches, and printer's devils for type lice brushes.

The main threat to the booze hidden in coal-cars was at the source, not at the destination. Free-lance liquor operators in the mining areas had sharp antennae for contents of cars being loaded with coal at any unlikely spot. Unless the shipper moved quickly and stealthily his precious cargo might be hijacked before it was ever sent on its way.

It might well have been that the decline in volume of business done by the drugstores in 1922, which the attorneys general reported with such satisfaction, was not really an indication that that problem had been brought under control. It might also have indicated that so much booze had been put in storage or was readily available from other sources that the drinkers were no longer compelled to pay drugstore prices for their booze. In any event, there is little doubt that in Manitoba at least conditions moistened radically after the 1920 plebiscite.

One factor which complicated the enforcement problem was the increase in the excise duty on alcohol in 1920. From a wartime level of $2.40 it was raised to $9 a gallon and this gave the homebrewing industry an incentive to expand. When bootleggers were paying $5 and $6 a bottle for their Saskatchewan Scotch, and selling it for $8 or $9 in Winnipeg, Regina, and Edmonton, it made the operation of an illicit still an attractive proposition. All this was foreseen some years before when the licensed distillers sought to sell their own brand of Temperance legislation. What was needed, they said, was a complete wipe-out of all the middlemen in the industry and a drastic reduction in taxes. This, coupled with highly restrictive governmental control, which would have permitted boozers to recharge their supplies only by direct purchase from the distillers, would starve the bootleggers out of business.[17] The illicit stills of western Canada were mainly small-scale operations with ten to twenty-gallon capacity.

With the whopping increase in the excise tax, even the hopelessly inefficient small-bore operators with their wash-boiler cookers and copper-coil condensers had a viable operation. They could produce bottom-quality alcohol for one dollar a gallon and potable stuff for a dollar fifty a gallon. Except for sugar and yeast, the main ingredients came right off the farms. The moonshiners who could unload their production on the bootleggers for five dollars a gallon could earn a modest profit, enough, almost, to pay the five-hundred-dollar fines imposed when the stills were seized by the R.C.M.P.

How many stills there were was anybody's guess, and guessing was a favourite game of the Wet propagandists. The *Leader Post,* in 1923, claimed there were more stills in Saskatchewan than in all the rest of Canada. It noted that the R.C.M.P. had investigated 962 illegal stills in 1922 and secured convictions in only 318 cases.[18] The Attorney General of Alberta put his estimate of the number of stills operating there at 1,140 and the moonshiners' profit at $1,140,000 per annum. To the Moderationists, these figures were completely unreal. At a Moderationist Rally in Regina one of the speakers estimated that for every still put out of business by the R.C.M.P. there were between twenty-five and fifty undiscovered. If there was any validity to such contentions then the academics have been sadly misled in their assessment of the causes of the agrarian discontent that swept the prairies in the post-war era; the farmers were not reacting to economic distress and disillusionment with Ottawa, they were in the throes of a long-sustained and incurable hangover from the moonshine they were distilling.

How it all ended—with governments as booze-pushers

Not the least curious of all the ironic aspects which attended the repeal of Prohibition on the prairies was that it was brought about by the Drys themselves. The Liberal governments of Alberta and Manitoba which had brought in Prohibition fell victims to the times in 1921 and 1922. They were driven from office by the organized farmers, who had been the staunchest supporters of Prohibition from the earliest days of settlement. It was the farmer governments which yielded to the pressure from the Moderationists and set up the plebiscites which the Liberals had refused to grant. The multiplicity of causes which pitchforked the farmers into power were deep-rooted enough and varied enough to downgrade substantially the liquor question in the order of their primary concerns.

In a sense the Liberal governments were destroyed by the mounting anger and frustration of the farmers with the Conservative government in Ottawa. Caught between falling prices and rising costs, their wishes flouted by a thirty-per-cent increase in freight rates, their future darkened by the Ford-McCumber tariff that shut Canadian cattle out of the United States market, the prairie farmers were in a cantankerous mood.[1] The Liberals just happened to be in the way when the explosions occurred.

The governments which replaced them in Alberta and Manitoba were governments by greenhorns and administrations operating largely from ignorance. Few of the farmer members had ever seen a legislative chamber before, let alone sat in one. John Bracken, who was drafted as premier of Manitoba, was a professional agrologist at the Agricultural College. Herbert Greenfield, who became U.F.A. premier of Alberta, had had considerable municipal experience in Ontario and Alberta but his ministry was largely composed of first-time members of the legislature.

Both governments came to power at a time of deep economic distress that was reflected in budget deficits as well as in dropping farm income. The farmers' movement was riven by the deep rivalry, bordering on hatred, between the followers of Henry Wise Wood in Alberta and those of T. A. Crerar in Manitoba. It was a movement pulled and shoved by those demanding a compulsory wheat board to market their grain, and those who saw solutions to their problems in free trade and Adam Smith economics. The farmer governments, moreover, were far more parties of protest than parties with programs. As they settled into office they found themselves wrestling with the mundane problems of keeping the ordinary machinery of government in operation and finding ways to meet the bills that piled up everywhere. The members of the U.F.A. and the U.F.M. may have been overwhelmingly Prohibitionist in outlook but they were also overwhelmingly tight-fisted by instinct and necessity. Their built-in prejudice against imposing increased taxes was as strong as their reluctance to pay taxes. Thus they became particularly vulnerable to the importuning of the Moderationist Leagues for plebiscites on the liquor laws.[2]

Reluctantly, one supposes, they began to put increasing credence in the Moderationist League argument that total Prohibition was impossible to enforce. Once that was conceded it became necessary to find a suitable alternative. The argument that carried was the endlessly repeated claim that government liquor stores would divert millions of dollars from the pockets of the bootleggers into the empty coffers of the provincial governments.

British Columbia became the shining example. In the first years of operation of the government stores, more than $1,400,000 profit was earned by the government. In one of his pre-election flights of mathematical fancy, Joe Boyle, the Alberta Attorney General, had come up with some calculations that proved there was an annual profit of $10,000,000 in the Alberta liquor trade.[3] The Moderationists naturally made the most of all such estimates, no matter how far-fetched they might be.

Nor was the financial argument limited to the provincial governments alone. To the hard-pressed city councils and country school boards it was suggested that the governments should share the booze profits with them. Just about anything an urban elector's heart could desire, from better streets to more schools and hospitals, could be his from the liquor profits.

John Bracken, from his knee-deep involvement in trying to master the intricacies of parliamentary government and cabinet decision-making, moved quickly to get the Moderationists out of his hair. He promised them a plebiscite as soon as he could get around to it. When he did so, he gave them not one but two. Then, doffing his mantle as premier, he jumped into the Dry campaign with both feet.[4]

The campaign in Manitoba took place in June 1923, and was followed by a similar one in Alberta in November. In some respects they were a throwback to 1915, except that the arguments now revolved around money and not social issues. The Moderationists were able to stand on end all the old-time Dry criticisms of the bars. The health of the drinkers was being undermined by the rot-gut booze that Prohibition was forcing on the public. Statistics were pulled out of the air to show that Prohibition was filling the jails with criminals. Far from reducing drunkenness, Prohibition was encouraging drinking in the high schools. Disrespect for the Prohibition law was bringing all law into disrepute. The authorities were turning their backs on enforcement of liquor laws. On and on and round and round it went and only two words were changed — "bars" was edited out of the script and "Prohibition" was edited in. In the end, however, the Moderationists always came back to money, and, of course, the claim that government control would put the boot-leggers and rum-runners out of business.

Indeed, government control was held out as a magnet which would bring thousands of tourists from the United States. They could come to Canada and once again experience the pleasure of discovering what good whisky tasted like. And if they decided to take a bottle or two home with them so much the better, for that would add to the provincial coffers and drive more nails into the coffins of the criminal rum-runners.

Toward the end of the campaign the money argument became rather ethereal. The Winnipeg Moderationists put the rock-bottom minimum government profit from booze at three million dollars a year. Rev. Charles McNally, a Baptist clergyman, embarked on a series of street-corner meetings to counter-attack the financial argument. He claimed that to earn that much profit the government would have to sell thirty million dollars' worth of booze a year, which, he said, would be such a drain on the economy that it would bankrupt most Winnipeg businesses in a matter of weeks.[5]

One notable new feature of the 1923 campaign was the rush to stand up and be counted by everybody in sight. The Wets in Mani-toba ran a huge newspaper advertisement filled with names. It included just about every holder of a military title above the rank of major, all the prominent leaders of the Conservative party, a sprink-ling of Liberals, and a handful of Independent Labor Party office-holders.

The Drys countered with a list that for the first time numbered a couple of highly placed Anglicans among the leaders of the move-ment. Included were Canon Bertol Heeney of St. Luke's and Arch-deacon McElheran of St. Matthew's, who were at least a balance for the support Archbishop Matheson gave the Wets. The largest public meeting of the campaign was the one that filled the Walker Theatre for the Drys to hear Louise McKinney and Nellie McClung from Alberta and a full complement of local business and religious celeb-rities, including Premier John Bracken.

The tip-off to the way the campaign was going was in the news-paper ads. The Wets had twice as many names as the Drys, and it was clear by the billboards and other advertising that the Wets were substantially outgunning the Drys financially. When the ballots were counted on June 23 on a straight question of sale of liquor under government control or not, the Wets won by 30,000 votes — 84,000 to 54,000. Just over 25,000 of that majority was rung up in Greater Winnipeg, while the arid southwestern corner of Manitoba stayed just as Dry as it had ever been.

So the question was decided in favour of government control and sale. But how? The second string to the Moderation League bow was sale of beer and light wines in hotels. Encouragement of beer drinking, it held, was a great Temperance measure because it weaned the boozers from their more potent libations. But so deeply ingrained was public antipathy toward the bars that when the beer and wine plebiscite was held on July 11 it was snowed under by 64,000 to 27,000, with Greater Winnipeg switching to the Dry side of the argument.

The decision in Manitoba made the work of the Moderation League in Alberta much easier, but the frugal Albertans, instead of having two plebiscites, decided to settle the question once and for all with a multiple-choice ballot. It broke into four parts as follows:

(a) For retention of Prohibition.
(b) Sale of beer in hotels.
(c) Sale of beer by vendors.
(d) Government sale of all liquor and sale of beer in licensed hotel premises.

The electors could, therefore, vote for Prohibition, period; or they could vote for Prohibition and the sale of beer in hotels; or for Prohibition and the sale of beer by vendors; or for proposition (d).

As it had done in Manitoba, the Moderation League concentrated its attention on the diversion of profits from the rum-runners and bootleggers to the government and came down strongly for a "Yes" vote for proposition (d), and the Drys chose this as their main target. In doing so they picked up a wholly unexpected new ally — the *Edmonton Journal*. In all the previous votes on the liquor question, the *Journal* had supported the Wets. By the time the plebiscite campaign opened in October 1923, it had changed its mind. Prohibition, it argued, had never been given a fair chance. Nevertheless it had been responsible for drastically reducing public drunkenness, and if the public would get behind it and support the efforts of the government, still greater gains could be made. It denounced proposition (d) as a return to the old bars and proposition (b) as an irreversible step toward that end.

To support its position, the *Journal* pointed to the experience of British Columbia, which had been allowing the sale of beer in hotels since the beginning of 1922. With the return to legal sale, prosecutions for liquor offences were skyrocketing in Vancouver, and with that development there had been a rapid rise in other criminal cases as well.[6]

But it was all to no avail. The money arguments of the Moderationists were too convincing and Alberta followed Manitoba back from eight years in the desert of Prohibition. The result of the balloting was:

Votes for

61,780 Proposition (a) Prohibition.
3,939 Proposition (b) Prohibition and beer in hotels
3,092 Proposition (c) Prohibition and beer in vendors
93,490 Proposition (d) government sale of all liquor, coupled with sale of beer in licensed premises.

Only Saskatchewan was left and it resisted the demand for a plebiscite until well into 1924. The Moderationists of Saskatchewan spent most of 1923 drumming up signatures on plebiscite petitions. The first petition submitted in March of 1923 contained 65,075 names but it was rejected because of challenges as to the authenticity of signatures. The next one was more expertly prepared and after it was accepted in December 1923 the government ordered a July 16 plebiscite with a ballot which contained three propositions, as follows:

(a) in favor of Prohibition;
(b) against Prohibition and in favour of sale by government vendors of all spirits and malt liquors;
(c) against Prohibition and in favour of sale by government vendors of all spirits and malt liquors, and sale of beer in licensed premises.

The Moderationists campaigned for proposition (c) while the distillers joined the Prohibitionists in campaigning for proposition (a). The Saskatchewan campaign was the first in which the cleavage between the distillers and the brewers came into the open. From the closing of the bars, the distillers had kept out of the spotlight, surfacing only occasionally to deliver a low-key pitch for direct sale by distillers to consumers under government control.

The Saskatchewan campaign was notable, as well, for the boisterous intrusion of religious animosity into the Wet-Dry argument. The Irish Catholic *Northwest Review,* in Winnipeg, continued its long campaign against the Prohibitionists. The *St. Peter's Messenger,* the official organ of the Roman Catholic Diocese of Humboldt, which was published at Muenster in the heart of the German-Canadian settlement, openly attacked the Protestant clergymen who were leading the Prohibitionist cause. They, said the *Messenger,* had devoted their lives to stirring up virulent hatred of the Roman Catholic Church and all who belonged to it. They had attacked the separate schools, assailed the head of the Church himself, and ridiculed the sacred tenets of the faith. Then, having ridiculed the foreigners and paraded their dedication to "one flag and one language", they turned around and appealed to Catholics to support their Prohibitionist campaigns.[7]

The temper of the *Messenger's* non-stop counter-attack on the Protestant clergy and Prohibition may be savoured from this extract from an editorial flailing the Liberal party for the Prohibitionist plank in its 1925 platform:

> Prohibition violated the fundamental rights of the individual. It is corrupt to the core. It is rotten in its essence, unsound in its nature, wrong in principle, unchristian in character and undermines the foundation on which all human liberty rests. It is conceived in ignorance, engendered in hypocrisy and bolstered up by a shameless distortion of facts. It is a curse to the nation, a blight to the country and a disgrace to the statute books wherever adopted. It breeds disloyalty to the flag, contempt of the power that brought it into being and generates wholesale disregard for the law. It shatters national unity, foments civil strife and would take 27,000,000 enforcers to make it effective.

St. Peter's Messenger, one could only infer, disliked Prohibition. Opposition of the Roman Catholics was not the only religious handicap to the Prohibitionist cause. The once impregnable united front of the Protestant churches was being cracked open by the great debate over church union. The rift within the Presbyterian Church between those favouring entry into the United Church of Canada and those intransigently opposed had reached a point where the factions were threatening legal action against each other. That dispute, and a drifting away of the Baptists in some localities, indicated a serious decline in the unity that had prevailed in 1915-16 and 1920.

When the votes were counted in Saskatchewan, the margin for the Wets was just about the same as it was in Alberta and Manitoba: 80,381 for Prohibition and 119,337 against. Unlike Alberta, however, Saskatchewan voted against the sale of beer in licensed premises by a very small margin.

One notable aspect of the votes in the three provinces was the way in which the Prohibitionists had maintained their strength over the years. The Dry decade had been one in which the Temperance laws had been flouted, ridiculed, attacked, and distorted without pause. Newspapers vied with politicians in publicizing the shortcomings of enforcement and the peccadilloes of the enforcers. The actions of the courts demanded corroborating testimony of witnesses to sales. Unpluggable loopholes made seizures of contraband all but impossible. Undercover agents were denounced as pariahs and stool pigeons by the whisky trade and the general public seemed to acquiesce in such destructive terminology. The abuse of privilege by a minority of the druggists and doctors was a long-continuing scandal. The brewers worked overtime to encourage their debtors to violate the law. All this might have destroyed the Prohibition movement. That it failed to do so is an indication of the firmness of the faith of the Drys who in the end were snowed under by the force of superior numbers, not by a weakening of their own convictions.

Thus ended the "noble experiment" on the prairies. After ten years it was again legal for any freedom-loving Canadian adult to drink himself into a stupor. Only now the action would rebound to the financial benefit of the provinces and not to the saloon-keepers. One of the great Canadian illusions, however, is that the end of Prohibition marked the end of the bootlegging era in the west. In point of fact, in Manitoba and Saskatchewan it marked the beginning and not the end, if the term bootlegging can be construed in its original context.

The word "bootlegging" goes back to the days of smuggling when thigh-length boots were the fashion, and contraband could be hidden in the boot folds. The word was adapted to the illicit liquor trade in the United States as early as the 1830s. Bootleggers were therefore sellers of booze by the drink, or at most by the bottle, rather than by the boatload. In this sense bootlegging bloomed like the flowers in May in Manitoba and Saskatchewan, and to a lesser extent in Alberta, with the establishment of the government vending stores.

The claim of the Wets that ending Prohibition would sound the death knell for bootlegging was quickly exploded. Indeed, it would have been difficult to devise a scheme that would turn out to be more conducive to the expansion of the illicit trade. The regulations in all three provinces were based on the theory that what was mainly wrong with boozing was where it was done, that drinking itself was less of an evil than the existence of the saloons, than the general environment in which the liquor was consumed. Out of this grew the notion that the social evils attending excessive drinking would be overcome if drinking was confined to the homes. The regulations contained a number of special provisions to achieve that objective.

It was contrary to law for anybody to drink in a public place, or to have liquor in his possession anywhere except in his private dwelling. In Saskatchewan and Alberta the liquor was sold in sealed containers and it was against the law to transport a bottle of whisky on which the seal had been broken. The thirsty citizens could buy their supplies but they could not sample them until they got home with them. In Manitoba regulations were even stricter. There the drinkers had to place their orders at the liquor stores and wait until the stores delivered it to their homes. In all provinces the stores closed at 6 p.m., so that if anybody developed a thirst in the evening there was no legal means available to abate it. The exception was in Alberta where the beer was also sold by the glass in the hotels which remained open until 11 p.m.

During the eight years of Prohibition the dedicated drinkers had evolved a new life-style which undermined the "do-your-drinking-at-home" program. Business and professional men were quickly able to adapt Prohibition to their tastes, rather than the other way around. The practice of keeping a bottle handy in the deep bottom drawers of executive desks spread rapidly. In the Winnipeg Grain Exchange, several of the vessel brokers filled up their vaults with imported Scotch and were able to survive the arid era without missing a drink. For the most part, however, the upper-crust drinkers relied on their friendly neighbourhood bootlegger to trot around with a bottle of the best when they telephoned.[8] The service charge exacted by the dealers seldom exceeded two dollars a bottle, which in itself was proof enough that few bootleggers got rich during the Prohibition era. It was a grubby low-status calling in which the dealers frequently drank most of their profits.

The delivery system served the needs of the management and professional classes, but fell far short of meeting the needs of run-of-the-mill thirsts. What was needed was a place where the rank and file could drop in for a libation or two after a ball game, after work, after a show, or after a fight at home. This need was fairly well filled by the brothels in the downtown apartment buildings and by the hotels, which locked up their unused barrooms and transferred sales of hard liquor to rooms set aside for the purpose, registered to a Richard Roe or a Mary Smith.

Drinking at home was not a habit that the general run of drinkers had acquired by the time the governments got into the business. Nor was the practice of keeping liquor on hand against an onset of drought. Instead it was the custom to finish a bottle once it was opened. All this meant that the drinking habits of generations had to be changed when the government went into the business.

Perhaps most important of all was that the government went into the liquor business midway in the women's liberation movement that grew out of the First World War. Women who had been recruited into business and commerce to overcome the labour shortages of wartime became wedded permanently to their new way of life. They rolled their stockings, shortened their skirts to unheard-of levels, learned to smoke cigarettes, and were prepared to share a drink or a rumble seat in the fancy new cars that were making their appearance. As one dance craze followed hard on another, the dance halls boomed and a flask on the hip was an essential part of a "with-it" cake-eater's ensemble. It was all described as part of a world-wide loosening of moral restraints.

In Winnipeg, with the nuisance of having to order liquor from the vendors and wait a couple of days for delivery, moral restraints could not be loosened all that easily. It was a lot easier for the gay blades to pick up a bottle from a bootlegger than to go through the nuisance created by the government. Besides, picking up a bottle at a boot-legger's, or dropping into Aunt Mary's Tearoom or Frank's Café to nurse a couple of drinks in a booth at the back enhanced any male's worldly image in his own eyes.

It all made for an environment with which the farmer governments were particularly incapable of coping. One thing they failed to realize was that the news of government-guaranteed quality booze being on sale for four or five dollars a bottle would become an over-night sensation in the bordering states. In a matter of a very few weeks the American liquor dealers located most of the cracks in the governments' regulations. When Alberta opened its liquor stores at Medicine Hat, Taber, and Lethbridge it was astounded to discover how much greater the demand was than anybody had expected. The Americans were coming north by the carload and loading up with liquor of all kinds.[9]

Far from welcoming the trade, the Alberta government viewed it with a bilious eye. It was perfectly legal for the Americans to come into Alberta and buy their supplies from the Alberta vendors. But to the strait-laced Albertans, there was something downright obscene in Americans, who could not legally drink at home, coming to Alberta to do so. And for them to load two or three cases of Scotch into their cars and sneak it back into the United States might have violated holy writ as well as the United States Constitution for the consternation it caused the law enforcers. So the Attorney General of Alberta rushed through enough changes in the regulations to discourage liquor purchases by the Americans.

In Manitoba one example will illustrate the warped approach of the government to the whole liquor problem. A group of American visitors checked into the Leland Hotel in Winnipeg and ingested some high-priced legal advice on the Manitoba Temperance Act. They then armed themselves with six thousand dollars in cash and ordered liquor to that value to be delivered to them at the hotel. When the load arrived they had a truck waiting and began transferring the liquor to it preparatory to taking it back to the United States. Down swooped a couple of enforcement officers, seized the liquor, and carted the Americans off to jail. The Americans were convicted of purchasing the liquor illegally and the entire load was confiscated.

Thirty years later, at a royal commission hearing in Winnipeg,

L. D. Morosnick, who had defended the hapless Americans, let loose
a blistering indictment of Manitoba morality. [10] Manitoba, he said,
was the only government in the world which undertook to enforce
the laws of a foreign power against citizens of that power who were
visiting Canada and doing what was legal under Canadian law. Instead of swindling the Americans by selling them liquor and seizing it
from them, he said Manitoba should have been encouraging the
Americans to buy its liquor. The more they bought the more money
Manitoba would make. But all this was thirty years after the fact.

In the Leland Hotel case the enforcement officers certainly acted
with speed and efficiency. But as a long-retired rum-runner told this
writer, the surprising thing about the Bracken government was how
long it took it to become aware of what was going on.

"I made more money selling booze to the Americans after the end
of Prohibition than I ever did before," he said. "And for the longest
time the permit system was a joke. You were limited to purchasing
twelve bottles at a time and as you ordered the twelve you were cut
off for two weeks. When you placed the order they entered the size
of the purchase in your permit. In the city they delivered the stuff to
your home but in the country you could have it sent to you by
express. Well, I had a dozen permits; one for Cartwright, one under
another name for Wakopa, one under another name for Pilot Mound.
I'd whip down there and pick up the booze and stash it away in a
barn down near the border and the guy I dealt with in Rollo, North
Dakota, would come up and get it. I tell you those government seals
on that booze made it really premium-priced stuff down there." [11]

The measure which put him out of business was the law passed by
Manitoba in 1926 which made it an offence to transport liquor
within the province of Manitoba without a special government
permit. A motorist convicted of having a bottle of liquor in his car
could get off with a fifty-dollar fine. If he had a case and was charged
with transporting the fine could reach as high as five hundred dollars.
It was an easy matter then for the Provincial Police to catch the
rum-runners by a simple system of road blocks and road checks.

"After that I used to run a load or two down to the States once in
a while just for kicks more than anything else," the retired runner
recalled. "I had a friend whose sister was a Catholic nun. Their order
had a convent or headquarters or something at Grand Forks, North

Dakota. This friend used to drive his sister and a couple of other sisters down to Grand Forks quite frequently. One time when his car was broken down I offered to take them. I loaded all the special compartments I had under the seats with booze and we whizzed through the customs at Noyes just like a damn, with those nuns sitting innocently on top of a dozen cases of Scotch. After that, whenever those girls wanted to make a trip to Grand Forks I was Johnny-on-the-spot."

In the period between the opening of the liquor stores in 1924 and the legalizing of beer parlours in 1927, there was to all intents and purposes a law-enforcement vacuum in the Greater Winnipeg area. The provincial government insisted it was the responsibility of the municipal police to enforce the liquor act. Winnipeg, St. Boniface, St. James, and Fort Garry all insisted that as the province took all the fines that were collected the responsibility for enforcement also belonged to it. [12]

A further complication was added by the federal government. Under the agreement between the provinces and the federal government, no distillery could be established in any province where there was a Prohibition law in effect without prior approval from the province. But was Manitoba a Prohibition province after it opened its liquor vending stores in 1924? Ottawa thought not and proceeded to issue a couple of distillery licences. Manitoba's protests went unheeded, even unanswered. [13] There was widespread suspicion that alcohol from the distilleries was leaking into competition with the liquor stores.

Rather substantial leakages also developed from the illicit stills, which grew larger and more numerous in the hinterland. The first years of government sales on the prairies coincided with a change in the moieties system of rewarding informers. As long as the informers could profit handsomely by snitching on their neighbours, the excise enforcers did not lack for tips on the location of illicit stills. Thus the officer in Brandon was able to locate and seize twelve stills in 1921. But when the reward was cut in half in 1925, his bag dropped to two, and in 1926 not a single moonshiner was located in western Manitoba. [14]

The biggest leak through any government dikes, however, was in Saskatchewan. There the operators of the Regina Vinegar Company had stumbled onto the trick of retrieving alcohol used to charge vinegar in the fermentation process. Alcohol that went into vinegar carried a duty of twenty-seven cents a gallon. If it went into beverage alcohol it was nine dollars a gallon in 1924. An official of the Customs and Excise Department was always on hand to measure the alcohol which was removed from the bonded warehouse and metered into the first-stage tanks of the vinegar-making process. Once he had his meter read he left and the vinegar workers pumped the alcohol out of the mix before it got into the generators, and then converted it into whisky. Nobody in the Customs and Excise Department at that time was aware that such a retrieval was possible. That was only discovered from the testimony of a former employee to the Royal Commission three years later. The Commission moved immediately to recommend suit be filed for the forty thousand dollars' estimated difference in the excise tax liability. [15] The unknown quantity of alcohol which became Scotch whisky in Zisu Natanson's blending plant had long since been consumed.

It was the breweries, however, which were responsible for the longest and most prolonged of hassles in Manitoba. Operating under federal licence, the breweries insisted they had a right to deal directly with the public and to deliver beer to the homes of customers, rather than to the Liquor Commission at a wholesale price for delivery by the commission. The brewers' attitude toward the Liquor Commission was one of an impatient belted earl toward his begging peasants. They delivered enough to the commission to meet its requirements and bootlegged the rest of their production directly to their customers, at twice the profit. The government laid information after information against the brewers, got repeated convictions against them, and appealed to Ottawa to cancel their licences. These appeals, like the protests against the establishment of the distilleries, went unheeded. [16]

In such an atmosphere bootlegging flourished, along quiet residential streets as well as in the downtown apartment buildings. Mike Shea, the *Winnipeg Free Press* sports editor, used to try to sleep most of Sunday to catch up for what he lost during the week covering night sporting events. He abandoned as hopeless a search to find a quiet apartment in the vicinity of the *Free Press* building where his Sunday slumbers would be undisturbed by drunken comings and goings. In the end he was able to reduce interruptions somewhat with a sign which he pinned to his door on Saturday night:

THIS IS NOT A BOOTLEGGERS
NO BOOZE HERE

In Manitoba at least, putting the government into the liquor business failed completely to achieve any of the ends which the Wets had promised. It did not end bootlegging and the net revenue which the government was able to wring from the trade fell far short of what had been promised.

By 1925 the Protestant preachers were beginning to become restive. Dr. F. W. Kerr charged that Winnipeg dance halls had become sinks of iniquity and blasted the police for ignoring the liquor traffic.[17] By 1927, W. R. Wood of the United Farmers of Manitoba charged that disrespect for law and order in Manitoba was worse than in the days of the open bars. He blamed the breweries for much of the drunkenness and debauchery, describing them as a menace to the nation.[18]

By this time Manitoba was in the throes of the beer-by-the-glass campaign which, the Moderationists now assured everybody, would destroy the bootlegging industry and usher in an era of civilized drinking. Its cause was sharply advanced by the bitterness of the controversy that raged over lack of enforcement. The preachers blamed the breweries; the Conservatives blamed the Bracken government for its hopelessly inept enforcement agency; the Attorney General blamed the federal government, the breweries, and the city police; the civic authorities blamed the provincial government. And the Winnipeg newspapers agreed that things really hadn't worked out as expected and perhaps something else should be tried.

L. St. George Stubbs, the country court judge who was an ex officio member of the Winnipeg police commission, said law enforcement was in such a mess that he wanted to be removed from the commission.[19]

The long impasse between the province and the city was basically about money, though not exclusively so. In company with police departments everywhere, the Winnipeg force took the most jaundiced view of being responsible for enforcement of morality laws. The more severe it became in cracking down on prostitution and bootlegging the less co-operation it got in its efforts to counteract serious crime. The sheer volume of work involved in policing the booze trade made it an impossible burden on the police department budget.

Yet the people of Winnipeg still looked to their own police department for assistance and for protection. They bombarded the city police with complaints about neighbours running blind pigs, about brothels which became established in their apartment blocks, about the heavy flow of traffic at all hours of the night into the house across the street. To all these calls the city police had a pat answer — call the provincial government. The things about which they were complaining were not considered criminal in Winnipeg.

The response of the provincial police was even less sympathetic. Usually they would send an undercover agent around to interview the complaining householders, not to gather evidence upon which to prosecute but to try to recruit the citizens into acting as observers, informers, and ultimately witnesses in court. The employees of the provincial liquor police were usually drop-outs from most other lines of employment. When not vainly trying to sell citizens on becoming informers, they seemed to have spent their off-hours as peeping Toms spying on suspected bootleggers and prostitutes. As one agent wrote in his report to a superior,

"I observed the suspect from 12 to 12.30. He was having sectional inter course with Mrs. Nolan." [20]

Eventually, after the beer-by-the-glass plebiscite passed, a peace treaty was signed between city and province and the Winnipeg police department again took up its truncheons against the liquor-law offenders. Nevertheless, the downtown apartment blocks still carried a full quota of boozeries — beer parlours or no beer parlours. Even if the customers had not become accustomed to the homely coziness of the so-called joints, the puritanical austerity of the beer parlours would have driven them to it. Official revulsion at the thought of any return to public bars dictated that the beer parlours be made as uncomfortable and unattractive as possible.

In Manitoba, no other law was enforced with quite the rigidity of the one against entry of women into beer parlours. Alberta had a law which separated men from women in the taverns, but women were at least permitted to quaff an ale or two in parlours set aside exclusively for them. Not in Manitoba, where the entry of a woman into a beverage room set the entire hotel staff into a panic, until she was ushered from the premises with the greatest of haste. As a result, a husband and wife going out on the town and seeking to share a drink had several choices. They could take their own liquor along; they could patronize one of the half-dozen cafés where booze was bootlegged quite openly to recognized customers; or they could take off for St. Boniface, which performed the same function for Winnipeg as Moose Jaw did for Regina in the 1920s. In the heyday of Chief Joe Gagnon, there were forty-one houses in St. Boniface where booze and/or sex were available.

Gagnon's free-wheeling fun city came clattering to its end from sheer inadvertence.[21] The distribution to charitable institutions of alcoholic beverages seized by the police was still being carried out in 1928. The system was to retain the booze at police headquarters until a sizable supply was collected and then distribute it. At each institution an official receipt was obtained which had to be filed with the provincial government. Sergeant Joe Baudry had happened upon a broken-down truck loaded with liquor on the street one day and the liquor landed in the St. Boniface police department's vaults. Chief Gagnon decided it should be distributed to the institutions. While the liquor was being loaded into the police department touring car the Chief decided the car needed an oil change. The driver was instructed to perform the operation. In doing so he neglected to tighten the drain plug. The oil leaked from the engine and the car seized up five miles away on Pembina Highway in Fort Garry heading in the general direction of the United States. The driver left the car and walked back to locate a telephone. While he was gone, the provincial police came upon the car, discovered the booze, and towed car and contents to their headquarters. Tracing the licence plates back to the St. Boniface police department, they set off such an uproar that Gagnon was blown out of office, along with all the aldermen.

Elsewhere, things went more smoothly for the police departments, except in Moose Jaw when the burghers at last lost patience with Chief Walter Johnson's benign reign over the River Street brothels and bootleg joints. In Saskatchewan generally the one-bottle-at-a-time cash-and-carry system of government vendors seemed to work well enough without beer parlours. Alberta, with its cash-and-carry stores and beer parlours, seemingly found a way of living with its liquor problems at last.

In any event, booze as a prime disturber of the public peace disappeared from the newspapers and the legislature debates. But most of all it lost its attraction for the reverend clergy. For them, the burning issues were becoming social rather than alcoholic. Such one-time inflamers of the public passion against booze as the Rev. Salem Bland and the Rev. A. E. Smith floated clear over into the backwaters of the Communist movement. The onset of the great depression insulated the minds of just about everybody from the booze problem. With mass unemployment and massive crop failures, booze ceased to be a problem. For the provincial governments, a different kind of a liquor problem began to emerge — how to maintain the flow of booze profits into the sadly under-supplied provincial treasuries.

And this, curiously enough, is the only permanently surviving aspect of the great booze debates of the 1920s, as much a concern of governments in 1972 as it was in 1925. Given the necessary purchasing power in the public's hands, the governments discovered an underlying alcoholic principle that was universal in application. That principle was:

Increased availability of liquor leads inexorably to increased consumption and increased abuse.

As the governments inched along the road that would lead them to the restoration of unrestrained boozing they discovered that it led through the wonderland of increased income. In such a wonderland how could the purveyors of the instant-money elixirs be expected to be concerned with the addictive nature of the stuff they sold? The needs of all governments for ever-expanding sources of revenue accelerated the drive toward making booze totally available to social drinkers, problem drinkers, and hopeless alcoholics alike, regardless of the social consequences.* Fifty years after the beginning of the Prohibition experiment, history was casting governments in the roles of the old-time bartenders who pushed booze at the customers with enthusiastic abandon to the accompaniment of the cash register symphony.

*For those interested in the supporting material for this statement a statistical appendix has been provided on pp. 222-6.

Fifty years after the Prohibitionists' experiment touched its driest point, the prairies were back to where they had been, on a comparative basis, in the lush years of 1913-14. Addiction to alcohol had become the major health problem there as it was elsewhere in North America, just as drunkenness had been the major social problem of the era before the wars. The difference was in terminology, not in fact. But there was a difference, and an important one, between the eras, and it is a difference which makes comparisons almost meaningless. The vast army of zealots who dominated the scene had vanished from the face of the earth and with them had gone the deep religious concerns that drove generation after generation of Protestant clergymen to relentless war on the evil Ambrosia with which the devil himself was imperilling the souls of men.

Sixty years after the "Banish the Bar!" sermon had been sent on its reverberating way across the prairies from a thousand pulpits all that remained in the all-encompassing silence was the fluttering of paper money onto the plates of the governments taking up the collection.

Appendix

Year	Convictions for drunkenness	Convictions against liquor acts	Liquor profits	Liquor sales
			(in thousands of dollars)	
1913	7,493	166		
1914	6,193	166		
1917	1,085	289		

MANITOBA - continued

1918	1,123	230		
1925	1,948	512	$1,200	
1935	1,054	792		
1945	2,040	1,429	4,379	
1948	2,829	1,922	6,980	
1956[1]	4,726	2,886	8,834	$37,000
1957	5,342	4,513	9,559	41,000
1958	5,531	4,097	10,637	44,000
1959	5,814	3,729	11,459	47,000
1960	5,803	4,479	12,880	51,000
1961	5,337	4,628	14,588	53,000
1962	4,261	5,402	15,042	55,000
1963	4,287	6,644	15,568	57,000
1964	5,966	7,581	16,673	60,000
1965	6,877	7,849	19,000	62,000
1966	7,132	8,256	21,000	65,000
1967[2]	7,608	9,062	23,000	71,000
1968	8,227	7,991	26,071	

[1] New liquor act enacted to permit cocktail lounges and sale of wine and spirits in restaurants.
[2] Closing time of all outlets extended by one hour.

Population		
	1914	530,000
	1925	632,000
	1935	711,000
	1951	776,000
	1956	850,000
	1961	922,000
	1966	965,000

Between 1918 and 1966 Manitoba population rose by 70%
Drunkenness rose by 550%
Between 1925 and 1966 Population rose by 50%
Liquor profits rose by 1,800%

SASKATCHEWAN

Year	Convictions for drunkenness	Convictions against liquor act	Liquor profits	Liquor sales
			(in thousands of dollars)	
1913	2,970	528		
1914	2,142	404		
1917	770	774		
1918	434	422		
1925	668	1,078	$1,126	
1935	379	506		
1945	1,010	1,406	4,162	
1948	1,392	2,311	7,920	
1956	4,441	4,539	10,250	$35,000
1957	5,116	4,286	11,252	38,000
1958	4,441	3,210	11,763	48,000
1959[1]	5,035	4,304	12,560	42,000
1960	3,691	4,046	13,352	44,000
1961	3,729	4,882	13,840	46,000
1962	3,603	5,639	14,150	45,000
1963	4,292	6,888	14,690	47,000
1964	4,959	7,672	16,100	50,000
1965	5,970	8,294	17,000	53,000
1966	5,972	9,652	18,000	56,000
1967	5,965	10,903	22,000	63,000
1968[2]	3,782	11,427	25,000	

[1] Legislation establishing cocktail lounges is passed. Authorized sale to Indians.
[2] Change in regulations for charging persons with drunkenness.

Population	1914	600,000
	1925	806,000
	1935	931,000
	1951	832,000
	1956	881,000
	1961	925,000
	1966	950,000

SASKATCHEWAN - continued

Between 1918 and 1966 Saskatchewan population rose by 58%.
Drunkenness rose by 1,500%
Between 1925 and 1966 Population rose by 15%
Liquor profits rose by 2,000%

ALBERTA

Year	Convictions for drunkenness	Convictions against liquor act	Liquor profits	Liquor sales
			(in thousands of dollars)	
1913	7,283	560		
1914	5,710	551		
1917	391	885		
1918	825	678		
1925	1,374	758	$ 1,600	
1935	692	472		
1945	1,515	1,454	6,026	
1948	2,580	2,670	9,971	
1956	8,888	6,867	16,250	$55,000
1957	9,770	8,961	17,881	59,000
1958[1]	9,634	9,281	19,056	63,000
1959	8,851	10,781	19,811	67,000
1960	9,867	11,805	20,080	69,000
1961	11,453	14,149	21,206	72,000
1962	11,858	14,700	22,465	76,000
1963	12,946	14,930	26,068	80,000
1964	12,928	17,048	27,435	83,000
1965[2]	13,548	18,272	28,000	85,000
1966[3]	16,291	20,679	31,000	95,000
1967	14,876	23,355	35,000	105,000
1968	15,565	23,393	41,580	

[1] Act revised to permit cocktail lounges and mixed drinking.
[2] Live entertainment permitted in beverage rooms.
[3] Indians permitted to drink.

ALBERTA - continued

Population: 1914   459,000
              1925   602,000
              1935   764,000
              1951   939,000
              1956   1,123,000
              1961   1,332,000
              1966   1,500,000

Between 1918 and 1966 Alberta population increased by 200%
                        Drunkenness increased by 2,000%
Between 1925 and 1966 Population rose by 150%
                        Liquor profits rose by 2,200%

Sources: Dominion Bureau of Statistics; Manitoba, Saskatchewan, and Alberta Liquor
Control Commissions; Alcoholic Research Foundation of Ontario.

Footnotes

Belly up to the bar, boys!

1. Tape-recorded interview, C.B.C. Archives, Regina.
2. Ibid.
3. *Winnipeg Times*, Jan. 6, 1882; *Macleod Gazette*, Sept. 19, 1884; *Lethbridge Herald*, Aug. 5, 1904; *Edmonton Journal*, July 22, 1912; Cypress River, *Western Prairie*, Mar. 2, 1916.
4. *The Manitoban*, Winnipeg, Mar. 8, 1873.
5. W. L. Morton, *Manitoba, a History*, Toronto, 1957, p. 159.

6. J. J. Hargrave, *Red River*, Montreal, 1871, pp. 270-4.
7. T. J. Healy, *Women of the Red River*, Winnipeg, 1923, p. 240.
8. Hargrave, *Red River*, p. 454.
9. *Winnipeg Times*, Jan. 26, 1883.
10. Ibid., March 1883.
11. Census, 1881, 1891.
12. *Winnipeg Times*, Mar. 1-21, 1883.
13. Charles Angoff, *A Literary History of the American People*, New York, 1935, Vol. 1, p. 278.
14. *Winnipeg Times*, Feb. 2, 1883.
15. Ibid.
16. Ibid., Apr. 28, 1883.
17. Morton, *Manitoba*, p. 303.
18. *Winnipeg Times*, Dec. 16, 1882.
19. Ibid.
20. Ibid., Jan. 11, 1883.
21. Ibid., June 18, 1883.
22. Ibid., July 1883.

The law and the prophets

1. J. K. Howard, *Strange Empire,* New York, 1952, p. 267.
2. J. P. Turner, *The North West Mounted Police*, Ottawa, 1950, Vol. 1, pp. 80-9.
3. Debates, House of Commons, intermittently, 1880-91.
4. Rev. Edmund H. Oliver, *The Liquor Traffic in the Prairie Provinces*, Toronto, 1923, pp. 166-7.
5. *Macleod Gazette*, Feb. 16, 1886.
6. *Lethbridge News*, Mar. 6, 1886.
7. *Annual Reports*, Commissioners, North West Mounted Police, 1880-90.
8. Ibid.
9. *Calgary Herald*, Sept. 16, 1884.
10. Ibid., Dec. 3, 1884.
11. Ibid., Aug. 10, 1884.
12. Ibid., December 1884, January 1885.
13. *Annual Reports*, N.W.M.P., 1880-91.
14. Eric Wells, unpublished manuscript, Winnipeg, 1967.
15. Various newspaper reports of sermons, 1880 to 1900.

The lesser breeds, and the wife-beaters

1. *Winnipeg Times*, May 14-24, 1883.
2. Ibid., February, March 1883.
3. *Edmonton Journal*, Sept. 13, 1907.

4. *Calgary Tribune, Calgary Herald*, March, April, July 1889.
5. *Lethbridge Herald*, Feb. 23, 1909.
6. Statutes of Saskatchewan, 1912, Chapter 12.
7. *Edmonton Journal*, Sept. 21, 1907.
8. *Medicine Hat News*, Apr. 13, 1911.
9. *Regina Standard*, Nov. 25, 1905.
10. Oral report to the author.
11. *Winnipeg Telegram, Free Press*, Sept. 19, 1904.
12. Robert Tyre, *Saddle-back Surgeon*, Toronto, 1954, pp. 97-8.
13. *Winnipeg Tribune*, Sept. 28, 1922.
14. Oliver, *The Liquor Traffic*, pp. 97-8.

What good were laws without loopholes?

1. F. S. Spence, *Prohibition in Canada*, Toronto, 1919, pp. 115-38; Oliver, *The Liquor Traffic*, pp. 80-102.
2. J. A. Stevenson, *Before the Bar*, Toronto, 1919, p. 79.
3. Norman Ward and Duff Spafford, eds., *Politics in Saskatchewan*, Toronto, 1968, pp. 124-43.
4. Robert Hill, *History of Manitoba*, Toronto, pp. 478-81.
5. J. W. Dafoe, *Clifford Sifton in Relation to his Times*, Toronto, 1931, pp. 52-5.
6. Spence, *Prohibition*, p. 261.
7. Ibid., pp. 247-8.
8. Joseph Schull, *Laurier*, Toronto, 1965, p. 373.
9. Oliver, *The Liquor Traffic*, p. 205.
10. Ibid., p. 107.
11. Ibid.
12. *Winnipeg Free Press, Tribune, Telegram*, Jan. 15 to Apr. 15, 1902.
13. Oliver, *The Liquor Traffic*, p. 134.
14. Ibid., p. 130.

The slogan that won the west

1. J. S. Woodsworth, *Social Surveys in Canada*, Toronto, 1914.
2. *Report of Royal Commission on Prostitution*, Winnipeg, 1910.
3. R. E. Popham and W. Schmidt, *Statistics of Alcohol Use and Alcoholism in Canada*, Toronto, 1958, pp. 48-51.
4. *Canadian Annual Review*, 1907, p. 286; *The Labor Gazette*, 1912, pp. 358, 360.
5. Oral report to the author.
6. Letter to the author.
7. *Labor Gazette*, 1912.
8. Promotional pamphlet, C.P.R., Glenbow-Alberta Institute, Calgary.
9. Letter to the author.

10. Oral report to the author.
11. Tape-recorded interview, Joseph Baudry, Museum of Man and Nature, Winnipeg.
12. Donald B. Chidsey, *On and Off the Wagon*, New York, 1969, p. 1.
13. *Winnipeg Free Press*, June 3, 1914.
14. Ibid., Aug. 5, 1913.
15. Ibid., June 25, 1914.
16. Details of this conspiracy were not revealed until the Royal Commission of 1916.
17. Erhard Pinno, unpublished Master's thesis, University of Saskatchewan, 1971, Saskatchewan Archives, Regina.
18. R. A. McLean, "Prohibition in Alberta", unpublished Master's thesis, University of Calgary, 1970, Glenbow-Alberta Institute, Calgary.
19. July 5, 1915.
20. *Edmonton Bulletin*, July 5, 1915.
21. *Winnipeg Free Press, Tribune*, Mar. 13, 1916.
22. Ibid.

Prohibition: where it worked, where it didn't

1. Popham and Schmidt, *Statistics*.
2. Letters to the editors, *Calgary Herald, Edmonton Journals, Winnipeg Tribune*, 1916-17.
3. *Annual Report*, Calgary Police Department, 1917.
4. *Calgary Herald*, July 9, 1918.
5. W. D. Bayley, *Brief #37 to Bracken Commission*, Winnipeg, 1952.
6. *Annual Report*, Royal Canadian Mounted Police, 1917.
7. *Calgary News Telegram*, July 3, 1915.
8. *Annual Report*, R.C.M.P., 1916.
9. Nov. 20, 1915.
10. Bayley, *Brief #37*.
11. Ibid.
12. W.C.T.U. pamphlet, Toronto, undated (*circa* 1922).
13. Tanner and Beaman, *The Reference Shelf*, New York, 1927, pp. 111-14.
14. *Six Dry Years*, Dominion Alliance, Toronto, pamphlet, 1922.
15. *Regina Morning Leader*, Feb. 17, 1916.
16. Letter to the author.
17. *Calgary Herald,* July 13, 1916.
18. Pinno, unpublished Master's thesis.
19. Royal Commission on Customs and Excise, proceedings, 1926-7, p. 11,699.
20. *Calgary Herald*, February, March 1918.
21. *Winnipeg Tribune*, July 20, 1922.
22. Royal Commission proceedings, pp. 9729-40.
23. *Winnipeg Tribune*, Oct. 27, 1922.

24. J. E. Brownlee correspondence, Alberta Archives, Edmonton.
25. Royal Commission proceedings, p. 8026.
26. Frank W. Anderson, *The Bootleggers*, Calgary, 1968, p. 48.
27. *The Albertan*, Calgary, Jan. 6, 1916.

Yorkton, where Harry planted the money tree

1. Philip Siekman, *Fortune Magazine*, November 1966, pp. 140-8.
2. Ibid.
3. Oral reports to the author.
4. Ibid.
5. *Henderson's Saskatchewan Directory*, 1908.
6. *Henderson's Ontario Directory*, 1910.
7. *Henderson's Manitoba Directories*, 1908-15.
8. Published by Distillers Corp., Seagrams Ltd.
9. Royal Commission Interim Report #10, pp. 52-4.
10. Oral reports to the author.
11. Ibid.
12. Ibid.
13. Royal Commission proceedings, p. 8527.
14. Oral report to the author.
15. Samuel Bronfman, Royal Commission proceedings, p. 23,040.
16. Ibid.
17. Oral report to the author.
18. *Winnipeg Tribune*, Oct. 27, 1922.

Here it is, you come and get it

1. Interview with the author.
2. Oliver and Johnston, open letter to *Saskatoon Star*, Nov. 14, 1921.
3. Acquitted at second trial, Regina, Sept. 13, 1930.
4. Sam Tadman, testimony at preliminary hearing, Regina, Dec. 19-23, 1929.
5. Interview with the author, August 1971.
6. Royal Commission proceedings, Ottawa, pp. 23,011-200.
7. Official returns to Saskatchewan Liquor Commission, Saskatchewan Archives, Saskatoon, January 1921.
8. Ibid.
9. Royal Commission proceedings, Regina and Winnipeg, January, February 1927.
10. *Winnipeg Tribune*, Oct. 16, 1922.
11. Ibid.
12. Letter to the author.
13. Cyril Knowles' testimony, Royal Commission proceedings, pp. 8500-700.

232 BOOZE

14. Letter to the author.
15. Tape-recorded interview, C.B.C. Archives, Regina, and interview with the author.
16. Ibid.
17. Ibid.
18. *Winnipeg Tribune*, Sept. 30, 1922.
19. C.B.C. interview.
20. Ken John, Estevan, interview with the author.
21. Royal Commission proceedings, p. 11,781.
22. Ibid.

Sue the bastards!

1. *Winnipeg Tribune*, Oct. 19, 1922.
2. Royal Commission proceedings, p. 23,806.
3. *Regina Morning Leader*, Nov. 17, 1921.
4. *Winnipeg Tribune*, Feb. 25-7, 1927; Royal Commission proceedings, pp. 11,680-798.
5. *Regina Morning Leader*, Feb. 19 to Apr. 19, 1925.
6. *Western Weekly Reports*, 1923, Vol. 1, p. 307.
7. Royal Commission proceedings, pp. 23,023-807.
8. Royal Commission Interim Report #10, p. 51.
9. Royal Commission proceedings, p. 23,821.
10. Ibid., p. 23,823.
11. *Western Weekly Reports*, 1924, Vol. 2, p. 1,165.
12. Ibid.
13. Royal Commission proceedings, p. 23,850.
14. Ibid., p. 23,849.
15. Ibid., p. 23,903.
16. *Supreme Court Reports*, 1929, p. 400.
17. S. A. Goldston, testimony, Leech libel trial, *Regina Morning Leader*, Feb. 22, 1925.
18. Ibid.
19. Ibid.
20. Ibid.
21. R.A.C. Manning papers, Manitoba Archives, 1918 reports.
22. *Regina Morning Leader*, Leech libel suit, 1925.

In the Customs Department, who told the truth?

1. *Winnipeg Tribune*, Nov. 30, 1929.
2. Royal Commission Interim Report #10, p. 55.
3. Ralph Allen, *Ordeal by Fire*, Toronto, 1960, pp. 262-74.

4. Royal Commission proceedings, Vancouver, December 1926.
5. Ibid., Winnipeg, February 1927.
6. Tape-recorded interview, C.B.C. Archives, Regina.
7. Dafoe, *Clifford Sifton*, p. xv.
8. Royal Commission proceedings, p. 8375.
9. Cyril Knowles' testimony, Royal Commission proceedings, p. 11, 784.
10. Ibid., pp. 11,798-816.
11. Ibid., p. 8589.
12. Ibid., p. 23,582.
13. Ward and Spafford. *Politics in Saskatchewan*, pp. 107-23; Gary Abrams, *Prince Albert*, Saskatoon, 1966, p. 279.
14. *Calgary Herald*, Oct. 8, 1920.
15. *Saskatoon Star*, Nov. 21, 1921.
16. *Regina Morning Leader*, December 1929, September 1930.

The first crack in the dike

1. Royal Commission proceedings, pp. 9544, 11,699, 11,735.
2. J. R. Boyle, *Calgary Herald*, Feb. 15, 1919.
3. The super-stars of the Chicago White Sox threw the 1919 World Series of baseball to the Cincinnati Reds.
4. Vancouver newspapers, October 1922.
5. *Edmonton Bulletin*, Oct. 16, 1922.
6. There is some confusion about the precise totals, depending on which source is accepted. These figures are approximate.
7. Oral reports to the author.
8. *Regina Daily Post*, Jan. 16, 1923.
9. *Edmonton Journal*, Oct. 20, 1923.
10. Royal Commission proceedings.
11. *Canadian Annual Review*, 1921, pp. 829-31.
12. Dominion Alliance leaflet, undated.
13. Newspaper reports of deaths from drinking canned heat appeared infrequently from 1921 to 1927.
14. *Canadian Annual Review*, 1921, pp. 829-31.
15. *Winnipeg Tribune*, June 4, 1923.
16. Oral reports to the author.
17. *Winnipeg Telegram*, June 26, 1919.
18. *Canadian Annual Review*, 1923, p. 713.

How it all ended — with the governments as booze-pushers

1. W. K. Rolph, *Henry Wise Wood*, Toronto, 1950, pp. 95-110.
2. Winnipeg, Calgary, Regina, and Edmonton newspapers, 1921-2.

3. *Canadian Annual Review*, 1921, p. 830.
4. *Winnipeg Free Press*, June 19, 1923.
5. *Winnipeg Tribune*, June 4, 1923.
6. *Edmonton Journal*, Oct. 20-5, 1923; *Moose Jaw Times*, Jan. 17, 1923.
7. Issues from 1923 to 1925, microfilmed, Saskatchewan Archives.
8. The author was employed in the Grain Exchange from 1922 until 1930.
9. Royal Commission proceedings, p. 8026.
10. Bracken Commission proceedings, Manitoba Archives.
11. Oral report to the author.
12. Manning papers, files 35 and 95.
13. Royal Commission proceedings, p. 9724.
14. Ibid., p. 11,430.
15. *Regina Morning Leader*, Feb. 8-12, 1927.
16. Royal Commission proceedings, pp. 9724-800.
17. *Winnipeg Free Press*, June 15, 1925.
18. Ibid., Jan. 11, 1927.
19. Manning papers. All Winnipeg newspapers, January, February 1927.
20. Manning papers, undated notes.
21. Baudry, tape-recorded interview.

Index

Aikins, J.A.M., 60, 61, 85
Alberta, 113; bootleg liquor in, 103-5, 202, 211; coming of Prohibition in, 67, 70, 82, 84, 86, 87; crime and drunkenness in, 70, 74, 90-1, 92; early settlement in, 34, 41; liquor policy following repeal, 211, 213, 218, 292; and the liquor traffic during Prohibition, 88, 98-9, 102, 105, 107, 119, 120, 132, 134, 138-9, 163; and the 1920 plebiscite, 107, 192, 195; prejudice in, 44; repeal campaign in, 197, 198, 203-5, 207, 210

Alberta Federation of Labor, 83, 262
Alberta Medical Association, 83
Alcoholism Research Foundation, 90
Allen, Ralph, 169
American Hotel, 5. *See also* The Dutchman's
Anderson, F.T., 136
Anderson, P.M., 185
Andrews, A.C., 135
Andrews, A.J., 157, 185
Anti-Treating League, 19, 66
Archibald, Adam, 23
Arlington Hotel, Brandon, 112

235

Arm River, Saskatchewan, 184
Army and Navy Veterans Association, 195
Arthur, Timothy Shay, 53-4
Assiniboine, Saskatchewan, 183
Assiniboine River, 11
Atlantic Import Company, 169
Atlas Shipping Company, 169

Bagshaw, F.R., 185
Balmoral Hotel, Yorkton, 113-14, 116, 118, 119, 129, 166
Banff, Alberta, 99
Banish-the-Bar Crusade, 70, 77, 78-9, 80-1, 86, 87, 90, 97-8, 105, 108, 195, 221
Barnblatt, L., 180
Barons, Alberta, 103
Bartenders' Union, 83, 85
Bassano, Alberta, 74
Bastedo, F.L., 157
Battleford, Saskatchewan, 93
Baudry, Sergeant Joe, 219
Beck, Levi, 117, 118
Begg, Alexander, 49
Bell, Nat, 132
Bell, W.J., 163
Bell Hotel, Winnipeg, 115
Belmont, Manitoba, 47
Berlin, Ontario, 53
Besserabia, 109, 110
Bienfait, Saskatchewan, 131,132, 142, 143, 145, 146
Biggar, Saskatchewan, 182
Bisaillon, J.E.A., 169-70
Black Sox scandal, 193
Blackfoot, the, 21
Blair, C.E., 186
Blake, Edward, 57
Bland, the Rev. Salem, 86, 220
Board of Licence Commissioners, Manitoba, 10
Boissevain, Manitoba, 136
Boivin, Wilson, and Company, 151
Bonfadini, Joe, 134
Bootlegging, 2, 92, 100, 105, 129, 187-8, 191, 196, 198, 201; and the Americans, 139; in British Columbia, 194; and the Bronfmans, 130, 132-3, 178; among Central Europeans, 45-6, 183, 199; encouraged by lack of law enforcement, 101, 103-4; following repeal, 206, 207, 211-13, 216-20; and gangsterism, 150; and official corruption, 162; quality of liquor, 124-5, 148-9; result of 1920 excise tax on, 201; and the Sairs, 141; widespread on the Prairies, 104

Booze: class distinctions in, 199; customs surrounding, 13-14, 16, 67, 71-4, 75, 211-13, 218-19; and farmers, 74-5; financial loss to the community through, 12-13, 15, 18-19, 34, 49; homemade, 103-4; and the hotels, 5, 6, 17-18, 29, 117; importance as issue in Canadian West, 1; importance to government of revenue from, 205, 214, 221; and the Indians, 1, 21, 24, 35; and the police, 13, 24-5, 27-9, 30; and politics, 1, 50-1; Protestant attitude to, 2, 40, 53; quality of, 30, 87, 100, 124-6, 148, 149, 153, 159-60; social conditions surrounding use of, 3, 10-11, 14, 19, 29, 31, 46-8, 50-1, 53, 64, 70-1, 73, 74, 74-7
Borden government, 3
Bowell, Sir Mackenzie, 57
Bowles, the Rev. R.P., 64
Boyle, J.R., 198, 205
Boynton Hall, Calgary, 26
Bracken, John, 204, 205, 206; government, 214, 217
Brandon, Manitoba, 29, 62, 63, 72, 79, 95, 174, 215; the Bronfman family in, 110-12, 114
Brandon Presbyterian Theological Seminary, 64
Brenton, Magistrate, 50
Brewers and Bottlers Supply Company, Winnipeg, 121, 151
British Columbia, 105, 165; bootlegging in, 104, 194; government monopoly of liquor trade in, 193-7, 205; and the liquor trade, 107, 119, 120, 133, 134, 171; and Prohibition, 58; results of repeal of Prohibition in, 208; and smuggling, 170-1, 193, 194; and "Temperance" beer, 161
Broadview, Saskatchewan, 131
Bronfman, Abe, 110, 111, 112, 113, 114, 115, 118, 135, 169
Bronfman, Allan, 112, 169, 179, 180
Bronfman, Ekiel, 109-12, 114, 115, 140
Bronfman, Harry, 135, 140, 145; arrest, 166; bootlegging, 171, 175-6, 178-9; bribery charges against, 165, 168, 176-7, 178, 180, 181, 184-9; early history, 110, 111-12, 114, 115; and the Harry Matoff murder, 147-8; and smuggling, 138-40; success as businessman, 128-30; whisky trade in Saskatchewan, 107, 118, 119, 121-7, 133, 134, 147-55 *passim*, 159-63 *passim*; in Yorkton, 107, 114, 116-18, 119
Bronfman, Laura, 110

Bronfman, Minnie, 109
Bronfman, Sam, 189; attitude to Yorkton, 117; and Chechik, 154-6, 158, 160; compared with Harry, 116; early life, 112, 114; and Knowles, 179, 180; in legal dispute, 126-7; as partner in whisky trade, 119, 121, 126, 134-5, 135, 154, 169; takeover of Bronfman business, 115
Bronfman, Yechiel. *See* Bronfman, Ekiel
Bronfmans, the, as business partnership, 122-4, 133, 134-5, 136, 141, 147, 149, 152, 156-9, 160-1
Brooks, Alberta, 83
Brooks Bulletin, 74
Browse's Hotel, Winnipeg, 5
Brunner, Frank, 80, 116
Buffington, E.J., 95
Bulman Brothers, 122, 123
Burdon, Magistrate, 50
Bureau, the Hon. Jacques, 169, 175, 179, 180, 181
Burgett, Archdeacon, 192
Burns, Major A.D., 196
Buscombe, Fred, 193

Cadillac Motor Company, 95
Calgary, 72, 125, 135; attitude to Indians in, 41-3; difficulties of enforcing Prohibition in, 32, 33, 99; drunkenness in, 30, 31; effects of Prohibition in, 92; growth of, 18, 29; as liquor centre during Prohibition, 132, 134, 135, 136; Prohibition crusade in, 84, 192; protest meeting at, 26
Calgary Albertan, 83
Calgary *Eye-opener,* 83
Calgary Herald, 26, 43, 83
Calgary House, 26
Calgary News Telegram, 83
Calgary Tribune, 42, 149
Calgary *Weekly Herald,* 42
Cameron, the Rev. A.A., 16-17, 30, 52
Canada Pure Drug Company, 118, 119, 122
Canada Temperance Act, 9, 107
Canadian Legion of the British Empire Service League, 195-6
Canadian Manufacturers Association, 169
Canadian Northern Railway, 113
Canadian Pacific Railway, 136, 153; Chinese as construction workers on, 43; drunkenness among workers, 49, 96; corruption on, 172-3; effect on development of towns, 18, 29, 74, 113; and liquor traffic, 113, 119, 120, 146; and the Manitoba-Ontario boundary dispute, 49; station in Winnipeg, 100, 111, 115; and work on Sunday, 8

Canora, Saskatchewan, 131
Capone, Al, 151
Carievale, Saskatchewan, 131, 143
Carnduff, Saskatchewan, 145, 180
Cartwright, Manitoba, 214
Ceylon, Saskatchewan, 131, 132, 144, 145
Charley Bull-Pup, 49
Chechik, Meyer, 150, 152-9, 160, 165
Chicago, 83, 84, 135, 151
Chicago Black Sox, 146
Chinese, the, 43-4, 194
Chown, the Rev. S.D., 78
Claresholm, Alberta, 192
Code, Abraham, 179, 180
Commercial Protective Association, 169
Congdon, Arthur, 85
Conservatives, the, 67, 135, 171; federal, 57, 181, 184, 193, 204; in Manitoba, 59, 60, 61, 62, 66-7, 79, 80, 84, 85, 174, 197, 217; and the repeal campaign, 197-8, 206; in Saskatchewan, 167, 181-2, 184-5, 187
Constantine, Superintendent, 35
Consul, Saskatchewan, 131
Costigan, J.R., 42
Cowley, Father Patrick, 17
Craik, Saskatchewan, 184
Creelman, Saskatchewan, 182
Crerar, T.A., 204
Crowsnest Pass, 104-5
Cuddy, Alfred, 92
Curran, S.D., 93
Customs and Excise Act, 185, 201
Customs and Excise Department, 104, 156, 169-71, 172, 175-6, 179, 180, 181, 216

Dafoe, J.W., 63, 174
Dagle, the Rev. J.A., 81
Dallin, Percy, 119, 120
Darrow, Clarence, 85
Darwin, Charles, 9
Davin, Nicholas Flood, 28
Davis, Attorney General T.C., 184
Dawson Trail, the, 22
Denton, William St. John, 187-8
Denver, 141
Dewdney government, 29
Diamond, Jack, 125-6
Diamond brothers, the, 132
Dillage, Lee, 146, 147
Dixon, Fred, 86, 94
Doe, Sid, 134
Dominion City, Manitoba, 47
Dominion Distributors Company Limited, 153, 156, 157, 161; warehouse operation, 148, 149, 159, 160, 163, 165, 178
Dominion Temperance Alliance, 17, 35

Drys, the. *See* Prohibition
Duff, Mr. Justice Lyman, 186
Duff, Saskatchewan, 46
Duncan, James, 30
Dunning, Premier Charles, 200
Dutchman's, The, 1, 5, 6
DuVal, the Rev. F.B., 79, 86
Dyke, the Rev. J.W., 26, 30

Edmonton, 30, 41, 72, 83, 84, 120, 132, 134, 135, 192, 202
Edmonton Bulletin, 42, 45, 83, 84, 92, 105
Edmonton Journal, 44, 83, 197, 207-8
Edwards, Bob, 83
Edwards, Jonathan, 9
Eighteenth Amendment to the U.S. Constitution, 95, 106, 188
Emerson, Manitoba, 112
Emmering, George, 5
England, 84
English Channel, 45
Estevan, Saskatchewan, 131, 140, 143, 145, 146, 147, 172, 186, 201
Evangelical Protestants, 17

Farrow, R.R., 179, 181
Fat Earl, 145
Felsch, Happy, 146
Fernie, Saskatchewan, 43
50th Foot Guards, 22
Fillmore, W.P., 135
Findlay, Walter, 193
First World War, 3, 90, 94, 115, 116, 137, 138, 140, 201, 212
Fisk, William, 42, 43
Flanders, 84
Ford-McCumber tariff, 204
Foresters, the, 40
Fort Dufferin, 22, 23
Fort Garry, 5, 22, 215, 219
Fort Macleod, 24
Fort Whoop-up, 22, 23
Fort William, 48
Fortune, the Rev. W.G.W., 66, 82
France, 91
Frank Slide, the, 44
French, Lt.-Col. George A., 22
Fullerton, C.P., 135

Gagnon, Chief Joe, 219
Gainsborough, Saskatchewan, 131, 141, 143, 145, 166, 175, 177, 180
Galicians, 44-5. *See also* Ruthenians
Gardiner, Premier J.G., 182, 184
Gellerman, Annie, 112
Gellerman, David, 178, 186-8

General strike of 1918, 101
General strike of 1919, 101
Germantown (Regina), 75
Germany, 84
Gladstone, William, 9
Gleichen, Alberta, 93
Glen Ewen, Saskatchewan, 131, 141, 143
Gordon, C.W., 86
Gordon, Dr. D.M., 17
Gorman, Mr., 154
Govenlock, Saskatchewan, 131, 134
Grand Forks, North Dakota, 214, 215
Grand Trunk Railway, 140, 173
Grassie, Lt.-Col. William, 196
Gray, Col. A.C., 196
Great War Veterans Association, 195, 196
Great West Express, 120
Greenfield, Herbert, 204
Greenway, Thomas, 56, 59, 60
Gregory, Major C.E., 185, 196

Hagel, Percy, 86
Halifax, 158, 169
Hamilton Times, 12
Hatton, Saskatchewan, 131
Hawkes, A.G., 163
Hawkins, J.H., 182
Heeney, Canon Bertol, 206
Henderson's Directory, 6
Henry, the Rev. E.Z., 64
Herchmer, Commissioner William, 26, 31, 35
Hirsch, Baron de, 109-10
Hudson's Bay Company, 4, 20, 63, 120, 126, 136
Hughson, J.H., 86
Hunter, Major W.T., 196

Icelanders, 4
Illinois Steel Company, 95
Independent Labor Party, 206
Indian Affairs Department, 42
Indians, displacement by white settlers, 21, 23, 24; and liquor, 1, 21, 35; prejudice against, 41, 42-3

Jackson, George, 85
Japanese, the, 44
Jews, the, 8, 45, 109, 110, 111, 152, 183
John, Ken, 132, 142
Johnson, D.C., 30
Johnson, Chief Walter, 219
Johnston, the Rev. H.B., 183

Kaleida, Manitoba, 136
Kamsack, Saskatchewan, 131

Keenleyside, E.B., 65
Kenora, Ontario, 49, 88, 118, 134, 135. *See also* Rat Portage
Kenora Wine Company, 134, 136
Kentucky, 121
Kerr, Dr. F.W., 217
Kerrobert, Saskatchewan, 131
King, Mackenzie, 170
Knights of Pythias, 40
Knowles, Cyril, 167, 171-2, 175-81, 184, 185, 186, 187
Krafchenko, Jack, 86
Ku Klux Klan, 182, 183, 185

LaCoste, Jimmy, 142, 146-7
Langevin, Archbishop, 79, 80
La Patrie (St. Boniface), 85
Lapointe, the Hon. Ernest, 181
Laurier, Sir Wilfrid, 57-60 *passim;* cabinet, 62, 63, 174; referendum, 66, 105
Leech, Chief Commissioner R.E.A., 163, 165
Leland, Henry M., 95
Leland Hotel, Winnipeg, 188, 213
Lethbridge, 24, 30, 43, 74, 84, 105, 134, 195, 213
Lethbridge Brewery, 197
Lethbridge Herald, 44
Lethbridge News, 44
Liberals, the, 67, 116; in Alberta, 82, 198, 203; federal party, 57, 184, 193; in Manitoba, 57, 59, 60, 62, 79, 80, 81, 84, 85, 197-8, 203; and the repeal campaign, 197, 206, 209; in Saskatchewan, 65, 80, 138, 163, 182, 184
Licensed Victualers Association, 80, 83
Lloyd, the Rev. George, 80, 183
Lloyd, Archdeacon T.G., 192
Lloydminster, Alberta, 132
Lloydminster, Saskatchewan, 131, 132
Locke, Mr., 126
Logan, Inspector George, 75
London, England, 84
London House, Winnipeg, 55-6
Lord's Day Act, 8
Los Angeles Times, 85
Louisville, 135
Loyal Orange Lodge, 40, 60, 79, 80, 182, 185. *See also* Orangemen

McCabe, Dominion Commissioner, 50
McClung, Nellie, 48, 79, 86, 192, 206
McCorvie, Archie, 134
Macdonald, Hugh John, 60, 62, 63, 67
Macdonald, Sir John A., 20, 21, 28, 60, 62; government, 9

Macdonald Act, 60, 61, 63, 82, 84
McDougall, the Rev. John, 21
McElheran, Archdeacon, 206
McGillivray, A.A., 185
Macgregor, D., and Company, 122
McIllree, Superintendent J.H., 32
McKillop, Charles, 30
McKinney, Henry, 5
McKinney, Louise, 192, 206
Macklin, Saskatchewan, 131, 132
McLean, Bella, 5
Macleod, Colonel J.F., 22
Macleod Gazette, 28, 41
McNally, the Rev. Charles, 206
McNamara brothers, 85
MacPherson, Major M.A., 168
Main Street, Winnipeg, 5, 72, 112, 115; fire on, 55; growth of, 4, 6; as trouble centre, 10, 12, 14, 64, 71, 73, 76, 94, 115, 200
Mair, Charlie, 6
Manitoba, 21, 54, 72, 82, 105, 111, 135, 181; attitude to liquor in, 9, 10; bank robberies in, 144; bootlegging following repeal in, 211; boundary dispute with Ontario, 49-51; and the Bronfmans, 111, 125, 134-5, 138; corruption in, 162-3, 174; crime and drunkenness in, 70; early settlement, 4, 6, 109; elite of, 11, 12; government control of liquor trade in, 10, 11; hotel policy in, 17, 18, 29, 112; liquor policy following repeal in, 211, 213-17 *passim,* 219; mail order houses in, 98; and 1920 plebiscite, 107-8, 120, 130, 191, 192-3; problems of enforcement of Prohibition in, 88, 102, 198; Prohibitionist sentiment in, 34, 35, 51, 53, 191; religious strife in, 78-80; repeal movement in, 196-7, 203-7, 208, 210; smuggling in, 29, 143-4, 175-7; social and economic problems in 1880s, 55-6; social conditions during Prohibition in, 90-1, 92; struggle for Prohibition in, 56-68, 78, 85-6, 89; temperance beer in, 161
Manitoba Liquor Commission, 216
Manitoba Provincial Police, 102, 176, 214, 218, 219
Manitoba Schools Question, 18, 56, 63
Manitoba Temperance Act, 87, 213
Manitoba Temperance Alliance, 9, 11
Maple Creek, Saskatchewan, 131, 132, 134
Mariaggi Hotel, Port Arthur, 114, 118, 188
Maritimes, the, 57, 135, 170
Marquette Review, 8
Martin, E.D., 85
Martin, Joe, 56
Maryfield, Saskatchewan, 131

Mason and Risch Piano Company, 96
Masonic Order, 40
Mather, Mr. Justice T.G., 92
Matheson, Archbishop, 17, 206
Matoff, Harry, 145-8, 149
Medicine Hat, Alberta, 30, 44, 213
Medicine Hat News, 44
Melville, Saskatchewan, 131, 182
Midland railway yards, Winnipeg, 114
Minneapolis, 141, 150
Minnedosa, Manitoba, 92
Minnesota, 4, 39, 134, 138, 144, 148
Minot, North Dakota, 141, 143, 146
Moderation Leagues, in British Columbia, 193-4; on the Prairies, 196-9, 200, 202, 203-8, 217
Montana, 29, 105, 111, 136, 138
Montreal, 33, 115, 117, 118, 126, 151, 166, 167, 168, 169, 188
Montreal Board of Trade, 169
Moose Jaw, 29, 30, 43, 72, 93, 131, 133, 134, 140, 162, 186, 187, 188, 219
Moose Jaw Times, 45, 182
Moosomin, Saskatchewan, 131
Moral and Social Reform Society, 78, 79
Morden, Manitoba, 92
Morosnick, L.D., 214
Morton, W.L., 11
Motherwell, W.R., 94
Muenster, Saskatchewan, 209
Mulligan, Al, the Bad Man, 49
Murdock, Mayor George, 26
Murray, D.B., 6, 10

Napovda, 110
Nares, Sir George, 13
Natanson, Zisu, 202-4 *passim,* 154, 160, 161, 165, 178, 187, 216
Nebraska, 148
Nesbitt, Len, 74
Neville, Saskatchewan, 96
New Brunswick, 58, 158
Newton, Chief of Police C.H., 135
Niven, D.A., 157
Norris, T.C., 79
North Dakota, 29, 111, 136, 138, 143, 144, 146, 148, 173, 175, 176; border, 181
North Portal, 143
North West Mounted Police, 1, 21-37, 55, 139, 175
North West Mounted Rifles, 21, 22
Northern Pacific Railway, 140, 173
Northgate, North Dakota, 173
Northgate, Saskatchewan, 140
Northwest Commercial Travellers Association, The, 93-4

Northwest Review, 85, 209
Northwest Territories, compared with Manitoba, 34, 35; Indians in, 41; liquor in, 26, 29-30, 32-3; Prohibition in, 23, 24, 26; settlement, 6, 29, 34, 51
Northwest Territories Act of 1875, 24, 31, 32-4, 35, 55
Northwest Territories Agreement, 63
Northwest Territories Council, 26-7, 31, 35
Nova Scotia, 58, 135, 159, 169

Oberhaltzer and Company, 53
O'Brien, Boston, the Slugger, 49
O'Brien, Dr. Murrough, 47
Olds, Alberta, 136
Oliver, the Rev. E.H., 183
O'Lone, Bob, 5
O'Lone's Hotel, 5, 6
Omaha, Nebraska, 141, 147
One Big Union, 192
Ontario, 39, 134, 168, 204; boundary dispute with Manitoba, 48-50; emigrants to West from, 4, 7, 16, 40, 51, 52; labour legislation, 73; liquor control act, 9; and the liquor trade, 107, 118, 120, 121, 170; N.W.M.P. recruits from, 22; and Prohibition, 57
Openshaw, Saskatchewan, 173
Orange Sentinel, 80
Orangemen, 40, 57, 78, 80. *See also* Loyal Orange Lodge
Order-in-Council of 1873, 23, 24
Order-in-Council of March 11, 1918, 105, 107
Oxbow, Saskatchewan, 81, 131, 140, 141, 143, 180

Palliser Triangle, 39, 136
Pantages Theatre, Winnipeg, 85
Paris, 106
Patrick, Principal, 64
Patterson, the Rev. J.H., 83
Peace River country, the, 105
Pembina Highway, Manitoba, 219
Picariello, Emilio, 105
Pilot Mound, Manitoba, 214
Pinkham, Archdeacon, 17
Piper, Constable C.B., 175-6, 180
Pitblado, Dr. C.P., 17, 52
Pitblado, Isaac, 85
Popham, Robert E., 90
Port Arthur, Ontario, 114, 115, 118, 135
Port of Winnipeg, 171, 179
Portage la Prairie, 11
Potts, Jerry, 23
Prairie Drug Company Limited, 151, 152, 158, 178

Presbyterian Theological College, Saskatoon, 183
Prescott Cavalry Regiment, 22
Prince Albert, Saskatchewan, 30, 52, 80
Prince Edward Island, 8, 58
Progressives, the, 184, 193, 198
Prohibition, 2, 3, 9, 19, 113, 116, 117, 150, 183, 190, 220-1; American business in Canada following repeal, 213; and the Bronfmans, 118; class aspects of, 135, 211-12; duration on Prairies, 89; enforcement crusade, 105, 163-5; enforcement in Northwest Territories, 24-7, 31-4, 35, 55-6; factors leading to repeal of, 196-211; at the federal level, 106-8; and the Laurier plebiscite, 57-60, 63, 66; loopholes in law, 97-103, 118-19, 210; movement in Alberta, 82-4; movement in Manitoba, 55-7, 60-5, 66-7, 79, 80, 84-6; movement in Saskatchewan, 65-6, 80-1, 86-7; 1920 plebiscite on, 191-3, 195; official attitude to, 34; positive effects of, 3, 90-7; repeal in Northwest Territories, 35; repeal of, 213-14; rise of opposition to, 149; strong support for, 2-3, 15, 34-5, 40, 50-1, 52-3, 54, 58-9; in the United States, 106-7

Quebec, 58, 107, 135, 168
Queen's Hotel, Winnipeg, 56

Rabinovitch, Harry, 150-1, 153, 154-5, 156, 157, 158, 159, 160, 165
Rat Portage, 49-51. *See also* Kenora
Read, W.H., 154
Red River, 11, 53; docks, 5; insurrection, 3, 4, 21
Red River Valley, 4, 5, 49
Reddy, Black Jim, 49
Regina, 187, 202, 219; the Bronfman operation in, 119, 129, 130, 135, 148-61 *passim;* crime and drunkenness in, 28, 30, 75; development of, 18, 29; and Harry Bronfman, 116, 117, 167-8, 178-9, 184-6; improved social conditions in, during Prohibition, 94; and the Ku Klux Klan, 182; as liquor export and smuggling centre, 130, 134, 140, 143, 146, 173; as market for bootleg liquor, 202; and 1920 plebiscite, 192; N.W.M.P. at, 35, 36; and Prohibition, 87; scandal regarding non-enforcement of Prohibition in, 163-5
Regina Junk Company, 178
Regina Leader Post, 202
Regina Morning Leader, 152, 161, 163, 164, 165
Regina Star, 184

Regina Vinegar Company, 215
Regina Wine and Spirits Company, 151, 152, 159, 160, 178
Repealers, the, 199. *See also* Wets, the
Retail Merchants Association, 85
Riel, Louis, 6, 85; insurrection, 3, 4, 21
Risburg, Swede, 146
Roach, Patsy, 70
Robertson-Ross, Colonel P., 22
Roblin, R.P., 59-60, 63, 64, 66, 67, 71, 78, 79, 80; government, 174; plebiscite, 63-4, 67
Roche Perce mine, 140
Rock Island, 169
Rock Lake Total Abstinence League, 52
Rodriguez, Mr., 154
Rollo, North Dakota, 214
Rosalie, 41
Rosetown, Saskatchewan, 172
Rossin House, Winnipeg, 55
Rouleau, Judge, 43
Royal, Joseph, 55
Royal Alexandra Hotel, Winnipeg, 115
Royal Canadian Mounted Police, 93, 102, 105, 147, 162, 167; and American bank robbers, 144, 145; liquor law enforcement, 98, 100, 104, 177, 202; and smuggling, 137, 175, 177
Royal Commission on Customs and Excise, appearance of Cyril Knowles before, 177, 180, 181, 183-4; appearance of Harry Bronfman before, 148-9, 168; appearance of Meyer Chechik before, 154, 155, 158; and brewery backing for Moderation Leagues, 197; and domestic sale of export liquor, 201; and the Regina Vinegar Company, 215
Royal Hotel, Winnipeg, 5, 6
Royal Hotel, Yorkton, 116
Russell case, 9, 11
Russia, 109, 140
Ruthenians, 25, 44, 91. *See also* Galicians
Rutledge, Dr. W.L., 17
Ryan, George, 85

Sabbatarians, the, 74
St. Boniface, Manitoba, 64, 72, 76, 79, 85, 86, 172, 195, 201, 215, 219
St. James, Manitoba, 215
St. Paul, Minnesota, 4
St. Peter's Messenger, 209
St. Regis Hotel, Winnipeg, 188
St. Valentine's Day massacre, 151
Sair, Isaac, 140, 141, 180
Sair, Jacob, 140, 141, 188
Sairs, the, 140-1, 152, 180-1
Saltcoats, Saskatchewan, 116

Sampson, H.E., 185
Saskatchewan, 2, 88, 89, 90, 102, 105, 116, 129, 138, 146, 149, 156, 159-60, 167-8, 197; and the Banish-the-Bar movement, 80-2, 84, 112; bank robberies in, 144-5; bootlegging in, 125, 202, 211, 215; the Bronfmans in, 124, 126, 133-4, 135, 165, 168; campaign for repeal, 208, 210; crime and drunkenness in, 90, 91, 93, 94, 128-9; early settlement in, 34, 109-10; enforcement of liquor laws in, 98; and the Harry Bronfman case, 184-9 *passim;* illegal obtaining of liquor in, 98-9; liquor traffic in, 107, 118-19, 120, 130, 132, 136, 147, 153-4, 159, 162, 170, 176; and the Prohibition debate, 65-71, 81, 86-7, 108, 191, 192, 195; racial and religious conflict in, 78-80, 181-3, 209; roads in, 138; scandal in the liquor trade in, 161-3, 197, 198, 200; smuggling in, 142-4, 148, 171, 173, 175, 180, 181, 201; system of liquor distribution in, 219-20; Temperance beer, 161-2; treatment of Chinese, 43
Saskatchewan Court of Appeals, 156, 158
Saskatchewan Liquor Commission, 139, 161-2, 164-5, 168, 200
Saskatchewan Temperance Act, 153, 158
Saskatoon, 72, 81, 87, 100, 129, 131, 132, 134, 136, 162, 171, 183, 192
Saskatoon Brewery, 197
Saskatoon Labor Council, 81
Saskatoon Phoenix, 93
Saskatoon Star, 45, 183
Saskatoon Temperance Colony, 51
Schmidt, Wolfgang, 90
Schultz, Dutch, 142, 151
Scotland, 119
Scott, Premier Walter, 65, 67, 81-2, 105
Scott Act, 53
Seattle, 92
Second World War, 90
Senate, Saskatchewan, 131, 132
Shea, Mike, 216
Shea, Pat, 135, 197
Shearer, the Rev. J.G., 78
Shea's Brewery, 197
Sheho, Saskatchewan, 116
Sherwood, North Dakota, 180
Sifton, Clifford, 56-7, 62, 63, 66, 174
Silcox, the Rev. J.B., 12, 17, 30, 31, 40, 52
Simpson, Colonel R.M., 196
Single Tax, 2
Smith, the Rev. A.E., 220
Smuggling, 2, 3, 91-2, 129, 130, 134-5, 171-3, 191, 201, 210-11; in Alberta, 105; by Americans, 141-2, 145-6; in British

Columbia, 193; and the Bronfmans, 133-4, 138-40, 151-2; economics of, 124; among farmers, 138; and gangsterism, 143-8; and official corruption, 169-71, 174-8, 180, 181, 189; and repeal of Prohibition, 206, 207, 213-15; and the Sairs, 140-1, 180
Snooks, Ginger, 76
Social Service Council, 79, 101
Souris River, 140, 173
Southern Exports Ltd., 188
Spalding, Inspector, 93
Sparling, Principal, 64
Spence, the Rev. Ben, 84
Spence, F.S., 86
Starr, the Rev. J.E., 17
Stewart government, the, 200
Stock Exchange Hotel, Winnipeg, 72
Stockyards Hotel, St. Boniface, 72
Strong Drink; and the Curse and the Cure, 53
Stubbs, L. St. George, 217
Stubbs, William, 180
Supreme Court of Canada, 158, 159
Sweatman, Travers, 135
Swift Current, Saskatchewan, 96, 131

Taber, Alberta, 213
Taché, Archbishop, 17
Tadman, Sam, 133, 186
Taylor, W.F., 178, 186
Temperance beer, 88, 99-100, 106, 161-2
Temperance movement. *See* Prohibition
Temperance and Moral Reform Society, 66, 82
Temperance Reform League, 196
Ten Nights in a Barroom, 53
Territorial Council. *See* Northwest Territories Council
Territorial Court en Banc, 32
Territories Prohibition Act, 28, 31, 32, 33, 35
Thompson, Sir John, 57
Titanic, the, 45
Toronto, 80, 84, 86, 96
Toronto Board of Trade, 96, 169
Toronto *Saturday Night,* 169
Total Abstinence League, 52
Trades and Labor Congress, 71
Trades and Labor Council, 78, 85
Trans-Canada Transportation Company Limited, 138
Tribune, Saskatchewan, 132
Tutt, Charles, 94
Tupper, Sir Charles Hibbert, 193
"Turf and Wine Vault", the, 11

Turriff, Senator J.G., 181
Tuxford, Brigadier G.S., 196
Tyrrell, Frank, 42

Union Government, 106, 119
United Farm Women, 192
United Farmers of Alberta, 82, 192, 198, 200, 204
United Farmers of Manitoba, 204, 217
United Grain Growers, 78, 83, 85, 138, 182
United States, 143-4, 175, 176, 178, 204, 219; and bootlegging, 211; and Canadian temperance movement, 53-4; effect of Canadian government control of liquor on, 206, 213-14; effect of Prohibition on, 96; and Eighteenth Amendment to Constitution, 106, 188; export of liquor to, 133, 138, 146, 152, 158, 164, 170-1; gangsterism in, 147-8; immigration to Canadian West from, 40, 52; importation of alcohol from, 148; and smuggling, 29, 107, 130, 137, 140, 141, 146, 191
University of Manitoba, 112

Vancouver, 44, 135, 173, 194, 208
Vancouver Export Company, 171
Vidora, Saskatchewan, 132
Ville La Salle, 169
Vivian, George, 72
Volstead Act, 107

Wabagoon Lake, 49
Waite, Ed, 161
Wakopa, Manitoba, 214
Walker Theatre, Winnipeg, 206
Walsh, Major J.M., 22
Wapella, Saskatchewan, 109-10
War Measures Act, 88, 107
Washington State, 171
Waterton Lakes, 136
Wesley College, 64
West, Inspector, 93
Western Prudential Investments and Trust Company, Ltd., 116
Wets, the, 197, 199, 207, 209; and bootlegging, 2, 202, 211; campaign against Prohibition in Alberta, 83, 84; campaign against Prohibition in British Columbia, 195; campaign against Prohibition in Manitoba, 85-6; and 1920 plebiscite, 191; and repeal, 206-7, 210; support by brew-eries, 196. *See also* Repealers *and* Moderation Leagues
Weyburn, Saskatchewan, 132, 146
White, F.T.G., 163
Whitemouth River, 49
White's Hotel, Bienfait, 145
Willard, Frances, 53
Wilson, W.F., 179, 180
Windle, Dr. A.C., 83-4, 86
Winnipeg, American purchase of liquor in, 213; and bootleg liquor, 201, 212, 217-19; Bronfman family in, 110, 112, 114, 117, 169; Bronfman dealings in, 121, 122, 123; campaign for Prohibition in, 53, 61, 63-4, 78, 85-6; conditions during Prohibition, 94, 100, 101; as Customs and Excise headquarters, 137, 178-81 *passim;* debate over Prohibition, 192, 195; as liquor centre for Northwest Territories, 29; and liquor during Prohibition, 88, 118, 120, 135, 176, 197; Meyer Chechik in, 150-1, 156, 157; religious conflict in, 79; repeal of Prohibition, 200, 206, 207; Royal Commission on Customs and Excise in, 171; social conditions in, before Prohibition, 3-19, 39, 48, 55, 70-1, 75-6
Winnipeg Free Press, 192, 216
Winnipeg Grain Exchange, 211
Winnipeg Times, 12-13, 15, 31
Winnipeg Tribune, 92, 124, 128, 167-8, 181, 197
Wolseley Expedition, 22, 53
Woman suffrage, 2, 3, 190
Women's Christian Temperance Union, 35, 44, 53, 58, 77, 82, 85, 97
Wood, Henry Wise, 82, 204
Wood, W.R., 217
Wynn, Sam, 116

Yorkton, Saskatchewan, 109, 129, 154; Bronfman beginnings in, 113-14, 116-37; as centre of Bronfman liquor business, 107, 118-22, 124, 126, 129, 130, 132, 135, 136, 138, 141, 148-9, 156-7, 159-60, 169
Yorkton Distributing Company, 124
Yorkton Enterprise, 117
Young, Superintendent G.F., 22
Ypres, 84